AF631500

Mixed-Income Housing Development Planning Strategies and Frameworks in the Global South

Mixed-Income Housing Development Planning Strategies and Frameworks in the Global South

BY

GEORGE OKECHUKWU ONATU
University of Johannesburg, South Africa

WELLINGTON DIDIBHUKU THWALA
Walter Sisulu Univesity, South Africa

AND

CLINTON OHIS AIGBAVBOA
University of Johannesburg, South Africa

emerald PUBLISHING

United Kingdom – North America – Japan – India – Malaysia – China

Emerald Publishing Limited
Emerald Publishing, Floor 5, Northspring, 21-23 Wellington Street, Leeds LS1 4DL

First edition 2024

Copyright © 2024 George Okechukwu Onatu, Wellington Didibhuku Thwala, and Clinton Ohis Aigbavboa.
Published under an exclusive license by Emerald Publishing Limited.

Reprints and permissions service
Contact: www.copyright.com

No part of this book may be reproduced, stored in a retrieval system, transmitted in any form or by any means electronic, mechanical, photocopying, recording or otherwise without either the prior written permission of the publisher or a licence permitting restricted copying issued in the UK by The Copyright Licensing Agency and in the USA by The Copyright Clearance Center. Any opinions expressed in the chapters are those of the authors. Whilst Emerald makes every effort to ensure the quality and accuracy of its content, Emerald makes no representation implied or otherwise, as to the chapters' suitability and application and disclaims any warranties, express or implied, to their use.

British Library Cataloguing in Publication Data
A catalogue record for this book is available from the British Library

ISBN: 978-1-83753-815-7 (Print)
ISBN: 978-1-83753-814-0 (Online)
ISBN: 978-1-83753-816-4 (Epub)

Printed and bound by CPI Group (UK) Ltd, Croydon, CR0 4YY

INVESTOR IN PEOPLE

This book is dedicated to our wives and children for their love and care during the period we were busy compiling the manuscript.

Table of Contents

List of Figures

List of Tables

List of Abbreviations

AMI	Average Medium Income
ANC	African National Congress
APNHR	Asia-Pacific Network for Housing Research
BNG	Breaking New Ground
CBO	Community-Based Organization
CCPR	California Centre for Population Research
CIA	Central Intelligence Agency
CLL	Common Law Leasehold
CoGTA	Department of Cooperative Governance & Traditional Affairs
CoR	Certificate of Right
COSATU	Congress for South African Trade Unions
CPF	Central Provident Fund
CSHA	Commonwealth State Housing Agency
CSIR	Council for Scientific and Industrial Research
DA	Democratic Alliance
DFI	Direct Foreign Investment
DPME	Department of Planning, Monitoring and Evaluation
DRDLR	Department of Rural Development & Land Reforms
FHA	Federal Housing Authority
FELDA	Federal Land Development Authority
ELCRA	Federal Land Consolidation and Rehabilitation Authority
FMBN	Federal Mortgage Bank of Nigeria
FPSG	Fixed Period State Grant
GDP	Gross Domestic Product
GRA	Government Reserve Areas
HDB	Housing Development Board

HOPE	Housing Opportunities for Everyone
HUD	Housing and Urban Development
ICESCO	International Convention on Economic, Social and Cultural Rights
IMF	International Monetary Fund
IRDP	Integrated Rural Development Programme
IUDF	Integrated Urban Development Framework
LAP	Land Administration Project
LITC	Low Income Tax Credit
MIRG	Mixed-Income Research Group
NAHA	National Affordable Housing Programme
NEP	National Economic Policies
NIMBY	Not In My Back Yard
NNHP	New National Housing Policy
NUSP	National Upgrading Support Programme
PIE	Prevention of Illegal Eviction
SACN	South Africa Cities Network
SERI	Socio-Economic Research Institute
SHHA	Self-Help Housing Agency
SPLUMA	Spatial Planning and Land Use Management
TND	Traditional Neighbourhood Design
TPC	Town Planning Complaint
UN	The United Nations
UNDP	United Nations Development Agency
VPADD	Voluntary Pro-Active Deal Driven

About the Authors

Dr George Okechukwu Onatu is a Staff and Senior Lecturer in the Department of Urban and Regional Planning, University of Johannesburg, South Africa. He completed his PhD in Engineering Management (Housing) at the University of Johannesburg in 2021. He was the former Head of Department from 2010 to 2016. His research interest lies in human settlements, informality, Spatial Planning, land use management, urban planning, housing provisions and property development as well as the Fourth Industrial Revolution and mix-use development. Some of his research works has been extensively published in recognized Journals and conference proceedings. He is a member of various bodies, including the editorial board of the Town and Regional Planning Journal South Africa and also support and assist in scholarly debates as a board member of the Association of African Planning Schools (AAPS). Dr Onatu is the author of over 40 published research articles in both local and international conference proceedings. He also assisted both the National Department of Human Settlements South Africa and National Homebuilders Registration Council (NHBRC) as a research consultant and policy expert specialist on housing issues.

Wellington Didibhuku Thwala is a Full Professor of Construction Project Management and Leadership at the Department of Construction Management and Civil Engineering at the Walter Sisulu Univesity. He is a Director of the DST NRF SARCHI Chair in Sustainable Construction Management and Leadership in the Built Environment. He is the Chairman of the Construction Management Foundation Advisory Board. Professor Thwala has varied research interest, including project management, construction management, supply chain management and leadership in the construction industry, health and safety, engineering design and management, 4IR, infrastructure delivery, business competitiveness and sustainable housing and local economic development. He is the Editor in Chief of the Journal of Construction Project Management and Innovation, Peer Reviewer of Built Environment Project and Asset Management, as well as Journal of Facility Management and has more than 1,700 citations and 490 publications.

Clinton Ohis Aigbavboa is a Full Professor at the Department of Construction Management and Quantity Surveying, University of Johannesburg, South Africa. Prof. Aigbavboa is the immediate past Vice Dean of the Faculty of Engineering and Built Environment, University of Johannesburg, South Africa. He has extensive knowledge in practice, research, training and teaching. He is currently the Director of the Construction Industry Development Board Centre of Excellence and the Sustainable Human Settlement and Construction Research Centre at the University of Johannesburg. He is also an author of 12 research books that were published with Springer Nature and CRC Press. He is currently the Editor of the Journal of Construction Project Management and Innovation (accredited by the DoHET) and has received national and international recognition in his field of research. He is rated by the South Africa National Research Foundation.

Foreword

It is a honour and privilege to be requested to write this foreword to this remarkable book on Mixed-Income Housing Development Planning Strategies and Frameworks in the Global South. With over 35 dedicated years of experience in teaching, conducting research and supervision of students of Urban and Regional Planning, I feel as the best person in a position to do justice to this request. Moreover, as the former Deputy Vice Chancellor of one of the Premier Universities in the continent, University of Nigeria, Nsukka, where I was instrumental in attracting many projects and organizing so many seminars and conferences which brought the University to visibility and to be ranked very high among the Universities in Nigeria. More also as one of the pioneering members of the Association of African Planning Schools (AAPS) and a member of the seven-man steering committee, the continental network comprising of 54 Universities where I met one of the authors in 2010, it gives me additional fulfilment to write about this important resource book on human settlements. Dr George O. Onatu is a seasoned scholar/Urban and Regional Planner as well as housing specialist who was instrumental in the growth and development of the Department of Urban and Regional Planning at the University of Johannesburg. He served as the Head of Department for two tenures. Prof C. Aigbavboa served as the Vice Dean Research and Internationalization of the Faculty of Engineering and Built Environment, University of Johannesburg with several other awards and is the Executive Director of Centre for Industrial Development Board (CIDB) and sustainable human settlements and construction management research. Prof D. W. Thwala is an NRF, DST and SARCHI Chair as well as top researcher for several periods with more than 25 years of teaching and research experience, with so many citations and Senior Fellow at a Centre and the Department of Civil Engineering, College of Engineering Science and Technology at the University of South Africa (UNISA). With this profile and diverse experiences of these scholars, they are all well grounded with multidisciplinary knowledge/skills to come up with this important resource book to showcase their valued contributions to the practice, teaching and research on housing.

Mixed-income housing development and implementations strategies are increasingly becoming one area of human settlements research that is gaining increasing attention and attractions. With the world population expected to reach an astronomical 9.8 billion by 2050 from the current 7.6 billion, informed by the addition of 83 million people every year on the planet, most governments and international organizations are facing considerable challenges as it relates to access to housing by these teaming population, exacerbated urban poverty and hunger, as well as environmental conservation and climate change issues. We cannot continue to fold our hands and stare. Hence, this book is recommended for all those who are interested in ensuring that the world moves forward with speed to cater for these rising population as it relates to shelter and necessary condition to attain sustainable human settlements. The framework so developed in the book is user friendly and will argue all current efforts, publications and policy gaps which need urgent solution on a global scale. The case examples drawn from both the developed and developing countries will serve as a sign post and road map to urban planners, construction economics, developers, researchers, community leaders, social scientists, private sector and all stakeholders as well as built environment students/engineering specialists/practitioners on how to approach the problems confronting human settlements and design strategies. You cannot wait further than to read this book that has come handy at this important period in the history of human race and associated challenges that at times resist solutions and appear not solvable. These problems are now noted and associated with hidden opportunities that are not so visible and are at times overlooked.

Yours sincerely,

Prof. Smart N. Uchegbu, PhD, MSc, BA, fnitp, fnes, meman, Rtp
Deputy Vice Chancellor Emeritus
University of Nigeria, Nsukka

Preface

The twenty-first century is noted globally as the urban century of unique character, dynamism, symbiosis and complexities because more than half of the world's population lives in cities. This population is projected to increase to 70% by 2050. South Africa is no exception to this phenomenal increase in urban population. More than 60% of South African population lives in urban areas, and this figure is projected to increase to 71.3% and 80% by 2030 and 2050, respectively. Access to human settlement by this teaming population remains a challenge/issue and undoubting task to the incumbent government and previous regimes. The problem of access to human settlements is compounded by historical apartheid's spatial geography characterized by racial segregation, fragmentation of urban space and separate development. During the apartheid period, settlement patterns were designed and planned in accordance with racial differentiation. This resulted to fragmented and dysfunctional residential settlements pattern that forced many people to travel long distances between place of work and home. Since 1994, the various housing policies, programmes and legislation have not been able to find solution to the spatial challenges that South Africa faces. The objective of this book is to investigate and unpack mixed-income housing development strategy and how this housing typology with a new framework can bring about spatial integration, improved access to social services, infrastructure and the promotion of social and economic inclusion. The research utilized the case study research design and employed the Delphi method for the investigation. It provides a step-by-step guide on how to use Delphi technique and Structural Equation Modelling (SEM) in human settlements research and planning. The findings reveal that proper coordination across all sectors of government and good working relationship between the private and public sectors will increase the sustainability of mixed-income housing development. This book for the first time brings together and synthesize the relevant theories and concepts that guide mixed-income housing development and human settlements in general. This book is also a reach out to support existing theories that mixed-income housing might not be able to bring about overall social integration, solve all housing problems, but it has the unique tendency, character and peculiarity in the South African case to address spatial imbalances by increasing the affordability of low-cost housing. This research book will provide important resource toolkit as it concludes that there is need for both inter-sectoral and intergovernmental collaboration as well as proper coordination/adequate urban planning to address the human settlement challenges in South Africa and for effective implementation of mixed-income housing development in both developed and developing economies. The use of case studies from the United States, Australia, the Netherlands, Brazil, Nigeria, Botswana and Ghana is noteworthy and serve as an important selling point.

Acknowledgement

We sincerely appreciate the contributions and cooperation of our colleagues at the Faculty of Engineering and the Built Environment, the Department of Urban and Regional Planning and the Department of Construction Management and Quantity Surveying. In this vein, we say thank you to Prof Daniel Mashao, Prof Morgan Dundu, Prof Charles Mbohwa, Prof Steven Ekolu, Prof Jeffrey Mahachi, Mr Zenzile Mbinza, Mr Aurobindo Ogra, Prof Trynos Gumbo, Prof Walter Musakwa, Dr Eric Makoni, Mr Jude Okafor, Ms Natasha Ntakana, Ms Sithembile Thusi, Adv Petrus Steyn, Dr Justice Agumba, Prof Innocent Musonda, Mr Nazeem Ansary, Mrs Mogodi, Mrs Corlia Jordan and Mrs N Mzobe. Our mutual sharing and working relationship over the years have not gone unnoticed. Finally, we would like to thank the following: the staff of Basil Reeds; Urban Dynamics Pty Ltd, the National Department of Human Settlements; the City of Johannesburg Metropolitan Municipality; Iyer Development Consultants, for their contributions to this book; our Statisticians, Mr Serge Malandala and Mr Elvis Ganyaupfu for data analysis. We also acknowledge the research work of Urban Institute in the United States on Mixed-Income Housing that also assisted us in building our argument. We are also very grateful to Africa Sustainability Infrastructure Mobility (ASIM) project of 2023 and Ardhi University, Dar Es Salaam, Tanzania where one of our colleagues spent time through staff exchange to finally conclude this book. Our sincere hope is that this book will serve these communities and the countries of global south and beyond.

Chapter 1

Introduction and Background

Abstract

The twenty-first century is noted globally as the urban century because more than half of the world's population lives in cities. This population is projected to increase to 70% by 2050. South Africa is no exception to this phenomenal increase in urban population. More than 60% of South African population lives in urban areas, and this figure is projected to increase to 71.3% and 80% by 2030 and 2050, respectively. Access to human settlement by this teaming population remains a challenge. The problem of access to human settlement is compounded by historical apartheid's spatial geography characterized by racial segregation, fragmentation of urban space and separate development. During the apartheid period, settlement patterns were designed and planned in accordance with racial differentiation. This resulted in fragmented, segregated and dysfunctional residential settlements pattern that forced many people to travel long distances between place of work and home. Since 1994, the various housing policies, programmes and legislations have not been able to find solution to the spatial challenges that South Africa faces. The objective of this book is to investigate and unravel mixed-income housing development planning strategy and how this housing typology with a new framework can bring about spatial integration, inclusive cities, improved access to services and the promotion of social cohesion and economic inclusion. This book utilized the case study research design and employed the Delphi method for the investigation. The findings reveal that proper coordination across all sectors of government and good working relationship between the private and public sectors will increase the sustainability of mixed-income housing development. This study also supports existing theory that mixed-income housing might not be able to bring about the overall social integration, and solve all housing problems but has the unique tendency and potential in the South African case to address spatial imbalances by increasing the affordability of low-cost housing. This book concludes that there is need for both inter-sectoral and intergovernmental collaboration as well as proper coordination/adequate urban planning policies to address the

---

Mixed-Income Housing Development Planning Strategies and Frameworks in the Global South, 1–8

Copyright © 2024 George Okechukwu Onatu, Wellington Didibhuku Thwala and Clinton Ohis Aigbavboa

Published under exclusive licence by Emerald Publishing Limited
doi:10.1108/978-1-83753-814-020231001

increasing human settlement challenges in South Africa and for effective implementation of mixed-income housing development.

1.1 Introduction

The intention of this work is to create and establish a mixed-income housing framework. The literature in this field is very less and this is because the isolation of the poor and poverty all put together give rise to other problems. There still remains certain grey areas that has not been fully explored and many open questions still need answers, such as, for example what is the best way and strategy to implement mixed-income housing development, especially in the global south? what other tangible outcomes/results should be expected from the projects and in what ways should the living standard and future housing be improved? In addition, with other scholarly works, Schwartz and Tajbakhsh (1997) notes that very few studies have taken the pain to carry out a detailed evaluation, assessment, processes of the prevailing circumstances of programmes, as well as the projects yet to be implemented. This calls for additional research studies, book of reading and scholarly investigation. In view of the legacy of previous apartheid government of separate development and fragmented city structures in South Africa, which to a large extent, skewed urban planning and housing development. Thus this book aims to contribute to the existing work, body of knowledge and debate. This will lead to adequate and affordable low-cost housing provision in Johannesburg as well as sustainable development.

This book for the first time brings together and synthesize the relevant theories and concepts that guide mixed-income housing development and human settlements in general. This book will provide important resource toolkit as it concludes that there is need for both inter-sectoral and intergovernmental collaboration as well as proper coordination/adequate urban planning to address the human settlement challenges in South Africa and for effective implementation of mixed-income housing development in both developed and developing economies. The use of case studies from the United States, Australia, the Netherlands, Brazil, Nigeria, Botswana and Ghana is noteworthy and serve as an important selling point. This book was able to compare the emerging innovative building approaches, policies and strategies as shared among these countries. This book will be of great relevance and resource material to policymakers, urban planners and practitioners as it contains all the relevant policies, planning framework and legislation that guide human settlements in South Africa and gaps identified. The developed framework establishes the interlink of Town Planning Approvals and Policies, Nearness to Social Services (NSS), Intergovernmental support and collaboration, Access to housing and affordability, Occupants Social Interactions and Community Involvement and Participation in the delivery and implementation of mixed-income housing development. This framework is for the first time developed and validated from very rigorous theoretical and empirical Structural Equation Model (SEM).

1.2 Background and Significance of the Study

Mixed-income housing development if properly implemented will play an important role for access to urban opportunities and decentralization of poverty. Research shows that the high concentration of urban poor households in high-poverty ridden neighbourhoods, rather than in mixed-income neighbourhoods, places additional constrain on economic mobility of the poor households (OECD, 2011:94). For the poor to be concentrated in high-poverty neighbourhoods is noted to lead to and result in joblessness, notwithstanding reliance and relevance of social networks to secure employment. The study is imperative because studies have shown that 'the high level of economic segregation in South African cities not only exposes the poor to finding a way to cope with their own poverty/situation, but also exposes them to lower quality schools, inadequate infrastructure and social networks with high level of unemployment'. The other significance of this study is to prove the point that lack of reliable information and quality data create problem to neighbourhood challenges to increase residential development and living condition in South Africa and other developing countries. Moreover, there still exist gaps in integrated human settlement studies and research of an effective instrumental framework that can be used to describe the focus of this research. Criticism arise on the ground that the current approaches and strategies is being pursued and promoted by various government for the wrong objectives/reasons (DeFillipis and Fraser, 2008). Though it is noted that a number of investigations and neighbourhood revitalization are occurring and taking place or even proposed, but what you still found is that we are only attracted to the ideal situation, basically in theory, but the reality on the ground is depressing. The significance of this book is to address these concerns and to provide empirical answers to the questions as enumerated below. The rationale is also to ascertain what are the aims and objectives behind mixed-income housing approaches and how it intends to try to accomplish noted gaps, especially in South Africa.

Relatively few researchers in the built environment have undertaken a more systematic evaluation of mixed-income housing development in the global south to determine their effectiveness in meeting specific housing and socio-economic development goals, as compared to taking a broad overview of a development. Furthermore, very little work has been done on the question of whether a mixed-income housing approach is necessary and if it is needed to revitalize distressed neighbourhood that encourages people of different social strata to reside together. Questions also abound in the literature as to whether other strategies can as well work better/or achieve the same goal with low-income population, but none has ever attempted to interrogate how it is planned and all the social partners involved in the implementation to accommodate people moving away from informal settlements. Most local authorities are running out of options on what type of housing strategies to adopt to tackle the increasing backlogs and challenges of affordable housing. Developers are not willing to release or accommodate low-income earners on the site earmarked for housing development if there is nothing beneficiary for them. This makes the planning and implementation of mixed-income housing very complicated and complex. Hence, this book provides a toolkit on how to plan and the need for intergovernmental collaboration together with other social partners. Secondly, there has not been any visible housing strategy on record to tackle the racial and segregated history of apartheid approach to urban planning and housing provision in South Africa. Low-income earners are forced to squat in most part of the global south in areas with no amenities and social facilities as well as sustainable infrastructure. This book provides a tool guide on how to go about accommodating people of different race, social profile and income groups in the same settlements for greater good of the new democratic states. For the first time, poverty alleviation strategies and the social ills associated with public housing programmes can now be reviewed with a different lens using mixed-income housing development strategies and an account given of its spillover effects in terms of local economic development (LED) and infrastructural provisions in global south.

1.3 Purpose and Objectives of the Book

A framework for mixed-income housing development that uses the Delphi method is rare and not much work has been done in this regard. Hence, the development of an empirical work on mixed-income housing development framework is needed and should be supported. Below are key objectives of this study that will be pursued:

1. To find out if large-scale urban revitalization can improve the socio-spatial and economic life of the low-income earners,
2. To find out the extent of intergovernmental support and collaboration in mixed-income housing development projects,
3. To study the ideals and significance of a new approach to housing on the ground,
4. Find out whether any lessons can be learnt from the best practices on strategies for mixed-income housing development from international experiences,
5. To find out the manner and ways that communities are developing while they are implementing mixed-income housing development,
6. The linkages between urban land use planning and housing policies in this regard,
7. To also find out why is that mixed-income housing is at times faced with a lot of challenges and difficult to implement and
8. Development of a framework to guide mixed-income housing.

1.4 Research Design and Methodology

In broad terms this can be categorized and separated in groups: One method is aimed at theory (or hypothesis) testing, whereas interpretative methods are aimed at theory building. In this research we focus on positive method. This is because, according to Jacobs and Manzi (2000), there is absence of theory testing in housing research. Hulse and Saugeres (2008), in a similar study in Australia, noted that Housing research in Australia and elsewhere has long been criticized on three related aspects: the strong but often inexplicable influence of positivism on housing research; the lack of explicit theory and failure to connect with theoretical developments in various disciplines; and the uncritical acceptance of constructs, questions and issues framed within housing policy debates. A mixed-income housing development framework is more than overdue as it will assist in guiding the implementation and decisions on human settlement strategies in South Africa and beyond as well as global south. Descriptive survey will be adopted in this research. Hence, Delphi method and Survey method is adopted. The design involves application of structured questionnaire and the utilization of SEM for data analysis. This approach is adopted to seek consensus among the experts on their view about mixed-income housing development.

1.5 Relevance of Work

Contribution into exiting knowledge is to hope for because very few works have attempted to look at the development of a framework. Furthermore, little emphasis is made on how much it costs to implement a given mixed-income housing and the implications thereof as seen in the project and whether it ends up placing additional burden to the communities. There is a need to develop a framework that can explain very well the suppositions, mechanisms, expectations and risks that underlie mixed-income housing development. Furthermore, the conceptual framework that will be developed from this book will add value to the existing debate by evaluating assumptions that is out there. In addition, this study will contribute to the discussion and solution to housing-related problems. While redevelopments of a neighbourhood are noted to create a physical space that can bring people close together, they do not always facilitate social interaction and community cohesion. Furthermore, the research intends to guide local authorities in charge of human settlement development. This book will broaden and expand the present knowledge base of mixed-income housing development projects and provide working guidelines for policy and managerial decision-making in this regard. This book will be of relevance to urban planners, estate agents, developers, housing practitioners, researchers and public servants and municipal officials, as well as all stakeholders working in human settlements space.

1.6 Implication

This book will help policy instruments to target and respond more meaningful to community needs. This book will go a long way also to assist in formulating an appropriate theoretical framework that can be used as a tool to advance knowledge and understanding of mixed-income development and strategies. Another implication of this book is to highlight how complex it is to tackle the spatial segregation and fragmentation of the South African human settlement environment, especially using mixed-income housing strategy. This study also provides useful insight on the need for private sector and public sector to work more closely together as well as other role players since South Africa's housing challenge is multidimensional and multi-complex, especially as it concerns the provision of low-income housing in current global economic challenges/situations.

1.7 Assumptions

The assumptions that guided this study were that participants will answer the survey honestly and that they would return each of the three phases of the questionnaire in a timely manner. It is also assumed that the information collected will be used solely as part of this book and that participants were representative of the opinions of all peers. The panellists are also assumed to have a very good idea about the issues that is investigated and have in depth knowledge of the field (Nworie, 2011:29). It is also expected that contextual issues and related drawbacks will not in any way influence the opinion of the panellists. Also, how reliable panellists will be in reporting back is of much importance (Ibid, 2011). Finally, those participants who chose to respond electronically will read, understand and respond to each phase of the survey that contributed to this book within a specified time frame without delegation of this responsibility to a subordinate.

1.8 Delimitation

The high rate of unemployment, wage differences, extreme poverty and inequality are the features of most cities. In view of this global crisis, most developed nations have adopted a housing typology to accommodate all classes, including the United States, the United Kingdom, Australia and the Netherlands. Similar trend is also emerging from the developing countries, including Brazil, Ghana, Nigeria, Botswana, Kenya and South Africa. This book is limited to South Africa because mixed-income housing development is an emerging issue, but insight will be drawn from the above-mentioned developed and developing countries. Due to time and cost, the sample stratum will be Johannesburg, as this metropolitan city is one of the major urban centres with high level of migration with attendant housing challenges. This region is very significant to this study because of the National Priority Project (NPP) on mixed-income housing projects at Cosmo City. Finally, based on the data collected, this book will develop a framework on mixed-income housing development project with a view of providing a reference empirical work that will guide the development both in South Africa and other places.

1.9 The Chapters Structure and Summary

Chapter 1: Introduction and Background: General background and introduction of the study is highlighted. It shows how significant the research is and the existing gaps in human settlements studies and development.

Chapter 2: Meaning, Goals and Implications of Mixed-Income Housing Development: Here, the various definitions and characteristics that inform and guide mixed-income housing development were explained. The goals and expectations of both government and developers as well as relevant stakeholders were highlighted.

Chapter 3: Mixed-Income Housing Development Research Theories and Concepts: This chapter discusses the relevant theoretical frameworks and the relationship to the study. The meaning of theory and how it illuminates the maturity of a discipline is explained. This chapter will further review the importance of theories in housing research in relation to explaining and predicting behaviour.

Chapter 4: Philosophical Perspectives Guiding Housing Research: The difficulties encountered by researchers are not only inherent from social sciences but also due to the complex nature of the discipline. This chapter will discuss the various philosophical perspectives and approaches that have been used in the study of housing, such as neoclassical, Marxist, socialist and neoliberal views. The differences and similarities in the approaches will be noted. This chapter also delves into the evolution of housing policies.

Chapter 5: Mixed-Income Housing Development in Developed Nations: We shall look at mixed-income housing development in the developed nations by reviewing the experience in these countries. The review will cover and compare the US, the UK, Australia, as well as the Netherlands. The objective is to identify the developed nations' mixed-income housing development strategies and how the policy has evolved over time as well as relevant shift in housing debate in these countries. This is necessary to derive lessons for the South African mixed-income housing approach.

Chapter 6: Mixed-Income Housing Development Model in Developing Nations: In this chapter, we shall look at housing development and policies in Brazil, Nigeria, Botswana and Ghana.

Chapter 7: South African Housing Policy and Legislative Framework: This chapter will review the negotiation process that underpins South African housing policy. It will also review the RDP, the Constitution, Housing Code 2009, Housing Act 1997, Breaking New Ground of 2004, NDP of 2012, SDG 11, SPLUMA 2013 and various legislations/policies that guide housing development over time.

Chapter 8: The Use of Delphi Study in Mixed-Income Housing Development: This chapter will look at the research design and methodology that is used in this book. It reviewed various arguments concerning case study and Delphi method. This chapter explains why Delphi method was chosen and the objective of Delphi Approach. It also highlights the advantages and disadvantages of Delphi as well as essential protocol observed in the compilation. This chapter will play important role in informing the development of the mixed-income housing development project framework model.

Chapter 9: Case Study Area, Cosmo City Johannesburg: This chapter looks at the survey case and response rate, the reliability of the scale and measurement of the validity of the result. This chapter also explains the unit of analysis as Cosmo City and the reason for the choice. This chapter also explains the Confirmatory Factor Analysis and variables. The dimensions, items contained in each of the Cronbach's alpha value were also shown.

Chapter 10: Mixed-Income Housing Development Framework for South Africa and Global South: This chapter presents the Mixed-income Housing Development Framework for South Africa. The compositions and variables include: Nearness to Social Services (NSS), Community Involvement and Participation (CIP), Town Planning Approval and Policies (TPAP), Occupants Social Interactions (OSI), Access to Housing and Affordability (AHA), Intergovernmental Support and Cooperation.

Chapter 11: Outcome of the Mixed-Income Housing Development Framework Findings and Results: This chapter delves into the rounds of Delphi questionnaire and the responses from the experts. The level of consensus and dissensus are also noted and analyzed. Result suggests that affordability and proper monitoring of the development pose a challenge to government. There is also high result for intergovernmental collaboration and relation in the planning and development of mixed-income housing.

Chapter 2

Meaning, Goals and Implications of Mixed-Income Housing Development

2.1 Introduction

Mixed-income housing is increasingly becoming a preferred model among academics, policymakers and practitioners for developing affordable housing. As noted by Galster (2007), there has been a longstanding concern by planners to encourage neighbourhood containing the appropriate 'social mix' and composition of residents. This chapter will provide explanation to the meaning, definitions, issues and concept of mixed-income housing. The examinations of the neighbourhood effects of mixed-income housing developments, low-income housing developments and coordination of neighbourhood populations exist in both sociology and economics literature (Schaeffer, 2007:5). Broadly speaking, economics analysis focuses, to a greater degree, on planning and coordination, whereas sociology addresses issues of socio-economic variables and group pattern identification. Convergence of these literatures is most apparent in urban planning and development, where both areas of social sciences inform public policy (Ibid, 2007). The emphasis here will be based on the convergence of the literature as relatively little research has been conducted to substantiate claims in both literature that mixed-income housing per se leads to positive benefits for low-income families.

2.2 Definitions and Meaning

We need to interrogate properly and understand to a great degree the meaning of mixed-income housing first and foremost in an attempt to review the body of existing knowledge in this field. The term mixed-income housing can refer to many different kinds of housing situations (Schwartz and Tajbakhsh, 1997:73). According to the findings from their research, mixed-income housing development vary in the number of income groups included, the amount of income mixing that occurs and the quality of housing occupied by various income groups. Unlike 'affordable' housing, 'mixed-income' does not carry a formal definition in the housing field (Johnson, 2006:13). Mixed-income housing is a broad term that carries different meaning for different

Mixed-Income Housing Development Planning Strategies and Frameworks in the Global South, 9–24
Copyright © 2024 George Okechukwu Onatu, Wellington Didibhuku Thwala and Clinton Ohis Aigbavboa
Published under exclusive licence by Emerald Publishing Limited
doi:10.1108/978-1-83753-814-020231002

audience (Smith, 2002). Most authors/scholars disagree vehemently in most occasions about the range of incomes, the grain of the mix (e.g. unit-by-unit mix, income-segregated floors within a single building, or income-segregated buildings on a single site) and the demographical make up, tenure mix, unit mix and scale required for a development to be considered 'mixed'. A study by the California Center for Population Research (CCPR, 2009) looked at mixed-income as an imprecise concept as it ranges from planned housing developments where households from diverse income strata live side by side with individual buildings and developments that follow a variety of formulas (for example, one-third low income, one-third mixed, one-third market-rated). According to them mixed-income housing is an extremely complex 'treatment' and any conclusions about its effects must be carefully qualified and analyzed by the larger circumstances under which they may occur. Only in hypothetical environment it is possible to think about the effects of mixed-income housing independently of the processes through which individuals and families come to live in mixed-income communities. The CCPR report concluded by noting that 'in actual urban environment, the success of mixed-income housing-both in its outcome and in the very possibility of establishing and maintaining economically integrated neighborhoods-depends on the social, economically, politically, culturally, and demographically milieu in which income mixing occurs' (CCPR, 2009:9). How individuals and families lived in mixed-income developments and neighborhoods (vs living in economically segregated areas) is the result of their complex motivations, experiences and opportunities. The Millennium, Housing Commission, academic authors and the wide range of practitioners each defined mixed-income housing differently. To some, a truly mixed-income development must include market-rated or close to market-rated units. For others, mixed-income development are exactly what the name implies, a mix of income without strict definition on how high or low the incomes of the residents are. Other scholars have categorized different properties by the nature of the funding that was used to produce the units. Some are based on the characteristics of the tenants, such as employment status and families with children, rather than simply the mix of incomes.

Levy et al. (2010) summed up the debate about the definition by highlighting in one of their research literature that mixed-income can be defined by considering issues that must be addressed in both the development and study of such communities. Issues include the scale and intent of mixed-income housing, the income mix, housing tenure and physical design, project nature and the sustainability of mixed-income housing. Regardless of the definition, mixed-income development varies greatly depending upon the same factors as any other housing development strategy: population served, location, tenure type, management and scale (Smith, 2002:15). This book will dwell more on the explanation provided by Levy et al. in their recent work in 2010.

2.2.1 Scale and Intentions

Mixed-income developments have no single definition in the literature. According to Levy et al. (2010:3), the scholars Varady, Raffel, Sweeney and Denson noted that even in 2005 HUD has yet to define mixed-income internally. However, to them the definition offered by Brophy and Smith captures key elements as previously highlighted by previous research (for example, Joseph et al., 2007). According to them, in their research Brophy and Smith (1997:5) defined mixed-income as:

> Deliberate efforts to construct and/or own a multifamily development that has the mixing of income groups as a fundamental part of its financial and operational plans.
>
> (Brophy and Smith, 1997, cited in Levy et al., 2010:3)

They also noted that Khadduri and Martin in their review of de facto rather than intentional mixed-income, Housing and Urban Development (HUD)-assisted multifamily housing developments (1997:37) refer to it as:

> Mixed-income housing must, at a minimum. Give poor children an opportunity to live close to families that are not dependent on welfare and instead belong to the mainstream working culture. Other motivations may be present and other objectives served, but we do not consider housing to be mixed-income if it serves mainly nonworking elderly or person with disability, or if it excludes the poor.
>
> (Khadduri and Martin, 1997:37, cited in Levy et al., 2010:3)

It is noted that although these definitions have not been featured and used by most other researchers, of interest is that most of the mixed-income researchers do include children in the definition as evidenced by the selection of study sites and discussions of benefits that do or do not accrue to low-income adults and children (Levy et al., 2010). Wilkins (2001 cited in Johnson, 2006:14) require that families with children be part of the mix. Moreover, mixed-income neighbourhood based on the HUD (1996) explanations can be defined by the degree of income diversity that is present in an area or the percentage of the poor households that resides within, regardless of the breadth of income mix (e.g. very low-income, low-income, moderate-income, high-moderate and very high-income) (Levy et al., 2010). Smith (2002) suggest considering projects along a scale of close to or farther away from purely market-rate units. His typology includes five categories, namely: (1) 'moderate-income inclusion' or projects that are predominantly market-rate but include some units for moderate-income households; (2) low-income inclusion', which are predominantly market-rate projects that include some units for low-income households; (3) broad range of incomes', which are projects that serve market-rate, moderate or low-income and very low-income households; (4) market-rate inclusion', which are developments that are predominantly low-income but include some market-rate units; and (5) 'affordable mix', which are development that are only mixed at the lower end of the income spectrum, including only moderate or low-income households and very low-income households. Galster et al. (2008) cited in Levy et al. (2010) characterized areas to be a mixed-income in terms of four degree of income diversity (high diversity, moderate diversity, low diversity and not diverse).

2.2.2 Income Structures, Tenure and Design

There is no general agreement or consensus among researchers on the optimal degree of income diversity, income tiers, tenure mix (rental or owner-occupier units) or development design (Levy et al., 2010:4). Sometimes decisions are made purely based on a mix of policy interests, financing streams and construction schedules. Researchers have discussed factors that ought to be taken into serious consideration when decisions related into income are made and this includes: 'Range of incomes and degree of income diversity among residents' (Ibid). Depending on the development, relatively higher income households have been defined as those earning anywhere from 51% to 200% of AMI. A development might have two income tiers or three or more. The percentage of units targeted to low-income families also ranges from a small percentage of all units to more than half (Brophy and Smith, 1997; Khadduri and Martin, 1997; Schwartz and Tajbakhsh, 1997 cited in Levy et al., 2010:4). On the other hand, the degree of income mix can affect residents' ability to bridge differences. Vale (2006) in a review of Hope VI argues that if gaps in income among residents are too great, it is unlikely that residents will be able to bridge their differences, especially in places with language diversity and any racial tensions. This point is also supported by Joseph (2006) who argues that in order to achieve stability, it is likely important to include a middle-income tier between the poorest and wealthiest residents. Subsequent research by Joseph et al. (2007 cited in Levy et al., 2010) noted the importance of income strata and the value of having an even mix of low-income, moderate-income and high-income households because people are more likely to mix socially with relative socio-economic peers. Decisions have also been based on 'goals and on an understanding of the mechanisms by which neighborhoods can effects residents' outcomes'. Galstar (2007 cited in Levy et al., 2010:5) rejects the idea of one optimal mix. He broadens the discussion of possible benefits derived from living in mixed-income communities by shifting to a consideration of mechanisms of influence. He focused on internal and external social interactions. The conclusion of the study is very valuable in the literature as it narrows down how the residents can be influenced either positively or negatively by the social dynamics in a neighbourhood or development.

The strength of the market and the economic conditions prevailing is also very crucial in explaining a mixed-income housing development. Brophy and Smith (1997) cited in Levy et al. (2010) noted the specific mix of income within any particular development should take into consideration market conditions. Stronger markets can support a wider mix of incomes rather than a weaker market. Specific design element and layout of the plan, e.g. designing units to be indistinguishable or by income tiers as well as placing units within developments in ways to integrate or segregate residents by income is another feature of mixed-income housing development. Briggs (1997, 2005 cited in Levy et al., 2010) discussed the theory of physical determinism which posits that the design elements can influence social interactions among diverse people. Design elements that enhance residents' interactions include, common areas with places to sit and narrow hallways as well as children play areas. Brophy and Smith (1997) cited in Levy et al. (2010) used the term 'seamless integration' to describe housing developments designed to make subsidized units indistinguishable from market-rate units. They argue that this homogenized a development and contributes to making residents to feel equal with one another.

2.2.3 Project and Neighbourhood

Mixed-income housing has been sponsored by public, non-profit and for-profit organizations and can include homeowners as well as renters (Schwartz and Tajbakhsh, 1997:73). According to these scholars any assessment of mixed-income housing must consider the variety of forms it can assume. Most mixed-income housing falls into four broad categories. First, some state and local governments foster mixed-income housing through density bonuses, inclusionary zoning ordinances and other land-use regulations that encourages developers to reserve a portion of the total amount of new housing (usually 20%) for low- and moderate-income housing. Secondly, public housing authorities have recently experimented with mixed-income housing. For example, the Hope VI, the Federal programme for the physical and social revitalization of distressed public housing, was aimed at promoting mixed-income housing. Thirdly, some State and local housing programmes require mixed-income occupancy as a condition for funding proposed developments. Finally, not all mixed-income housing originates with government programmes designed to encourage this type of housing; some results from the independent efforts of individuals and agencies. Rosenbaum et al. (1996) provide the most in-depth study to date of a mixed-income housing development – Lake Parc Place in Chicago – which happens to be one of the best known. In their conclusion, they noted that the success of the project is principally its ability to attract moderate-income working households and that after several years in operation it is considered safe and without serious management difficulties.

2.2.4 Sustainability of the Project

Fraser and Kick (2007) in their comparative study of two mixed-income developments argue that for mixed-income housing to be successful in attracting a range of residents and achieving benefits for low-income families, four key groups of stakeholders need to develop share goals and to build capacity across their groups. Fraser and Kick identify key stakeholders as investors, local government staff, non-profit staff and community residents. Vale (2006) also noted that establishing a mix of incomes among residents early on in the life of a development is insufficient to the longer term sustainability of income diversity. The mix needs to be 'monitored and managed for decades'. Quality schools can be a factor in the retention of higher income families. Khadduri and Martin (1997) observed that it is difficult to attract and keep relatively higher income households with children to mixed-income developments. They stated that a good school system can help retain families that have housing options.

Overall, the definition of 'mix' in studies and in developments is individually determined and operationalized (Johnson, 2006:17). The composition which results is due to a wide range of factors including the local housing market, the availability or requirements of financing programs and legislative efforts and the goals of the developer, whether public or private. The complexities and wide variety of developments can pose a serious challenge in the definition and evaluation of any given mixed-income housing.

In this book, no rigid strict definition of mixed-income has been adopted but the emphasis is on the need to include the poorest of the poor, low-income residents, medium income and high-income residents for a truly mixed-income housing.

2.3 The History of Mixed-Income Housing Policy

The promotion of safe and adequate housing has persisted since the late 1800s in the United States, when the early interventions focused on tenement reforms. The federal government did not enter into housing question until 1937 when Congress passed the Wegner – Steagall Housing Act, which launched the federal public housing programme that still exists till today (Ellickson, 2010). This Act is formally known as 'United States Housing Act of 1937' which provided for subsidies to be paid from the government to local public housing agencies (LHA) to improve living conditions of low-income families. The act created the United States Housing Authority within the United States Department of Interior and built on the National Housing Act of 1934 (Ibid, 2010). With so many reforms and re-organization, the act was later transformed to United States Department of Housing and Urban Development (HUD). The HUD manages *Section 8 of the Housing Act of 1937*, often simply known as section 8 with several amendments. It authorizes the payment of rental housing assistance to private landlords on behalf of approximately 3.1 million low-income households in the United States. Tenants pay about 30% of their income for rent, while the rest of the rent is paid by federal government. The largest part of the section is the *Housing Choice Voucher* which pays and provides 'tenants-based' rental assistance, so a tenant can move from one unit of at least minimum housing quality to another or to apply their monthly vouchers towards purchase of a home (HUD, 2006). Historically, public housing as described sought to achieve the goals that efforts of mixed-income housing developments seek today, including mixing diverse residents, improve neighbourhood services and creating a ladder out of public housing (Vale, 2006).

The desire for neighbourhood to be more 'mixed' or 'balanced' is not new. It can be traced back at least as far as the nineteenth-century designers and visionaries who gave rise to the Garden City Movement and, ultimately, to Town and Country Planning (Chesire, 2007:7). One of the first development reflecting this new impulse was Bradford Park, in Chiswick, in Western London, which began with the construction of the District Line of the Underground in 1871 (Ibid, 2007). It was designed to provide a community within easy reach of London and as a home for liberal professionals and artists, with cottages as well as substantial middle-class homes, in order to ensure 'social balance'. Homestead Garden Suburb, started in 1910 by two disciples of Ebenezer Howard, was intended to be a 'balanced community' (Chesire, 2007). Mixed-income housing started to emerge in the mid-1960s and 1970s with some federal programs and when local authorities initiated inclusionary zoning (Ellickson, 2010:992). In 1983, the New Jersey State Supreme Court determined that inclusion of affordable housing would satisfy a municipality's state constitutional obligation to house the poor, and then in 1986, US Congress authorized the Low-Income Tax Credit (LITC) programme, which provided a tax credit to private developers who included affordable housing in their developments. Mixed-income housing became a popular policy strategy in the 1980s and 1990s in an effort to de-concentrate poverty and redevelop urban neighborhoods (Ibid, 2010). Wilson (1987) identified a problem of social exclusion, with significant harmful effects associated with living in neighbourhoods in which poverty was concentrated. This was part of the argument for ODPM (2005) that:

> People living in deprived neighbourhoods are less likely to work, more likely to be poor and have lower life expectancy, more likely to live in poorer housing in unattractive local environments with high levels of antisocial behaviours and lawlessness and more likely to receive poorer education and health services. Living in deprived area adversely affects individuals' life chances over and above what would be predicted by their personal circumstances and characteristics.
>
> (ODPM, 2005:6)

The 1992 Hope VI programme emerged as the pinnacle of this interest and to address the above concerns. In the next sections we shall discuss the goals of this housing typology.

2.4 The Goal and Implication of Mixed-Income Housing

Relatively few researchers have undertaken a more systematic evaluation of mixed-income developments to determine their effectiveness in meeting specific goals, rather than taking a broad overview of a development. Furthermore, very little work has been done on the question of whether a mixed-income approach is necessary (Bratt cited in Smith, 2002; Levy et al., 2010). Question abounds in the literature as to whether other strategies can as well achieve the same goal with an all-low-income population? The goal of this section is to synthesize some of the insight into both the effectiveness and necessity of mixed-income approach as this is normally underevaluated in most policy research.

2.4.1 Goal 1: Improvement in Social Network and Avoiding Negative Behaviour

One of the principal and disturbing characteristics of the high-poverty neighbourhood or housing development is the incidence of negative social behaviour, such as violent crime or drug use and gang activities. In *The* Truly *Disadvantaged* (1987), William Julius Wilson presented his highly influential description and analysis of a new urban poverty, which was characterized by the geographical concentration in certain neighbourhood of high rate of joblessness and welfare dependency; high proportions of female-headed households, out of wedlock birth and teen pregnancy; and high level of social disorganization, violence and crime. Wilson's work, and that of other scholars, formed the basis for a new view of urban poverty that helped to explain the growth in high poverty neighborhoods between 1970 and 1990 resulting in an 'underclass' culture (Crane, 1991; Jargowsky and Bane, 1991; Massey and Denton, 1993; Richetts and Sawhill, 1988; Spencer, 1993; Tienda and Stier, 1991; Wilson, 1987).

Joseph et al. (2007) identified four ways in which mixed-income environment are thought to improve the socio-economic positions of poor people locked in these neighbourhood through improved social network: whereby poor people expand their job-search and acquisition networks; improve social control, where the presence of higher income people leads to higher levels of accountability to establish norms and rules followed by increased order and safety; promote behaviour effects, in which higher income residents model alternate lifestyle and norms, which in turn promote behavioural change and increased self-efficacy among low-income residents; and promote political economy of space, in which the presence of higher income residents will create new market demands and effective political pressure that will lead to higher quality goods and services for all residents. Smith (2002:22) noted that for low-income Americans, overcoming the barriers of a limited education, low-performing local schools for one's children, a lack of employment opportunities and racism present a significant challenge by any standard. Mixed-income housing is seen to offer a solution to reducing these negative behaviours because the higher income households will not tolerate crime or drug trafficking in their housing development. The argument is that higher income households will either place more pressure on management or police to address the problem, will refuse to live in the development (thereby posing de facto pressure on management) or will confront tenants engaged in negative behaviours.

2.4.2 Goal 2: Addressing the Shortage of Affordable Housing

The provision of affordable housing has been a persistent problem in American housing market and even other parts of Global South over the years. The market place if left alone cannot meet and satisfy all the demand for housing that is affordable to low-income and moderate-income households (Johnson, 2006:19). The federal government does provide direct housing assistance to about 5 million households, but only one in three are eligible to receive it (Smith, 2002:12 cited in Johnson, 2006:19). One reason for this is (Not in My Backyard) NIMBY attitude towards subsidized housing in many communities across the country. As Smith (2002) (cited in Johnson, 2006:19) puts it 'being poor is a proxy for being minority and vice versa, and being either is a proxy for not wanting them in your neighbourhood'. Affluent neighborhoods are resistant to affordable housing due to fears of crime and damage to property values, while lower income neighborhoods argue that they already have more than their fair share of affordable housing and are resistant to the construction of additional units. Consequently, affordable housing is politically unpopular among a variety of constituencies at every level of government. Housing subsidies are very expensive for government, and when combined with political battles over where to locate the needed housing units, affordable housing often becomes a political casualty (Johnson, 2006). Mixed-income housing can provide both direct and indirect responses to some of these challenges of providing affordable housing. Mixed-income development can also contribute indirectly to an overall increase in the availability of affordable housing by generating high-quality housing to win neighbourhood approval, overcoming political barriers, and providing incentives for developers to include affordable units. URI (2003:14) concluded in one of their studies that 'the market place needs help to supply enough housing, especially for working families; mixed-income developments can alleviate that need, providing housing that is safe, livable, and close to employment centers'.

2.4.3 Goal 3: To Mitigate Property Value and Community Concerns

Mixed-income housing developments if not properly monitored and implemented can face enormous challenge from NIMBY neighbours protesting – 'Not In My Back Yard' because of concerns about the perceived fiscal, social and environmental impacts of affordable housing units (Urban Land Institute, 2003). Smith (2002) (cited in Johnson, 2006:20) also noted that 'investment of time, a commitment to quality, and outreach to build community support, it is difficult [for developers] to overcome deep-rooted fears about the effects of low-income housing and its residents'. Subsidized – especially 'public housing' has a reputation for being very poor quality. While this is certainly true of some projects, this perception is largely a stereotype (Johnson, 2006:20). Study carried out from 1998 to 1999 by HUD survey of subsidized units (both publicly and privately owned) revealed that 82% of inspected units were in good or excellent condition. Though some units are stigmatized because they have the appearance of 'projects' or simply do not look like the rest of the surrounding neighbours, for instance, in low-income areas, residents feel burden with the feeling of cheap, low-priced housing. Whereas, in high-income areas, people have the fear that subsidized housing units will cause a major decline in the value of their property (Johnson, 2006). Mixed-income – as opposed to purely subsidized low-income housing units can allay this community fear. According to Urban Land Institute (2003) in a study in San Francisco of 3,000 sales of low-cost, for sale home built by the BRIDGE Housing Corporation, an affordable housing development company in the Bay Area, showed no decline in the values of property nearby over a 4-year period. They concluded by noting that new affordable housing can improve neighbourhood stability and appeal, and in so doing, can actually boost nearby property values. Mixing more affordable housing types with high-end residential development also can generate concerns about property values, such as the perception that multifamily housing will have negative effects on the property value of neighbouring single-family homes. They concluded by noting that there is no evidence that multifamily communities have led to a devaluation of single-family home nearby. This conclusion is also supported by American Housing Survey that showed no evident difference in the appreciation of value of single-family homes located near apartments or condominium and that are not (ULI, 2003:18). Similar study conducted in the Twin Cities, Minneapolis by Maxfield Research also examined how affordable rental tax-credit developments affected adjacent property values (Ibid, 2003:19). The research concluded that: 'there is little or no evidence to support the claim that the tax-credit family rental developments in the study eroded surrounding home values but rather the markets surrounding the tax-credit developments became stronger as a group compared with the Twin Cities overall.' This point is also supported by Smith (2002:34) who noted that 'including a mix of incomes appears to be an effective strategy in overcoming community objections to affordable housing, and may be a necessary strategy in many communities. However, it may result in fewer needy families being served in the most desirable developments or locations.'

2.4.4 Goal 4: Developing High-Quality Housing

There is a saying that when people think of affordable housing, they may imagine the drab, monolithic, concrete high rise that characterize some of the most visible public housing projects of the mid-twentieth century (URI, 2003). The reality today is different because most designs of today's affordable housing – housing that meets the users' needs is responsive to its contents, enhances its neighbourhood and is built to last and widely accepted by the benefiting communities. For mixed-income developments, good residential design is often a competitive selling point to attract market-rate residents. Developers are now competing among themselves to improve the quality of the units due to increasing awareness of the previous stigma attached to low-income housing development. Smith (2002:28) noted that 'Painfully aware that the image of troubled public-housing projects is linked to low-income housing, many affordable housing developers and designers have focused on building their housing to a very high standard'. Based on his personal interview with developers it emerged that: 'Good design can alleviate any stigma associated with low-income housing'. This is also necessitated by the market pressure to serve higher income population and hence compel developers of mixed-income housing to ensure high standard of the end product. Concerned about social problems and associated poor quality accompanying most low-income housing, developers are now forced to design developments that meet a high standard and can last the test of time without traceable negative visual effect to surrounding neighborhoods. Mixed-income housing and good design are a winning combination that has demonstrated the capacity to encourage faster project approvals, attract the support of future residents and overcome the fears of neighbours who are uncertain about the prospects of affordable housing next door (URI, 2003:12). The growing awareness of the popularity of the new urbanism since the early 1990s also has influenced the design of affordable and mixed-income housing. Smith (2002:28) highlighted this by noting that 'while a mixed-income approach may be effective in building high-quality housing, community pressures may be as important as market pressures in holding the housing to a high development standard, including extra amenities such as pools or fitness centers'.

2.4.5 Goal 5: Addressing Negative Social Behaviours

One of the most disturbing and reoccurring phenomenon associated with high-poverty neighbourhood or housing developments is the incidence of negative social behaviours and associated violence, crime and grime. Mixed-income housing according to Smith (2002) is offered as a solution to reducing these negative behaviours because the higher income households will not tolerate crime or drug trafficking in their housing development. The theory is that higher income households will either place more pressure on management or police to address the problems or will refuse to live in the development (thereby imposing de facto pressure on management), or will confront tenants engaged in negative behaviours. Rosenbaum et al. (1998) in their study of Lake Parc Place in Chicago reported that the higher income tenants were more likely than the public housing tenants to support all of management's rules and evidence also show significant reduction in crime rate. In the same vein, studies have also shown that mixed-income housing development may have unanticipated and negative consequences. As mixed-income redevelopment lowers crime in one area it may shift it to other area, either through the movement of people or the movement of drug or gang-related activity (Halasz, 2008, cited in CCPR, 2009:41). With respect to management and attempt to ensure proper behaviours, developers have resorted to 'strict screening of prospective applicants'. According to Smith (2002) in reviewing the criteria for Hope VI 'residents must be in good standing and pass credit checks'. While the practice of strict screening and management appears to be effective in reducing negative behaviours in a property, it is also likely to serve those who would have the best chance of attaining housing, albeit at higher prices. In addition to reducing negative behaviours, mixed-income housing is intended to encourage positive, upward mobile behaviours. This positive behaviour together with new outlook to life occurs for low-income families through both observation of and interaction with higher income families. Contrary to this assertion, CCPR (2009:14) noted in one of its research projects that 'the higher proportion of poor families in mixed-income housing may have both positive and negative effects on both poor families and their non-poor neighbors'. While the negative effects and limited opportunities that accompany large concentration of poverty are clear, the method and approach to be adopted in transferring positive influence, as well as the type of influence, from higher income to lower income families within housing development is very contentious. Some scholars consider the possibility of role-modelling, creation of job networks and social capital with the hope that 'higher-income households within the residential environment will influence the goals, perception and opportunities of low-income households towards greater labor market participation and mainstream behavior' (Smith, 2002:23). Although mixed-income housing may be a means of improving the quality of life and perhaps even social mobility of poor families as highlighted above, it may nonetheless have negative effects on families as well. Poor families may encounter such challenges as increase stigma and both formal and informal monitoring, a sense of relative deprivation and a loss of local power and influence (Briggs, 1997; Patillo, 2007).

2.4.6 Goal 6: Attracting Political Support for Affordable Housing

Mixed-income housing development is considered an effective instrument to build and strengthen political constituency for affordable housing. The high quality of mixed-income housing development may help to create more favourable impression of affordable housing (Smith, 2002). This could result in more funding for affordable housing and more willingness among communities to allow affordable housing to be built in their areas. Johnson (2006:22) argue that rather than appearing to be a waste of taxpayers' money, good quality mixed-income housing both aids needy households and may be perceived as a community asset. Well located mixed-income projects can help to raise standard for good design of affordable housing generally (Urban Land Institute, 2003). Simply stated tax-payers and politicians or policymakers are more likely to support housing when a significant number of its residents are people who 'work hard and play by the rules' (Wilkins, 2001:3 cited in Johnson, 2006:22). It is also highly debated in the literature that mixed-income housing is an essential tool that can aid in attracting broad political support for affordable housing. Ensuring a good support base for affordable housing requires expanding the political constituency for housing assistance to include working-class and middle-class households (Ibid, 23). As Vale (1998:754) puts it that 'only by reconceptualising as a seamless integrated part of more economically diverse communities will public housing be able to attract further and broader funding'. This scholar ended up noting that 'income mixing may be the only political necessity to save public housing' (Ibid, 756).

2.4.7 Goal 7: Providing Economic Advantage

Apart from being considered a political effort towards the provision of affordable housing, mixed-income housing may be an economically attractive housing solution as well. According to Joseph and Feldman (2009) mixed-income can be a way to leverage private sector resources when creatively financed through government incentive programs. Developers may find that offering a wider variety of housing products at a range of price points can reduce the overall risk of the project and help increase absorption rates by widening the scope of the target market. Density bonus as offered to a private developer in US can enable the provision of affordable units in their project (Ibid, 2009). This point is also noted by Khadduri and Martin (1997) together with Schwartz and Tajbakhsh (1997) that rent collected from market-rate units can provide part of the subsidy needed in the lower income units, reducing the financial input required from the government. In areas with tight, competitive housing markets and high market rent (such as Boston or San Francisco), cross-subsidy is theoretically possible (Brophy and Smith, 1997). Cross-subsidization is more feasible for non-profit developers who have a small profit threshold than for-profit developers. In other words, most developers claim that mixed-income projects are more cost-effective than all subsidized developments because higher income households are less expensive to serve. The cost of the extra amenities demanded by high-income households, as well as the additional market expenses, can make mixed projects actually more expensive than all-subsidized developments (Smith, 2002). It is also argued that developers value more the low turnover and the guaranteed rent provided by subsidy programs.

2.5 The Challenge and Implication of Mixed-Income Housing Development

Scholars have come out strongly to challenge the potential benefits of mixed-income housing developments (DeFelippis and Fraser, 2008; Schwartz and Tajbakhsh, 1997; Smith, 2002; Wyly and Hammel, 1999). In an extensive evaluation of these policy document, DeFelippis and Fraser (Ibid, 9) noted that one of the central issues is that these programmes do not produce their hypothesized results and there is a little evidence that the expected benefits will be realized. They concluded by noting that 'poor people do not seem to benefit much from 'Mixed-income housing neighborhoods (MIHN)'. The failure of mixed-income housing neighborhoods is noted too often, it 'leave poor people in places without the social networks and informal social support of prior neighborhoods'. Despite assumptions to the contrary, poor urban neighborhoods have dense networks of social support that have been created largely out of necessity because services that are commodities in wealthy neighborhoods (childcare, for instance) must be negotiated as non-commodified when the participants do not have money. Empirical studies have found out that relocated public housing residents have a difficult time rebuilding social networks (Clampet-Lundquist, 2004), leading to higher degree of social isolation for children as well as adults in many situations (Curley, 2005; Gibson, 2007; Goetz, 2003). Moving the low-income people into mixed-income residential neighbourhood also leaves the poor without acceptable institutional services and capacity to support their prior neighborhoods, and puts them in new places within a precarious situation. Mixed-income policies have also failed to create social mixing, networks and interaction – that is, social capital (DeFelippis and Fraser, 2008). In a review of HOPE VI, they noted that the development based on an organizational framework sort people based upon subsidies versus market-rate status. There have been many documented cases where impoverished public housing residents have been excluded from having any real power in the decision-making process (Elliot et al., 2004; Smith, 2000). Instead, city power brokers have been largely in control of the HOPE VI redevelopment process (Bayor, 2003; Keiting, 2000). Greater resident participation requirements might be a step towards improving mixed-income development projects as this relates to residents' hopes and goals. While conceptually the mixed-income housing redevelopment is purported to promote both positive neighbourhood change and opportunities for low-income households, thus serving both people and place-based objectives, some urban scholars have noted that the 'benefits of HOPE VI [mixed-income] have chiefly been placed-based: reclaiming particular neighborhoods, reducing criminal activities in those areas and significantly upgrading the physical environment'. In many cases, this redevelopment has spawned of facilitated gentrifications (Goetz, 2005).

2.6 Gentrification

An important fact that is widely considered in the literature that is related to the economic impact of mixed-income housing development is Gentrification. Gentrification according to Joseph and Feldman (2009:29) is composed of two related processes: 'class-based colonization of the lower-priced residential neighbourhoods and reinvestment in the physical housing stock'. According to Merriam Webster Dictionary, Gentrification is the 'process of renewal and rebuilding accompanying the influx of middle-class or affluent people into deteriorating areas that often displaces poorer residents' The term was first used in 1964, by Ruth Glass to describe a working-class London neighbourhood. It is also recognized by Chicago School as an aspect of middle-class succession and suburbanization or a new form of neo-liberal urban policy (Burgess, 1925; Newman and Ashton, 2004). Gentrification is also loosely used as a term to describe the arrival of wealthier people in an existing urban district, a related increase in rents and property values, and changes in the district character and culture. The term is also used negatively to explain the displacement of poor communities by rich outsiders. The fact is that it does exist and continue to cause major changes to the physical and social landscape of the urban areas (Joseph and Feldman, 2009). The effects of gentrification are complex and contradictorily it is argued by some scholars. This has led to long-standing and overlapping debates over the appropriate definition of the phenomenon, its causes and whether it is positive or negative for cities. Initially confined to western cities, gentrification has now spread globally. Rérat et al. (2010) provided an academic explanation of gentrification as 'the movement of relatively wealthy in-migrants (gentrifiers) and lower income out-migrants (displacees or evicted population) in urban neighbourhoods'. These migratory flows is as a result of the outcome of public policies and/or the strategies of private actors in the housing market as well as the result of changing residential aspiration of affluent households.

2.7 Problems Raised in Mixed-Income Study

The first problem encountered in the study of mixed-income housing development is the variation of opinion in the definition of mixed-income housing. Scholars as shown in Section 2.2 hold different opinions with respect to the definition. However, like any other real estate development, Smith (2002:15) noted that the market determines to a great extent what mix of incomes is possible. A mixed-income development located in a very soft market will have a difficult time renting market units to high-income households. Furthermore, it is crucial to point out that not every mixed-income development or funding programme places the same priority on the various goals as highlighted above. Some may place top priority on building units with a low amount of subsidy, while others are most concerned with providing greater life chances for their low-income residents. The priority given to different goals also helps to shape the mix of incomes in the development. Thus, a combination of the market and the priority given to the goals results in the mix of incomes served. The second problem as noted in the literature is that of how to manage the informal social network built over the years and enjoyed by low-income residents in their prior neighbourhood before moving to the new mixed-income housing development. This is worthy to be considered by policymakers and researchers as moving the low-income households into mixed residential neighbourhood with all its good intentions and objectives might put them in a precarious situation without this social network which they do not pay for but enjoy freely by mutual sharing and support. The third issue that is noted as part of the problem associated with mixed-income housing development is that of political support and for it to serve as an asset to the community. This is relevant and will be interrogated further in this research as the determination of the scale of the development, composition, location, tenure types and funding mechanisms are all politically influenced and motivated. Very few studies engage strongly on this debate and this will be looked into in the case study areas covered in this research. The final problem associated with mixed-income research is on the acceptability of the affordable housing units provided. Most development are hindered on the question of the ratio of the subsidized components of the housing provision and the location. This issue as highlighted in the literature is very relevant to this study and will be investigated further.

2.8 Conclusion

In this chapter, the assumptions and guiding principles characterizing mixed-income housing development is highlighted. Important points noted in this chapter, includes the failures and success of mixed-income housing development in various countries and the inherent lessons thereof. The goal of mixed-income housing development as it relates to affordable housing, social network, increase opportunities and favourable political support for its development are also noted. Also noted in this chapter is the attempt to use mixed-income housing development to address social and economic characteristic facing neighbourhood with high concentration of low-income households. It is also highlighted that the mechanism to manage the informal social network built over the years and enjoyed by low-income residents in their prior neighbourhood before moving to the new mixed-income housing development might pose a serious challenge. Policymakers and researchers are cautioned based on the literature review that moving the low-income households into mixed residential neighbourhood for whatever motives and objectives might put them if proper measure is not taken in a precarious situation without this social network which they do not pay for but enjoy freely by mutual consent. The issue of NIMBY factors and the need for improved good design and high-quality housing as 'competitive selling point' is also cautioned as an approach to be explored. This chapter concludes with the point that priority should be given to different goals to shape the mix of incomes in the development. Thus, a combination of the market requirements and the priority given to the goals results in the mix of incomes served.

Chapter 3

Mixed-Income Housing Development Research Theories and Concepts

3.1 Introduction

This section explores the relevant theoretical framework that informs this book. A theoretical framework is relevant to any research endeavour because it has the ability to (a) focus a study, (b) reveal and conceal meaning and understanding, (c) situate the research in a scholarly conversation and provide a vernacular and (d) reveal its strengths and weaknesses. In this chapter, it is imperative for us to look at the main theoretical framework that informs this book. We shall also consider the implication of this debate for planning and for the management of urban change. The most important theories influencing public housing policies and ultimately contemporary urban renewal, including mixed-income housing trends, are categorized into four subheadings: physical determinism, cycles of disadvantages, concentrated poverty and social inclusion/exclusion (Walker et al., 2003:3). Before we discuss each of the theories, it is necessary to interrogate the need for theories in housing research.

3.2 Theory and Its Importance in Housing Research

The term 'theory' is used in a variety of different ways, but its most common meaning is as an explanation of observed regularities (Nueman, 2006:21). Theories are also seen as sets of systematically interrelated constructs and propositions intended to explain and predict a phenomenon or behaviour of interest, within certain boundary conditions and assumptions (Bhattacherjee, 2012:14). Characterizing the nature of the link between theory and research is by no means a straightforward matter. Theory is important to the social researcher because it provides a backcloth and rationale for the research that is being conducted. It also provides a framework within which social phenomenon can be understood and the research findings can be interpreted. Before we can discuss the use of theory in this book, we must understand what 'theory' is. The word comes from the Greek root '*theos*, to see, implying the ability to look within oneself as well as without' (Malnar and Vodvarka, 1992:7). Theory as will be used in this research seeks to describe, explain, or predict observable

Mixed-Income Housing Development Planning Strategies and Frameworks in the Global South, 25–40
Copyright © 2024 George Okechukwu Onatu, Wellington Didibhuku Thwala and Clinton Ohis Aigbavboa
Published under exclusive licence by Emerald Publishing Limited
doi:10.1108/978-1-83753-814-020231003

facts and events. This is in line with the general agreement by researchers that a complete theory must define *what* (variables), *how* (relationship), *why* (underlying dynamics that provide rationale) and *who-when-where* (conditions that set the boundaries of the theory) (Whetten, 1989 cited in Steggell et al., 2001:89). Theory plays an essential role in research, and its use may be an indicator of the maturity of a discipline. This argument is supported further by Steggell et al. (2006:5) who noted in a review and analysis of the use of explicit theory in housing research as published by *Housing and Society* from 1974 to 2003 that 'quantifying the use of theory in housing research may provide indicators of the state of the discipline'. They concluded by noting that vast majority of housing research acknowledge explicit theory or theories, but that few used the theories to directly design the study or to interpret findings. Moreover, there is general agreement in the literature by scholars that the use theory is essential to systematically organize and synthesize information, discover relationships among variables and guide the discovery of new facts to move research forward (Creswell, 2003; Touliatos and Compton, 1988). Without theory-based research, it is argued that a discipline chaotically moves in all directions with lack of purpose (Mitchell and Jolley, 1992). The relationship of theory to research methods has been linked to a road map to driving. Without it, all roads look the same; you can never tell for sure where you are, you waste a lot of time making wrong turns and getting lost and when you get where you are going, you may not know it (Guy et al., 1987:64). In this study, theories are also used because according to Touliato and Campton (Ibid:12), both concluded that 'the maturity of an academic discipline is generally gauged by the extent to which it has developed a solid foundation for the construction of theories'. This follows the caution provided later by Steggell et al. (2006:5) that 'theory is present in all research, even if a recognized theory has not been named'. Hence, housing research has a need for theory as used in this study due to 'too much information and numerous disconnected pieces of empirical research which, in effect, become counter-productive' if not properly organized (ibid:19). Theory, therefore, is noted to allow us to 'explain and predict behaviors, it also dictates which and whose behaviours are worthy of study and which should be excluded from study' (Lennon and Burns, 2000:221).

3.3 The Physical Determinism

3.3.1 The Right to the City Model

In 1967, the French philosopher and sociologist Henry Lefebvre wrote 'La Droit a la Ville', or 'the Right to the City', a passionate plea for a new and radical kind of urban politics (Boer and Vries, 2009:1321). Lefebvre states that the right to the city can only be conceived as a 'transformed and renewed right to urban life' (Lefebvre, 1967:132 cited in Ibid:1321) and explains the concepts by discussing different aspects of this right. A central theme in his work is the perception of the city as a collective artwork of all inhabitants and users of a city. They can contribute to the collective shaping of the future of urban space and by inhabiting their urban environment actively, for example by participating in the public life of their community by the appropriation of both time and space of their city. The emphasis on the appropriation is based on

Levebvre's opinion that everybody has the inalienable right to use all spaces of the city in order to provide themselves with the necessities of daily life. According to him, the appropriation of space is more important than the domination of those who own space. Therefore, the use value of space has the priority above the economic value, which means that the social function of space is always more important than the profit that can be made by its exploitation or selling (Levebvre, 1967 cited in Boer and Vries, 2009). These rights to the city need to be fought for even if it requires confrontation. In recent times, the right to the city has been interpreted to mean 'to radically rethink the social relations of capitalism, the spatial structure of the city and the assumptions of liberal democracy' (Purcell, 2008:92). According to this scholar, two concepts are central to the right to the city: participation and appropriation. Harvey (2003:393) adds to the debate by pointing out that it is our fundamental human right to take control of urbanization and urban transformation and 'to change the city after our hearts desire'. Both Harvey and Dikec emphasize that the right to the city does not belong to a single individual but should be perceived as a certain relationship between an individual and the rest of the society. It is an 'enabling right' that offers all inhabitants of a city the possibility to participate in public life, which is much more than the well-known participatory planning. It leads to a city as a political collectivity, where the public welfares are permanently redefined and realized through political struggle (Dikec, 2001; Harvey, 2008). Both the most radical and more reformist interpretation of the right to the city can be very broad with respect to the scope of their analysis or proposed solutions. The reformist agenda on this usually contain extensive lists of rights that should be included in the city, such as access to housing, access to education and the job market. Likewise, certain public spaces, such as political spaces, are also crucial: parliament, the executive power, state agencies, etc. The right to the city is, therefore, far more than a right of individual access to the resources that the city embodies: it is a right to change ourselves by changing the city more after our heart's desire. It is, moreover, a collective rather than an individual right since changing the city inevitably depends upon the exercise of a collective power over the processes of urbanization. Lefebvre, Harvey, Purcell, Dikec and others in their opinion advocate different roads to establishing full participation of inhabitants and users of the city. The right to the city provides a terrain for the assertion and exercise of these rights:

> The right to the city, complemented by the right to differences and the right to information, should modify, concretize and make more practical the rights of the citizen as an urban citizen (citadin) and user of multiple services. It would affirm, on the one hand, the right of users to make known their ideas on the space and time of their activities in the urban area; it would also cover the right to the use of the centre, a privileged place, instead of being dispersed and stuck in ghettoes (for workers, immigrants, the 'marginal' and even for the 'privileged'.

While many contributors to the academic debate seem to assume that both approaches are mutually exclusive, or at least conflicting, not much is known on how the radical and reformist approaches interact in practice (Boer and Vries, 2009:1323).

In view of the case study, there are clear obstacles in current South Africa governance practice towards establishing a 'full right to the city'. From the radical perspective, current practices systematically ignore minority interests. The right to the city seems realized when – in a liberal democracy – a majority of the people agree with the present policies, plans and changes regarding their urban environment. The right to the city as used in this context appears to be a very useful concept and functions as a framework in which all connected groups can cooperate and pursue their goals (Purcell, 2002, 2008). It is also responsive to competing expectations regarding the use of space, especially mixed-income environment and appropriate normative behaviours to the negotiations of these expectations in the context of safety, order, what constitute public space and the right to use it (Chaskin and Joseph, 2013). The right to the city it is argued also offers the possibility to bring together different groups within a social issue, especially housing, mixed-income housing specifically. It can form an important link to bring together actors and stakeholders with different socio-economic, ideological or ethnic background to cooperation. As Balibar (1968 cited in Goonewardena et al., 2008:261) remarks, the advancement of a right to the city calls for major changes in the structural dynamics that produce urban space. Unless the forces of the free market, which dominate – and shape to a large extent – urban space, are modified, the right to the city would remain a seductive but impossible ideal for those who cannot bid for the dominated spaces of the city; those, in order words, who cannot freely exercise their right to the city. The notion of the right to the city implies a change not only of spatial conceptions but of society; the ways in which the notion is conceived and justified depend very much on society itself. The use of the right to the city as a model in this book is because it is a very flexible model and 'broadly used' (Boer and Vries, 2009:1324). Its discourse is extensive; it is characterized by a broad conceptual framework and can be interpreted in many ways for different agenda.

3.3.2 The New Urbanism

New urbanism adheres to spatial principles but at the scale of the local neighbourhood. Like so many city planning schemes of the twentieth century, New Urbanism struggles to meet its objectives. This is because it promotes a vision of cities with fine-grained mixed-use, mixed housing types, compact form, an attractive public realm, pedestrian-friendly streetscapes, defined centres and edges and varying transport options (UN-Habitat, 2009:17). Facilities such as health, libraries and retail and government services cluster around key public transport facilities and intersections to maximize convenience. Arguments in favour of compact cities revolve around claims that they are more efficient, inclusive and sustainable (UN-Habitat, 2009:158). The costs of providing infrastructure are lower, there is better access to services and facilities since threshold are higher, the livelihoods of the urban poor are promoted and social segregation is reduced. The time and cost of travelling is also lower. The new urbanism calls for an urban design that includes a variety of building types, mixed uses, intermingling of housing for different income groups and strong public realm. Despite the unequivocal goal of income diversity as expressed in the Charter of the Congress for the New Urbanism, one of the more significant challenges facing the movement according to Johnson and Talen (2008) has been the creation of socially diverse neighbourhoods, especially ones that include a mix of income. Fainstein (2005) earlier highlighted on this and noted that the basic unit of planning is the neighbourhood, which is limited in physical size, has a well-defined edge and a focus centre. The daily needs of life are accessible within the 5-minute walk (Kunstler, 1996:117).

According to Hasic (2000), there are four most important frameworks guiding New Urbanism: the centre of each neighbourhood should be defined by a public space and activated by locally oriented civic and commercial activities; each neighbourhood should accommodate a range of household's types and land uses; the importance of cars should be kept in perspective; architecture should respond to the surrounding fabric of buildings and spaces and to local traditions. Compact cities are less reliant on cars and minimize distances travelled and, hence, fuel use, and have less impact upon farmlands and environmental resources. As a consequence, they are theoretically more resilient in the context of climate change and have fewer harmful impacts (Chen et al., 2008). Critics, however, question several of these claimed benefits and argue that compaction is contrary to market forces towards sprawl, the decentralization of work and residents' desires, and hence, is not politically feasible or even desirable. Higher density, they argue, is associated with congestion and pollution, higher crime rates, and puts greater pressure on natural resources. Containment policies push up land costs and also encourage development beyond restricted zones (Ibid, 2008). Much of the debate has focused on cities in developing countries, where high car ownership rates in an era of low fuel costs have propelled low-density sprawl (Newman and Kenworthy, 2000). Although research showing that higher density cities use less fuel has had its detractors (Gordon and Richardson, 1997; Mindali et al., 2004; Simmonds and Coombe, 2000), the relationships established are remarkably robust (Breheny, 1995), and there seems to be clear association between higher densities and public transport, and between low densities and reliance on cars (Bertaud, 2004). Nevertheless, high densities only provide the conditions for public transport; they do not guarantee it. Nor do they prevent rising car ownership and use, even where public transport systems are relatively good as, for example Japan (Taniguchi and Ikeda, 2005). Some research has found that higher densities are associated with less usage of the motor car for some trips, but not for all (Simmonds and Coombe, 2000), and that households in places designed along new urbanists lines may nevertheless drive elsewhere to work, shop and use facilities (Handy, 2005). The complexities of these relationships (and of urban forms) mean that many attempts to prove the benefits of compaction statistically are weaker and more equivocal than expected. Bradbury et al. (2014) describes this as an era where 'Comprehensiveness continues to resonate as we try to escape modernity'. The New Urbanism orientation resembles that of the early planning theorist Ebenezer Howard, Frederic Law Olmsted, Patrick Geddes – in their aim of using spatial relations to create a close-knit social community that allows diverse elements to interact (Fainstein, 2005). Fundamental to its development has been a critique of American surburbia:

> In the postwar era, surburbia became the lifestyle of the choice for most Americans. While this new way of living has many advantages, it also fragment our society ... separating us from friends and relatives and breaking down the bonds of community that had served our nation so well in earlier times....
>
> (Katz, 1994:ix cited in Fainstein, 2005:11)

3.3.3 The Relevance of Compact Cities in Developing Countries

It is important to understand that there is a direct link between mixed-income housing development programme and the desire of urban planners and policy makers to address broader questions of urban management and sustainability. In this context, the notion of compact city is thus important to provide a theoretical analytical framework for mixed-income housing development. Compact city is, therefore, defined as 'relatively high-density, mixed-use city, based on efficient public transportation system and dimensions that encourages walking and cycling' (Burton, 2000:1970 cited in Matjiya, 2009:47). There are various definitions and views as to what the compact city should focus more attention on. This is reflected in the ideas from various authors such as Goodchild who focused on population density, to Williams et al. (1996) whose attention was on mixed use development and Elkin et al. (1991) who focused on nature and quality of the development (Matjiya, 2009:48). It is widely accepted, particularly in land use planning policy (for example, DoE and DoT, 1994 cited in Williams et al., 2000: 19) noted that the most effective solution to achieving sustainable urban form is implementation of the compact city idea, that is, advocacy of high density, mixed-use urban form. The claimed advantages of the compact city have been well documented – they include: conservation of the countryside, less need to travel by car, thus reducing fuel emissions; support for public transport and walking and cycling; better access to services and facilities; more efficient utility and infrastructure provisions; and revitalization and regenerations of inner urban areas (William et al., 2000). The geographical sprawl of South African cities is both disadvantageous to the poor and economically dysfunctional. Hence the emphasis of the National Development Plan (NDP) is on compact cities, which implies much more infill and multi-storey development (DA, 2013:5). However, to date, there is little evidence to support such claims, and the sustainability of the compact city continues to be contended (Breheny, 1992; Williams et al., 1996).

Access to land and housing has been a major challenge to the urban poor in most developing countries over time. This is most pronounced in areas where the pursuit of housing development around areas of high economic opportunities have tendered to push the urban poor to the periphery as they cannot afford the high rent and land cost. Yet, the benefits of urban densification, at least for the inner-city poor, are apparent: while housing costs are high and they have less space, they have greater livelihood opportunities (particularly in the informal sector) and access to employment. Transport costs are low, and they are able to rely to a greater extent on non-motorized transport (Brown and Lloyd-Jones, 2002). In many respects, dense areas in cities of developing counties, including informal settlements, are living versions of compact city ideas. Planning and public policy might most appropriately work with these processes of change to consolidate the position of the inner-city poor and to support existing processes of informal upgrading and improvement of infrastructure and services (UN-Habitat, 2009:159). In Brazil, participatory informal settlement upgrading – including the provision of a range of social services and facilities – has helped to improve living conditions in Rio de Janeiro's favelas. Avoiding displacement or forced relocation of slums, as has often occurred through modernist planning in the past, is also important.

3.3.4 Critique of the New Urbanism

The new urbanism is vulnerable to the accusation that its proponents oversell their product, promoting an unrealistic environment determinism that has threaded its way throughout the history of physical planning (Fainstein, 2005:12). Some scholars have continued to praise the theory but with caution. David Harvey (1997:1) praises certain aspects of the new urbanism … its emphasis on public space, its consideration of the relationship between work and living, and its stance towards environmental quality. Nevertheless, he also noted some mix feelings:

> But my real worry is that the movement repeats at a fundamental level the same fallacy of the architectural and planning styles it criticizes. Put simply, does it not perpetuate the idea that the shaping of spatial order is or can be the foundation for a new moral and aesthetic order………? The movement does not recognize that the fundamental difficulty with modernism was its persistent habit of privileging spatial forms over social processes.
> (Harvey, 1997:2)

As a result of its spatial determinism, the new urbanism runs into certain dangers. It is accused of merely calling for a different form of surburbia rather than overcoming metropolitan social segregation. Though scholars have tendered to defend this, e.g. Duany who calls for planners to build better suburbs. The movement is less convincing in its approach to social injustice (Fainstein, 2005: 12). Harvey fears that the new urbanism can commit the same errors as modernism… of assuming that changing people's physical environment will somehow take care of the social inequalities that warped their lives. This argument is also supported by Johnson and Talen (2008:584) who noted that New Urbanism as currently practiced is not typically affordable for households at the lower end of the income spectrum. The new urbanists are, therefore, encouraged to work with private developers to build and finance their visions. The new urbanism with its main focus on physical form tends to ignore diversity, and this also perpetuates segregation in neighbourhoods and municipalities (Fainstein, 2005:12).

> The reification of physical models is used by the architects of New Urbanism as a strategy to create local community, by reproducing a physical environment that fosters greater casual social contact within the neighbourhood. However, these architects fail to sufficiently consider segregation within the greater urban area according to class, race and ethnicity, and may, in fact, help perpetuate it.
>
> (Lehrer and Milgrom, 1996:15 cited in Fainstein, 2005:13)

Only a publicly funded effort to combine social groups through mixing differently priced housing with substantial subsidies for the low-income components can produce such a result. Hence, this research on mixed-income housing development is imperative. This is based on increasing recognition in the literature that expanding the range of affordability in New Urbanism cannot be achieved by design alone but rather requires a better marriage between policy and design (Deitrick and Ellis, 2004, cited in Johnson and Talen, 2008:585). New Urbanism developers contend that affordability is a casualty of various forces beyond their control, including market dynamics, soaring construction costs, community resistance to affordable housing and diminishing sources of public subsidy. New Urbanisms are unclear about what they should be doing to further the objectives of social diversity. While diversity is generally thought to be a key ingredient for successful urbanism, there is no agreement in most literature on how it should be accomplished, what form it should take or how far New Urbanism should go to promote it. Talen (2002) confirms this by noting that mixed-income housing policy incorporates the philosophy of New Urbanism at a broader level with aims and objective of advancing three social goals: community, social equity and the notion of the common good.

3.3.5 Path Dependency Theory

Path dependence is an idea that has been used, and sometimes hotly debated, in a number of different social science disciplines, including economics, politics and sociology (Malpass, 2011). The definition that attracts a lot of attention is the one given by Sewell that path dependence tends to show that 'what has happened at an earlier point in time will affect the possible outcomes of a sequence of events occurring at a later point in time' (quoted in Mahoney, 2000:510). This notion is supported by Pierson (2000:251) who noted that path dependence is used to support a few claims 'specific patterns of timing and sequence matter; starting from similar conditions, a wide range of social outcomes may be possible; large consequences may result from relatively small or contingent events; particular courses of action, once introduced, can be virtually impossible to reverse; and consequently, political development is often punctuated by critical moments or juncture that shape the basic contour of social life'. In his own argument, Levi (1997) contended that path dependence if it is to mean anything, that once 'a country or region has started down a track, the cost of reversal are very high. There will be other choice points, but the entrenchments of certain institutional arrangements obstruct an easy reversal of the initial choice' Path dependence is a way to narrow, conceptually, the choices set and link decision-making through time. It tends to emphasize stability and continuity between events. The idea is that 'small events or decisions can have big consequences over time and what distinguishes the possibly small but influential events at a critical juncture from other is the timing' (Malpass, 2011:308). To explain path dependence further, Streeck and Thelen (2005:31) base their argument by explaining how rapid changes, be it in policies or programme precipitate a step down a path and increases the likelihood of further steps in the same direction. They list the following:

(1) Displacement: slowly rising salience of subordinate relative to dominant institutions;
(2) Layering: new elements attached to existing institutions gradually change their status and structure;
(3) Drift: neglect of institutional maintenance in spite of external change resulting in slippage in institutional practice on the ground;
(4) Conversion: redeployment of old institutions to new purposes; new purposes attached to old structures; and
(5) Exhaustion: gradual breakdown (withering away) of institutions over time.

The above is seen to have a lot to do and offer to the explanation of continuity and change in housing (Malpass, 2011:308). In looking at this more closely, especially using the Nordic countries as basis of analysis, Bengtsson et al. (2006) found that 'Though housing policy in all five countries has been "social" in the meaning that an important goal has been to provide decent housing to households of lesser means, the institutional arrangements chosen to achieve these goals differ fundamentally'. They also agree in their finding using this concept that the five countries have experienced the same sequence of four phases of policy over the last 100 years. Malpass (2011:310) also used this model in the United Kingdom and noted that many years, the housing policy has been based on two key assumptions: that the ultimate aim is to provide a decent home at an affordable price for every household, and that the role of the state is to underpin the market, which can be expected to provide for most people most of the time. The conclusion drawn from this study is that in terms of the explanation of the observable and enduring differences between the housing systems of different countries, path dependence is clearly of some use. Since dynamism is a feature of national housing systems, the use of path dependence theory in a given country like South Africa can be more effective in analyzing the historical development of housing policies. According to Malpass (2011), the use within countries (as distinct from between countries) needs to be formulated in a way that can ensure the understanding of both the causes of both change and continuity. This is very relevant to this research on mixed-income housing development, especially in view of the several changes in policies and legislation that has occurred in South African housing since 1994 before this new trend.

3.4 The Cycles of Disadvantages and Concentrated Poverty of the Urban Poor

3.4.1 The Urban Underclass Theory

William Julius Wilson in his book 'The Truly Disadvantaged: The Inner City, the Underclass, and Public Policy' outlined the problems for those living in neighborhoods of concentrated poverty. Wilson (1987, 1991a, 1991b) and others (Jenks and Peterson, 1991) on urban poverty and the underclass have provided the immediate impetus for much of the recent work on the effects of neighborhoods and communities on poor children and families. Wilson argued that the concentration of male joblessness, poverty and female-headed households which have resulted from the job losses and the middle class's flight from inner-city neighbourhood, may have led to social isolation and to a shift in neighborhoods' social and cultural norms.

According to him, the persistent problem of the prevalence of violence out-of-wedlock births, female-headed households, and welfare dependency in inner-city neighborhoods, and lack of role models with sustainable jobs and advanced education all characterize American urban environment. Wilson's text has been called the 'most influential scholarly book on contemporary American poverty' (Katz, 1993:17 cited in Johnson, 2006:68), and its authors 'easily the most influential contemporary analyst' of the lower class (Hughes, 1989:188). Wilson's contributions were to help return poverty to the national agenda and revive research topic that had been previously dormant since the publication of the Moynihan report (Johnson, 2006:68). His emphasis on the 'structural thesis' of urban poverty represented the strongest argument against the notion of a culture of poverty to date. Wilson specifically defines the 'underclass' as:

> Individual who lack training and skills and either experience long-term unemployment or are not members of the labour force, individuals who are engaged in street crime and other forms of aberrant behaviours, and families that experience long-term spells of poverty and/or welfare dependency.
>
> (Wilson, 1987:8)

This term has generated a lot of debate in the literature. The term was coined by journalist Ken Auletta who emphasizes the behaviour and values of those deemed to be members of the 'underclass', though without claiming that these were necessary the cause of their plight. He categorizes them into four: the passive, who are long-term welfare recipients; the hostile, who are street criminals, dropouts and drug addicts; hustlers, who earn their living in the underground economy; and the traumatized, a group which includes drunks, addicts, drifters, 'bag ladies' and the mentally ill homeless (Katz, 1993, cited in Johnson, 2006:68). Christopher Jenks in one of his writings suggested three different kinds of 'underclasses', and these are: an economic (those of working age unable to get steady job), a moral (those with deviant behavioural norms) and an educational (those lacking in cultural and social skills). However, there is still no single agreed definition of the 'underclasses' and different definitions tend to reflect whether the definer subscripts to a structural of behavioural/cultural explanation of its cause (Murray, 1996:3). Prosser, a senior policy adviser in the Bush administration, concludes his review of the state of the debate and the evidence in the United States with the observation that, despite the volume of research undertaken, 'we still do not have agreement on what we mean by the underclass, much fewer what factors are associated with its growth' (Ibid, 1996:6).

3.4.2 The Culture of Poverty

Oscar Lewis in his study of poverty and family life in four slums of Greater San Juan in Puerto Ricans in 1965 noted that there are many poor people in the world. The poverty of two-thirds of the world's population who live in the underdeveloped counties has been rightly called 'the problem of problems' (Lewis, 1965:21). He identified 70 traits that characterized poor communities and noted that wherever these conditions prevail the way of life among some of these people is classified as 'culture of poverty'. The principal ones may be described in four dimensions of the system: the relationship between the subculture and the larger society; the nature of the family, and the attitudes, values and character of the individual (Lewis, 1965:21). According to this theory, the disengagement, the nonintegration, of the poor with respect to the major institutions of society is a crucial element in the culture of poverty. It reflects the combined effects of a variety of factors, including poverty, segregation and discrimination, fear, suspicion and apathy and development of alternative institutions and procedures in the slum community (Lewis, 1965:23). The people do not belong to labour unions or political parties and make little use of the banks, hospitals, departmental stores or museums. A relief system that barely keeps people alive perpetuates rather than eliminates poverty and the pervading sense of hopelessness. People in a culture of poverty produce little wealth and receive little in return. Chronic unemployment and underemployment, low wages, lack of property, lack of savings, absence of food reserves in the home and chronic shortage of cash imprison the family and the individual in a vicious circle. Thus, for lack of cash, the slum family makes frequent purchases of small quantities of food at higher prices (Lewis, 1965). The slum economy turns inwards; it shows a high incidence of pawning of personal goods, borrowing at usurious rates of interest, informal credit arrangements among neighbours and use of secondhand clothing and furniture. Along with disengagement from the large society, there is hostility to the basic institutions of what are regarded as the dominant classes. There is hatred of the police, mistrust of government and of those in high positions and a cynicism. That extends to the church (Lewis, 1965). The culture of poverty thus holds a certain potential for protest and for entrainment in political movement aimed against the existing order. The individual who grows up in this culture has a strong feeling of fatalism, helplessness, dependence and inferiority (Ibid, 1965). Hence, this tendency tends to perpetuate itself from generation to generation because of its effect on children. Lewis regards the culture of poverty as applicable to only Third World countries, or countries in the early stage of industrialization.

3.4.3 Criticism of the Culture of Poverty Concepts

But Sociologist American Michael Harrington argues that the culture of poverty can apply to an advanced industrial society. Another Anthropologist Walter Miller (1976) also argues in this way claiming that the American lower class has its own set of focal concerns that emphasizes masculinity, living for the present and luck rather than effort as the basis of success. He regards this class subculture as self-perpetuating and an adaptation to lower skill occupation. Kenneth Little's study of West African urban communities shows that the poor do participate in many voluntary associations. William Mangin's study of *pueblos jovenes*, people living in shanty towns, shows a high level of community and political involvements and a great deal of 'self-help'. J. Schwartz also finds in his study of slum areas of Venezuela little evidence of apathy and resignation. Jones and Luo (1999) also conclude in their study that there is little support for the traditional culture of poverty arguments. They found out that poor people do have work ethics and that their motivation is more related to worsening personal economic conditions and what the future holds. Townsend's (1979) definition of poverty that is both materialistic and idealistic also challenges Lewis assertion. According to his findings, and this is also supported by UNDP (2006:5), poverty as a public policy concern, whether at the global, national or community level, should be widely considered to be a multidimensional problem. Poverty is also considered as a complex set of deprivations and reflects failures in many dimensions of human life – hungers, unemployment, homelessness, illness, healthcare, powerlessness and victimization and social injustice; 'they all add up to an assault on human dignity'. Poverty he further writes 'is the lack of the resources necessary to permit participation in the activities, customs and diets commonly approved by society' (Townsend, 1979:88). To him, some other varieties of inequalities include assets, private income in kind and employment benefits. More significantly, criticism of Lewis theory is that his data and conclusion do not match (Valentine, 1968). It is also noted that it is very difficult to operationalize most of the traits mentioned by Lewis, and therefore, it is quite difficult to do research about the culture of poverty. The concept is also noted to 'blame the poor for their conditions' and thus connotes negative implications about poor people.

3.5 Social Cohesion and Social Capital

Social cohesion refers to the extent of connectedness and solidarity among groups in society (Berkman and Kawachi, 2000). According to Durkheim, a cohesive society is one that is marked by the abundance of 'mutual moral support', which instead of throwing the individual on his own resources, leads him to share in the collective energy and support of others when his own got exhausted (1897, 1977, p. 210 cited in Berkman and Kawachi, 2000). A cohesive society is also one that is richly endowed with stocks of *social capital*. Social capital is defined as those features of social structures – such as levels of interpersonal trusts and norms of reciprocity and mutual aid – which acts as resources for individuals and facilitates collective action (Coleman, 1990; Putnam, 1993 cited in Berkman and Kawachi, 2000:175). Social capital thus forms a subset of the notion of social cohesion. Social cohesion refers to two broader, intertwined features of society, which may be described as: (1) the absence of latent social conflict – whether in the form of income/wealth inequality; racial/ethnic tensions; disparity in political participation; or other forms of polarization; and (2) the presence of strong social bonds-measured by levels of trust and norms of reciprocity (i.e. social capital); abundance of association that bridge social divisions (civil societies); and the presence of institutions of conflict management (Ibid:175). Social cohesion and social capital are both collective, and ecological, dimensions of society, to be distinguished from concepts of social networks and social supports, which are characteristically measured at the levels of individual. James Coleman was one of the first Social Scientist to attempt a formal definition of social capital (1988, 1990). According to Coleman, social capital consists of those features of social structure that facilitates the actions of members within them. This definition is 'functionalist' and implies that social capital can take several forms. In reviewing this explanation further, some important generalization is drawn about the nature of social capital:

(1) It is social. The distinct feature of social capital is that it is external to the individual – i.e. it is not lodged within the individuals (as is human capital) nor in the means of production, rather social capital inheres in the structure of social relationships and of ecological characteristics (Ibid:176).
(2) Social capital is a public good. Any action or service by any member is not for personal glorification but to the benefit of all. It does not exclude anyone in the consumption, and it is different from physical capital, which is a private good.

3.6 Social Control

The physical environment in which families live, in particular the design and condition of dwelling units, has an effect on the manner in which they live. Among the effects of architectural design which have been identified by previous research is that of the physical proximity. There is strong evidence for the relationship between levels of socio-economic status, homeownership and residential stability and the level of social organization in a community (Joseph, 2006:387). In their analysis of the British Crime Survey, which includes almost 11,000 respondents across localities, Sampson and Groves (1989 cited in Joseph, 2006) noted that lower levels of community socio-economic status had the largest effects among other variables on the extent of unsupervised peer groups. In turn, the rates of unsupervised youth had a large and significant effect on self-reported personal and property victimization and rates of offending. In a mixed-income environment, higher income residents will raise the socio-economic status and homeownership rates of the community. Though available evidence is mixed about whether increased levels of social control have been observed in existing mixed-income developments and, if so, the sources of that increased control. Moreover, an increase in socio-economic status and homeownership rates should be associated with increased informal social control by residents, stronger accountability to norms and rules and lower levels of deviant and antisocial behaviours (Ibid:388).

3.7 Political Economy of Place

The use of politics as an exchange approach to explaining the emergence of mixed-income developments does not rely on the superior knowledge and benevolent interests of the government planners to identify which group or characteristics are going to produce a better neighbourhood (Schaeffer, 2007). The political economy of mixed-income developments examines both the intuitional features and the strategies played out within those rules structures that lead to the creation of mixed-income development. Joseph et al. (2007:378) also noted that individual and external leveraging of external resources leads to higher quality local services and infrastructure, thus directly promoting an improved quality of life for local residents. Feasible exchange between politicians and special interest groups determines the outcomes observed. The institutional context of rules and enforcements under which the neighbourhood develops influences the types, persistence and durability of residential patterns (Schaeffer, 2007). Once neighbourhood coordination problems are viewed as spontaneous orders, the questions then turn to consideration of the institutional environment within which these complex orders emerge. The rules of the game influence the strategies that individuals find in their interest to pursue and determine how agents learn strategies and correct poor ones. Mixed-income development policy is predicated on not only alleviating the effects of concentrations of poverty but more importantly of doing so where those concentrations have developed in a context of public ownership.

3.8 Spatial Segregation

Spatial segregation is a feature of metropolises from San Diego to Boston, from Santiago to Cape Town and from Belfast to Bangalore (Greenstein et al., 2000). In some places, the segregation is associated primarily with racial groups, in orders places, ethnic or religion, while in still other places, income status. Residential segregation also has different meanings and consequences depending on the specific form and structure of the metropolis, as well as the cultural and historical context (Ibid, 2000). The forces that contribute to spatial segregation are many and varied. While government evictions and legal framework are explicit mechanisms for creating urban spatial segregation, more subtle mechanisms also have been used to create or enforce spatial segregation (Ibid, 2000). According to these researchers, the policy consequences of spatial segregations is a very serious issue because of the complex interactions between land and housing market on the one hand and their connections to local revenue and the distributions and quality of local services on the other hand. The result of this is poor inner-city enclaves where children attend substandard schools, which in turn limits their life chances. Spatial segregation of the poor often occurs within informal settlements that are viewed as aberrations, but scholars increasingly understand informality 'as a result of the normal functioning of land and housing markets, not as part of a duality of formal versus informal economies' (Greenstein et al., 2000). Spatial segregation is both a reflection of the existing social structure and a mechanism to enforce that structure, thus raising the question of how and when segregation should be addressed. There is a need to improve the understanding of the social problems in these segregated areas in order to adequately design and implement appropriate policy responses that are necessarily 'multi-dimensional' (Greenstein et al., 2000). According to UN publication Urban Society, many of the world cities have ended up with internal unstable residential patterns with the carving out of ethnic–cultural enclaves along socio-economic lines in cities, thereby threatening the very foundation of urban culture. To achieve or combating social problems in segregated areas requires a multidisciplinary rather than ad hoc approach (UN, 2009). Studies also show that 29% of cities in developing world have areas considered inaccessible or too dangerous to the police.

3.9 Conclusion

In this chapter, various theories and frameworks that inform and guide this research were highlighted. Theories are seen as systematic and important propositions that enable researchers to predict behaviours of interests guided by specific assumptions. The use in this chapter was to show the maturity of housing research and to systematically assist in the organization of collected information. The right to the city is argued to shape the participation and transformation of our urban space. These rights are not reserved or belong to an individual per se but are seen as a collective design. The New Urbanism calls for an urban design that includes varieties of buildings, mix uses and strong public realm is critically assessed. In spite of some consensus, various scholars caution that the New Urbanism though supported by Ebenezer Howard, Patrick Geddes and Frederic Law Olmsted might not commit the same error as modernism in terms of breaking down the bond of community relations, not to worsen the fragmentation of our society and the separation of people based on race, gender and social profile. The chapter also touched on the link between Path Dependence theory with emphasis on rapid changes in housing policies and programmes. This is relevant to this study in view of the background of South African Housing Policies to be explained in subsequent chapters. The use of urban underclass to highlight the increasing level of urban poverty, especially housing and associated deprivation, is considered imperative for national agenda. The argument that poverty is a complex phenomenon is supported in this study and resonates on the high level of unemployment, homelessness and social exclusion that characterized the case study areas. The chapter concludes with the relevance of social cohesion and social capital based on the interpretation that this is 'naturally occurring social relationships among persons which promotes coordinated action of society'. This relation is further investigated in this study, especially in relation to mixed-income housing development projects.

Chapter 4

Philosophical Perspectives Guiding Housing Research

4.1 Introduction

This chapter will clarify the status of housing studies as a field of studies in relation to other social sciences. Housing research faces difficulties partly because of its multi-disciplinary nature. To this end, any investigation into housing research should aim at re-integrating housing into the broader issues of social structure and related housing debates in the social sciences. This is necessary because housing studies have been undergoing a slow metamorphosis, and there is a growing conceptual and theoretical awareness in housing research. This chapter will discuss the various philosophical perspectives and approaches to housing that have been used in the study of housing, such as neoclassical, Marxist, and socialist and neoliberal views. The differences in the approaches tend to point directly to the functions and roles of the housing within the frame which housing developed over the years (Soliman, 2004).

4.2 Philosophical Perspectives

Housing research is guided by some philosophical perspectives, and these include: neoclassical perspectives, neo-Marxist perspectives, the non-Marxist (liberal) perspectives, and social and institutional perspectives.

4.2.1 Neoclassical Perspectives

The neoclassical economic perspectives on how individuals' interaction has dominated the academic history of the field and has influenced policymakers as noted by various scholars. The neoclassical models have historically assumed, explicitly and implicitly, that human beings are 'rational' agents (Whitle et al., 2014:17). This means that people act in ways which maximize their expected 'utility' (happiness) within the full set of information available to them. When making decisions, people reflect on available information to ensure their choice to enter a market truly reflects their needs, as they perceive them. In housing market, the heterogeneous nature of

Mixed-Income Housing Development Planning Strategies and Frameworks in the Global South, 41–50
Copyright © 2024 George Okechukwu Onatu, Wellington Didibhuku Thwala and Clinton Ohis Aigbavboa
Published under exclusive licence by Emerald Publishing Limited
doi:10.1108/978-1-83753-814-020231004

houses in terms of size, conditions, orientation, location, modifications, attachments, etc. make this a challenging condition. The neoclassical theorists hold that if the price of housing reflects its value as an asset and a source of shelter (home), people will also address price formation by employing the allied 'Efficient Market Hypothesis', which is associated with Adam Smith (1759) publications. The efficient market is hypothesized to hold that humans are both utility maximizing individuals and rational in their price formation. Neoclassical economists argue that changes in interest rates have profound effects on adjustable-rate mortgages (Madsen, 2012). This effect is mostly felt in the disposable income of households. The decisions by households to move are purely based on rational decision. They are an expression of the deliberate employment of means in order to reach ends. So, people move if they feel they can improve their situation by doing so or (as economists would say) if they expect a higher 'place utility' at the new location. A recent work by Smith and Shawky (2011) tried to answer whether other disciplines, especially behavioural economics, can clarify and help to understand housing market dynamics. Though the researchers all focused on house prices and residential mobility, they differ as it relates to the emphasis on housing market model and price model since they argue the need to include and incorporate psychological perspectives to enable a better understanding of the function of housing market. The central elements of a neo-classical approach centres on understanding the nature of demand, supply and price both in the housing market as it relates to both land and finance market. Chapham et al. (2012:117), in support of this argument, note that 'understanding these relationships has continued to be the core agenda for mainstream economic research in housing and the most positive legacy of neo-classicalism'. There is now increasing criticism of neoclassical economics. Several writers (such as, Tversky and Kahnemann, 1974 cited in Whitle et al., 2014; Kahneman and Tverky, 1979) criticize the assumption that people act as rational agents and claim that asset-pricing models based on rationality cannot explain patterns that are observed regularly by economists.

4.2.2 Neo-Marxist Perspectives

Marxism is the economic and political theories of Karl Marx and Friedrich Engels. These two philosophers believed that human actions and institutions are economically determined, that class struggle is needed to create historical change, and that capitalism will ultimately be superseded by communism. The Marxist view defines housing in terms of three fundamental dimensions. According to Soliman (2004), these include: firstly, housing is a necessary good meaning that housing is obviously a means of survival that is necessary for the reproduction of the labour force and, therefore, a good whose cost enters directly or indirectly into the production of all commodities. Hence, it is an aspect of capitalist's social formation. Secondly, housing is a fixed good. As a fixed good, the material precondition for producing a house requires that it has to occupy land in a specific location. Land in this context cannot be reproduced at will; it is a limited product, and rights to land and its use are preserved in legal rights to property. Thirdly, in a capitalist society, housing not only has a use value but also an exchange value.

Housing can become a product whose consumption can only be realized by those with a housing need and who can afford to purchase it. The neo-Marxists view in addition to the above focused on the role of the state in the process of capital accumulation, including its role in housing (Smith, 1999:18). To them, the poor are necessary to capital accumulation in the sense that they ensure the cheapening of the cost of labour reproduction through the provision of a large and cheap labour pool. The state's role in this process is twofold: to support capital accumulation and to maintain social stability (legitimation). These two stated objectives were used by Marcuse (1979 cited in Smith, 1999) to categorize the state housing policies (Bassett and Short, 1980:225). It is from this theoretical tradition that Burgess engaged in a long debate with Turner on self-help housing (Smith, 1999). Burgess argued that self-help leads to commodification of housing, thereby linking poor households with inequality and exploitation by the capitalists (Burgess, 1978, 1982). Self-help housing production consumes products and labours with an exchange value, and thus have both use value itself and exchange value (Smith, 1999:18).

4.2.3 The Non-Marxist (Liberal) Perspectives

The non-Marxist perspective sees housing in four dimensions. Firstly, housing is distinguished as a 'noun' and a 'verb' (Soliman, 2004). As a 'noun', housing is defined as a physical structure, and in view of this, it does not put up with any effect on the mechanism of the housing market. As a 'verb', housing becomes a dynamic process that proceeds according to the needs of the residents. Secondly, housing is attached to and interactive with the community members. Housing is considered among the basic components that go into the improvement of the environment due to elements, materials and services to relate to different activities. It is considered as an investment with spin off effect that is reflected in the process of economic development. Thirdly, housing is defined in terms of the major function it performs in a community which affects, and is affected by, the residents. The fourth dimension relates to the freedom to build a housing unit, and this is considered as one of the most important priorities and needs of the residents. Turner (1966) further expounded on this by noting that 'the failure of policies and programmes for public housing and for the control of urban growth are partly due to misunderstanding of the nature of housing'. The common mistake is to evaluate housing quantitatively in terms of its objective appearance and that this is unrealistic; instead, the 'value of a house, or, rather, of the dwelling environment, is the qualitative of its responses to the life-situation of the person in the family and in the local community'. To this end, the project type most commonly employed to solve the housing problems (of failing to respond properly to the life situation of their intended inhabitants) tends to compound the social, economic and political problem rather than solve them. In his 'third sector approach', Turner advocated for self-help housing (Smith, 1999:15). Turner was inspired by his observation of squatter settlements in Peru. Writing in the period from 1967 to 1969, Turner and Mangin laid the foundation for the subsequent debate that influenced the World Bank housing policy (see Mangin, 1967; Turner, 1967, 1968; Turner and Fichter,

1972). Turner developed a model of migrant categories in cities in developing countries that assumed that 'the socio-economic position of (migrant) households determines their particular housing conditions and that upward social (or occupational) mobility will result in rather predictable housing careers' (Van Lindert, 1992:158). Out of the three migrant categories identified by Turner, the two longest established types (consolidators' and status seekers') whose housing priorities were tenure and amenities, respectively, relied mainly on self-help to satisfy these priorities (Smith, 1999). Based on this model, Turner articulated a critique of conventional mass housing (including Reconstruction and Development Programme (RDP)) as was being implemented in several developing countries at the time. These include:

- The users know their own needs better than bureaucrats and experts and should not be hindered by state-imposed standards,
- The users can use scarce resources, producing cheaper and more affordable houses than commercially built units,
- Self-help housing results in better architecture because it is built for its use value and not for its exchange value,
- Residents in self-help housing neighbourhoods have a better position for improving their economic situations than those in monofunctional mass housing estates.

These arguments were used by Turner to advocate for 'low-cost housing', and this was a means of self-fulfiling people's aspiration without reliance on the state. His criticism of supply-driven housing provision was addressed to both centralized state socialism and capitalism (Pugh, 1997:93–94). Turner further expressed the view that communities should control decisions that affect their neighbourhoods, including mixed-income housing, while the state must ensure access to resources that will allow the implementation of these decisions. In addition, Turner envisioned a role for a third party between community and state, which was referred to as the 'third system', which comprised community-based organizations (CBOs) and non-governmental organizations (NGOs) (Smith, 1999:17). Turner's proposals, according to Nientied and van Der Linden (1988:141), are considered of little appeal since they do not question the economic and social structure shaped by capitalism. By separating and opposing use value and market value, Turner fails to appreciate their dialectic interactions. Turner is also criticized because he overlooked the fact that industrialism is just an aspect of capitalism (Ibid:141). The squatter does not build outside the sphere of capital circulation; rather the capitalist is part of the specific circuit called 'petty commodity production', which is an integral part of the capitalist system. It is noted that Turner depoliticize both the housing problem and the state (Nientied and van der Linden, 1988).

4.2.4 Social Perspective and Approaches

Social perspective in housing studies is related to sociological perspective. Sociological perspective is the study of human life and social interactions and how those interactions shape groups and society (Giddens, 2006). Social perspective is increasingly one of the salient features of western European nations. Here housing policymakers see enhancing the social diversity of residential environment as an important goal, although how 'diversity' is defined by national context (Anderson and West, 2006; Klienhans, 2004) differs. The emphasis of this perspective centres on social opportunities that housing can provide either by mixed-income housing or social housing (Galster, 2007). It is also aimed at combating economic, social and ethnic segregation through housing by way of social mix. The post-war development (e.g. in Sweden, France, the United Kingdom and the Netherlands) were efforts aimed at greater diversity that were based on widespread restructuring of large, homogeneous, post-war neighbourhoods and housing estates (through selective demolition, infill construction and sale of social housing). According to Kemeny (1992), housing research tends to neglect the fact that housing is so deeply embedded in social relations and structures that trying to theorize it independent of other aspects of society is doomed in failure. The most important thing in the name *Housing, Theory and Society* is the comma between 'Housing' and 'Theory'. Housing research, therefore 'needs both to draw more extensively from debates and theories in the social sciences and to contribute to such debates with studies of housing'. In contributing to the debate, King (2009) notes the phenomenological analysis of what people do as users of housing. He referred to this as private dwelling: activity in which we use dwelling to meet our ends and fulfil our interests to such an extent that this singular dwelling becomes meaningful to us.

4.2.5 Institutional Perspective

Institutions comprise of both sets of formal rules (like constitutions) and informal norms of behaviour (North, 1998). The function of institution is to provide certainty in human interaction, and this is accomplished by the inherent features of rules and norms. Thus, Guy and Henneberry (2000) assert that the institutional approach to housing offers an alternative to the positivist theories, which identifies, idealizes, and isolates economic structures and individual behaviour. One way of theorizing the institutional perspective in housing analysis is to define a housing system (Murie et al., 1976) or structures of building provision, as suggested by Ball (1998). The latter identifies historically contingent networks of relations (structures) associated with the provision of types of buildings. These networks, Ball (1998) claims, are historically contingent, and they imply that the pattern of networks is shaped by history and is an empirical question. According to Clapman (2001), the argument is that there can be no general theory of how markets work, but each context must be approached separately with reference to the historical interaction between actors and institutions.

It is difficult to pinpoint the most acceptable housing theory because of a number of factors. According to Ruonavaara (2012), the basic reason for the impossibility of a Theory of Housing is that housing itself is not a research topic but a common denominator of a number of research topics: housing policy, housing provision, housing organization, housing choice, housing mobility, housing tenures, use of housing, meaning of housing, politics of housing, etc. Therefore, the borders of housing studies are fuzzy and unclear – research under its broad umbrella can be seen as belonging to one or more specialisms. Housing, as noted by Ruonavaara (2012), indeed is embedded in society to the extent that it is a common denominator of several research topics that often are connected to questions that concern wider range of issues than just housing. A sensible strategy for theorizing housing research is to make use of the concepts and ideas developed in more general research specialism as well as general research approaches developed within disciplines. Apart from just applying theories developed elsewhere, housing researchers should pay back the debt to other fields by trying to contribute to them with the ideas and concepts they have developed while investigating housing issues. This is the reason behind the development of conceptual model for mixed-income housing development in this study. Before this research, look at this; the next section will first review the evolution of housing policies and the impact of the perspectives.

4.3 The Evolution of Housing Policies

According to Clapham (2016), housing policy may be defined as government action to achieve housing objectives. These objectives could be an improvement of the quality of the housing stock, dwellings or dealing with homelessness. This definition is supported by the City of Winnipeg, Canada, that defines housing policy as: 'A standard that measures housing conditions on whether the dwelling is safe, has basic plumbing and heating, and is in a reasonable, habitable state of repair according to accepted standards for residential dwellings such as those established by the City-By-Laws' (The City of Winnipeg, 2013:2). Another definition argues that housing policy is more of 'government intervention in housing field'. The difference is that some interventions in the housing field may be directed to objectives outside the field. This definition is supported by Angel (2000:11) who argues that in the absence of a clear and acceptable definition of what constitutes housing policy and who attends to it, we can only speak of housing environment. Housing policy environment is defined as: 'the set of government interventions that have critical and measurable effects on the performance of the housing sector'. This definition is considered 'open and inclusive' as housing is not a discrete entity. Housing production is part of the construction sector, housing investment is a part of overall capital formation, residential property is a part of the real-estate sector, housing finance is a part of the financial sector, housing subsidies are a part of the social welfare expenditures, and residential development is a part of urban development (Angel, 2000:11). They are, no doubt, large parts, but they still are parts of many larger wholes, each with its own bundle of policies. The housing environment, therefore, consists then of a set of interventions in the housing sector by different government agencies. In another vein, housing policy is seen as a guideline provided by the government through negotiation of various bodies in a country as put together by the government (Agbola, 1998, cited in Aigbavboa and Thwala, 2013:126). Housing policies provide a guide which defines action and sets goals and, in most cases, specify strategies for achieving the goals. The evolution of housing policies in the developing world can be grouped into three phases: 1950–1971 (Phase 1), 1972–1981 (Phase 2) and 1982–1991 (Phase 3).

The two decades from 1950 to 1970 saw the political independence of many former European colonies in Asia, Africa and Caribbean and a new economic independence emerging from the significant industrialization of many Latin American countries that occasioned dramatic rates of urbanization (Wakely, 2014).

The first post-colonial governments of newly independent Asian and African countries, anxious to be perceived as 'progressive' and 'modern' by their electorate and internationally set in train programmes for the clearance of 'unsightly and unhealthy urban slums' that tended to include all urban informal settlements and the construction of impressive 'modern' apartment blocks and housing estates resembling those of the recent post-war reconstruction of European cities, employing all the tenets of the then fashionable functionalism of the Modern Movement in architecture that offered a good vehicle for such gestures (Wakely, 1988 cited in Wakely, 2014).

4.3.1 Self-help Housing

The gap between the supply of and the demand for affordable housing in developing countries is huge. In view of this, the immediate future housing demand, governments must pay much attention to the powerful factors that self-help housing can be, or in the words of UN-Habitat (2005b:166):

> Assisted self-help housing is the most affordable and intelligent way of providing sustainable shelter. It is cheap because it is based on minimum standards and incorporates a substantive amount of sweat equity. It is useful because individuals and communities engaged in it acquire precious skills. It is practical because it responds to peoples' actual need and levels of affordability. It is flexible because dwelling units are often designed to be able to expand over time. But all construction, and particularly incremental upgrading, requires a suitable supply of building materials, components and fittings.

4.3.2 The Origin of Self-help in Housing

Much has been written on the origin of self-help in housing (see Gumbo and Onatu, 2015; Harris, 1998, 1999b, 2003; Pugh, 2001). Self-help housing is as old as humankind (Pugh, 2001). In many cases, the idea of government support to enable families to build their own houses came from the people themselves, and not from governments or international experts (Harris, 1998, 2003 cited in Marais, Ntema and Venter, 2008). Various researchers have indicated that self-help has been a common phenomenon for centuries in a number of countries (Harms, 1992; Ward, 1982; Parnell and Hart, 1999, cited in Marais et al., 2008), and that aided self-help was lobbied for, and practised, long before the rise of the ideas of Turner in the 1960s and 1970s (Harris, 1998, 1999a). Thus, as pointed out by Harris (1998, 2003), the formulation of ideas on self-help may well be the result of western writers following, rather than leading, international trends. Harris (1998:185, 2003:257) cites the examples of Puerto Rico and India in the late 1930s and 1940s to illustrate this point. At the same time, aided self-help and the renewed emphasis on this approach in the 1960s and 1970s cannot be considered in isolation from the drive for government involvement in housing, especially in South Africa. Studies have shown that few countries have actually managed to address their housing problems by means of state-driven approaches (Hardoy and Satterthwaite, 1997). Against this background, Turner's work in Latin America became known (Turner, 1976). As already pointed out, scholarly works have indicated that Turner was certainly not the first person to lobby for self-help, and that self-help had been conventional wisdom in some parts of Latin America before Turner committed his ideas to writing (Harris, 1998, 2003 cited in Marais et al., 2008). Yet there can be little doubt that Turner's beliefs influenced policy, and he is probably the most frequently cited author on self-help (Harris, 2003). Turner based his work on a number of principles in respect of housing (Turner, 1976). Turner viewed housing as a 'verb'. Firstly, he emphasized that housing should be regarded as a process: thus, housing takes place over time, with due consideration of the income of the household, the life cycle of the inhabitants and the needs of those who occupy the house (Marais et al., 2008). Secondly, Turner (1976) also argued that a house should not be considered in terms of its physical characteristics. In his view, the importance of housing lies not in 'what it is', but in 'what it does'. The fact that housing will be upgraded over time ensures that the physical characteristics of the house will most likely improve, should people be given the 'freedom to build'. Thirdly, the value of the house to the user was related to dweller control, according to Turner, rather than to its physical characteristics.

In this regard, he argued that the main criterion in respect of housing was whether the owner was in control of the construction process – although not necessarily as a participant in the actual building activities. Harris (2003:248) summarizes Turner's contribution in an excellent manner, in the following words: 'By self-help Turner has always meant not only the investment of sweat equity by owners in their homes but also the processes of owner design and management'. Ward (1982) quotes Turner's statement that many of his critics too easily equate self-help with self-construction rather than dweller control. In evaluating Turner's contribution concerning dweller control, Harris (2003) also points out the irony of the fact that although dweller control was probably the most novel idea that Turner brought to the housing debate, it is also the idea which has received the least recognition in policy development. The argument is that this idea has received very little attention in the practice of self-help, either internationally or in the South African context – most probably because of the association of Turner's broader ideas with neoliberal policy thinking.

The practical implication of Turner's work is that governments should not provide those aspects of housing which people can provide for themselves. Consequently, Turner was a proponent of site-and-service schemes (referred to as 'aided self-help' schemes) in terms of which governments had to take responsibility for the provision of basic services, and individual households were responsible for the construction of the housing unit (Pugh, 2001). However, it should be noted that Harris (2003) argues that Turner actually also had some reservations in this regard.

Turner's ideas were heavily disputed by Marxist scholars, who argued that self-help leads to the commodification of housing, that it is a mechanism aimed at disciplining the workforce, and that it prolongs the working day for low-income workers (Burgess, 1977, 1978, 1982, 1985). The labelling of Turner's self-help ideas as 'inherently capitalistic' received further momentum when the World Bank started to propose site-and-services as a policy direction despite the fact that the World Bank followed an inherently different point of departure – Turner was in favour of dweller control, whereas the World Bank's approach was based on the economics of housing, with a view to the reduction of labour costs (Harris, 2003; Pugh, 2001). Harris (2003:248) summarizes these discrepancies and similarities in the following words: 'Some of Turner's arguments about self-help are consistent with a conservative brand of political economy, but his thinking has always been most strongly informed by the philosophy of anarchism'. In the process, Turner's ideas regarding the link between housing satisfaction and dweller control became part of and were lost to sight in a political economic debate.

4.3.3 The Enable Market Work and Government Interventions

The enabling debate and the interventionist strategies have been the focus of discussion on strategies for African development during the 1980s, a debate not restricted to housing but to economic development as a whole (Angel, 2000:13). The World Bank and the International Monetary Fund (IMF) decided to focus attention to structural adjustment – the liberalization of the African economies through shrinking public spending, privatization of state enterprises, removing price control, removing rampant subsidies and increasing the capacity of government for managing market-based economies (Angel, 2000). The key argument advanced by the liberalization school is that the role of the state is to create an enabling environment for the market to work by relinquishing control over the economy. This is because of the failure of the market to meet basic needs, the inability of the private sector to raise sufficient capital to compete in international markets and the domination of the national market by foreign concerns (Ibid, 2000). The criticism level around the World Bank enablement housing strategies is associated with the inappropriateness of reassessing public housing policies from the developed world to the developing world (Moser et al., 1997; Pugh, 1997). There was also an issue with the dominant emphasis on Modernization Theory with the presumed adoption of the attributes of the West to address the need of the developing countries (Marais and Venter, 2006).

4.3.4 Conclusion

This section looks at the philosophical perspective guiding housing research, especially as it relates to broad issue of social structure. The neoclassical perspective views housing in the context of demand, supply and prices as it impacts on land and finance market. While the neo-Marxist focuses on the role of the state in the process of capital accumulation and housing, the liberal on the other hand sees self-help and its use value against exchange value context. Though the liberal has been criticized on every front as their proposition was considered to lack appeal in some areas, especially the questioning of the both the economic and social structure shaped by capitalism. This chapter discussed the social opportunities that housing provides either in the form of mixed-income housing or social housing. In reviewing the evolution of housing from 1950 to 1990, the chapter brought out an interesting argument as it relates to future housing demand as highlighted by UN with emphasis on assisted self-help. It is seen as not only providing sustainable shelter but also incorporating a substantive amount of sweat equity. The enablement strategies of the 1980s as experimented by World Bank in Africa development trajectory was not the focus on housing alone but on the continents entire economic development. The chapter concludes by noting that the policy shift of the late 1990s onwards advocates a strong 'community development capacity' and to re-equip engineers, architects, town planners and construction project managers with advisory and instructor skills in order to enable them be able to advise non-technician community leaders and householders on how to plan and build economically and efficiently, or how to instruct and supervise small (artisan) builders. The next chapter will look at the housing development strategy that requires this cluster of professionals in the implementation and management.

Chapter 5

Mixed-Income Housing Development in Developed Nations

5.1 Introduction

Quigley and Raphael (2004) in their research on housing unaffordability in the United States argue that concern of the people when it comes to housing should be viewed from multiple sources. To start with housing is considered to constitute very significantly to the item in the monetary expenditure tables of both an individual and families in today's world. According to these findings, most families in Europe and the United States set aside about 25% of their annual income to housing-related issues. This is noted to have adverse effects in both the maintenance of the house or mortgage cost as well as other associated consequences in the household well-being (Quigley and Raphael, 2004). A second point that is highlighted is that consumers' housing needs and location do tend to influence and impact on urban life quality, including items such as transport, schooling, employment consideration, social activities and general neighbourhood access to social amenities (Quigley and Raphael, 2004). The third point considered is that other external factors do tend to contribute and determine the type of housing consumed by households. Apart from the social and physical isolation of the poor who live in low-income residential neighbourhoods, other identified issues that are worthy of note are the social capitals and the political participation of households who are the owners of their homes (Quigley and Raphael, 2004). According to Darcy (2010) though, the United Kingdom, the United States, and Australia do show some areas of similarities and differences in the typology, formation, characteristics and the nature of tenant populations in their housing systems they are noted to have engaged in the redesign and redevelopment of old buildings to fight social injustice and marginalization by replacing areas with mixed-income development. The previous chapter discussed the theoretical and philosophical perspectives that inform housing research over time. In this section, we shall look into mixed-income housing development as practiced in developed nations through the revision of experiences and practice in these countries. The purpose is to identify the developed nations' mixed-income housing development strategies as well as how the policies evolve over time. This is necessary to derive lessons for the South African mixed-income housing approach.

Mixed-Income Housing Development Planning Strategies and Frameworks in the Global South, 51–69
Copyright © 2024 George Okechukwu Onatu, Wellington Didibhuku Thwala and Clinton Ohis Aigbavboa
Published under exclusive licence by Emerald Publishing Limited
doi:10.1108/978-1-83753-814-020231005

5.2 Mixed-Income Housing Development in the United States

Mixed-income housing development took hold across the United States as an urban redevelopment strategy. According to Bennett et al. (2006 cited in Guenther, 2015:7) mixed-income housing in the United States is an 'attempt to undo years of hostility, racial segregation and discriminations in housing'. Since the mid-1990s, mixed-income housing development has gained increased attention from policy-makers and local developers, particularly as a tool for transforming failed public housing developments (Bohl, 2000; Boston, 2005; Briggs, 1997; Brophy and Smith, 1997; Epp, 1996; Goetz, 2003; Khadduri, 2001; Popkin et al., 2000, 2004; Rosenbaum et al., 1998; Schwartz and Tajbakhsh, 1997; Smith, 2002; Turbov and Piper, 2005; von Hoffman, 1996). One view of mixed-income housing developments is that they are about more than building quality housing: they are about rebuilding urban neighbourhoods. The central goal should be about 'building community' (Chaskin et al., 2009:1). Mixed-income developments are the new wave in low-income housing policy. This policy replaces the existing ruins of public housing projects by granting private producers subsidies predicated on building developments that maintain a pre-determined ratio of subsidized to market rate tenants. The policies of the US government explicitly target the mal-effects and underlying problems associated with concentrations of poverty produced by the traditional government projects. Government housing facilities ended up becoming centres of crime, violence, juvenile delinquency, substance abuse, and an array of other social ills that imposed costs on the recipients and the community (Coulton and Pandey, 1992; Crane 1991; Polikoff, 1994; Quercia and Galster, 1997). Additional costs associated with concentrated poverty are externalities that are harder to capture in the traditional sense, including stigmatization, alienation, and withdrawal from private capital and connections to the neighbourhood (Leavitt and Loukaitou-Sideris, 1995; Massey and Kanaiaupuni, 1993). For example, some scholars have found out that the stigmatization of deprived neighbourhoods as noted in some American cities may lead employers to discriminate against workers because of their residential location (Zenou and Boccard, 2000). Market failure arguments also implicitly or explicitly underpin these planning proposals, even when acknowledging the failures of public housing programmes. In his own argument Ellickson (2010:987) noted that the quality of the United States housing stock has improved markedly since the beginning of the 20th century. Despite the relative stinginess of the United States housing aid, the United States housing compares favourably in quality, even at the low end, to that found abroad. Members of American households in the bottom quintile of the national income distribution have 855 square feet of living area per capital. This is roughly double the per capital living area available to members of average-income households in France, Germany and the United Kingdom.

5.2.1 The Implications of Public Housing Programme

The results of past housing programmes, social conditions and policy changes all combined to signal that new strategy is needed for addressing the nation's affordable-housing problem. Smith (2002:7) notes that mixed-income owes much of its resurgence in America to the following factors: (1) adverse effects of concentrations of poverty, (2) poor perceived quality of subsidized housing and (3) shortage of affordable housing.

5.2.1.1 Adverse Effects of Concentrations of Poverty

The degree to which neighbourhoods with high concentrations of poverty proliferated due to the exodus of middle-class families from urban areas is startling. In 1970, only one neighbourhood in Chicago had a poverty rate of over 40%, but by 1980 that number had grown to nine. In the nation's five largest cities, the number of poor families living in such neighbourhood grew by 182% during this time period (Wilson, 1987). Bruce Katz of the Brookings Institution asserts that researchers have "found a direct correlation between these neighbourhoods of high poverty and such key social indicators as declining school performance and relatively high rates of criminal activity, family fragmentation, substance abuse and teenage pregnancy (Katz, 1999). Some of the key report and findings for individuals living in neighbourhoods with very high concentration of poverty, particularly those with poverty rates of greater than 40% according to Smith (2002), include:

- *Poor School Performance/Drop Out:* One study report that when the percentage of high-status workers in a neighbourhood fell below 5.6%, the dropout rates of African American teenagers rose dramatically.
- *Low Wage and Employment Levels:* One study found out that at least one quarter of the gap in education and earnings of African American men due to background differences can be accounted for by differences in neighbourhood quality.
- *High Teenage Pregnancy Rates:* A review of empirical research found that almost all studies indicate a negative relationship between neighbourhood poverty levels and sexual activity or pregnancy among adolescents.
- *High Incidence of Crime:* Studies indicate a strong association between violence and low neighbourhood socio-economic status.

Several theories exist as to why these negative factors grow more prevalent in communities with high concentrations of poverty, and why it is more difficult to break a cycle of poverty in such circumstances. One reason is that fewer opportunities exist in high-poverty communities to encourage skill development and income growth. Schools are often poor, local employment opportunities are scarce, and community institutions are weak or non-existent (Smith, 2002). There is also emphasis on economic isolation. William Julius Wilson argues that social isolation of residents of high-poverty areas constraints their access to job networks, marriageable partners and exposure to conventional role models. 'Ghetto-specific culture is a response to these structural constraints and limited opportunities'. Oscar Lewis, have asserted that the negative behaviours of poor persons in high-poverty areas are not only a response to their environment, but represents an endemic culture of poverty, 'passed down from generation to generation'. While the role of social and strictly economic factors in perpetuating a cycle of poverty can be debated, the underlying findings are clear that families residing in high-poverty areas face a tremendous difficult path to escaping poverty.

In reaction to the abject conditions found in both neighbourhoods and public-housing developments with high concentration of poverty, many policy-makers have concluded that these concentrations must be broken up at all costs. The boldest step in this direction and one with the most resources has been the HOPE VI programme administered by HUD from 1993 to 2002. The goal of these developments is to create mixed-income communities that tackles the social ills of the prior development. Since HOPE VI legislation was passed in 1992 mixed-income housing has become the dominant form of public housing delivery in the United States and the great hope for making cities more liveable and equitable place (Guenther, 2015:7).

5.2.2 The Homeownership and Opportunity for People Everywhere (HOPE) VI Programme

The housing problem in America involves people under 30% of area median income, sometimes called extremely low – income households (Wilkins, 2001:2). HOPE VI (Homeownership and Opportunity for People Everywhere) programme is a plan by the US Department of Housing and Urban Development (HUD). It is meant to revitalize the worst public housing projects in the United States into mixed-income developments. Its philosophy is largely based on the new urbanism and the concept of defensible space. The new urbanism is an urban design movement which promotes walkable neighbourhoods containing a range of housing and jobs types. It arose in United States in the early, 1980s, and has gradually informed many aspects of real estate developments, urban planning and municipal land use strategies. It comprises of principles of traditional neighbourhood design (TND). It is also related to regionalism, environmentalism and smart growth. It also supports regional planning for open spaces. It now has a charter that covers issues such as historical preservations, safe streets, green building and the re-development of brown fields land. According to Yan (2004) the Hope VI exposed again the federal role in low-income housing delivery and contributed significantly to a landmark piece of legislation in the Public Housing Reform Act of 1998.

5.2.3 The Concept

HOPE VI makes use of new urbanism, meaning that communities must be dense, pedestrian-friendly, and transit-accessible. Housing rarely comes in the form of apartments. Instead, private houses, duplexes, and especially for public housing projects, row houses are preferred, because these buildings directly interact with the street. Similarly, houses always stand close to the street, with small front yards. It is common to see porches on the buildings, as well as small apartments for single residents built over garages or on the ground floor. By applying defensible space, most communities are specifically designed or remodelled with private property, emphasizing security. Buildings are low-rise and often integrated directly into failing urban areas, to revitalize them. Private custodianship, with individuals taking care of their assigned part of the project, is a critical element. Likewise, providing residents with high-quality materials and houses is believed to encourage pride in the space and an interest in keeping things in good condition. The plan focusses on the economic and social needs of the residents (Johnson, 2006:291). This, theoretically, mitigates vandalism. In general, much of the philosophy comes from a theory that apartment buildings are not healthy spaces for human habitation. Only with substantial wealth can an apartment building maintain the characteristics of security, social networking, and urban integration that the designers feel is necessary for a healthy community. Instead, the lower-rise, urban feel with a sense of safety in the built environment satisfies that need.

Many of the elements of the programme do not involve construction of buildings at all. More funding goes to housing assistance vouchers than in previous programmes. As with the strategy of constructing in-fill housing in middle-class neighbourhoods and providing new housing for market-rate buyers, this element helps integrate residents into existing neighbourhoods to produce cohesion. It aimed at making recipients of public assistance more self-sufficient by linking them with training, employment where possible, transportation and childcare through housing provisions (Johnson, 2006:296). In almost all implementations of the programme, housing authorities and non-profits have provided resident-assistance information programmes for new homeowners, teaching them and their neighbours how to take care of a house that they must protect.

5.2.4 The Criticisms

Some have criticized the plan for having the right goals but not accomplishing them, or not going about them in the right way. The National Housing Law Project issued a joint report saying, 'HOPE VI has been characterized by a lack of clear standards, a lack of hard data on programme results, and misleading and contradictory statements made by HUD'. The report said:

> HUD's failure to provide comprehensive and accurate information about HOPE VI has created an environment in which misimpressions about the program and its basic purposes and outcomes have flourished – often with encouragement from HUD. HOPE VI plays upon the public housing program's unfairly negative reputation and an exaggerated sense of crisis about the state of public housing in general to justify a drastic model of large-scale family displacement and housing redevelopment that increasingly appears to do more harm than good.

Some have criticized the new developments, because they do not require a 'one-for-one' replacement of the old housing unit – the new unit does not have to house the same number of tenants, which results in a net loss of housing for the poor. The one-for-one replacement policy was repealed by Congress in 1998, separately from HUD's implementation of HOPE VI. The Urban Institute reported that the number of units receiving a federal subsidy and available for the deeply poor to live in is cut in half in developments arising from the programme. The National Low-Income Housing Coalition has said that no HOPE VI grants should be allotted without requirements for one-for-one-unit replacement.

The NLIHC maintains that to acquire federal grants, local housing authorities have 'demolished viable units and displaced families.' The programme has been called 'notorious' for its allotment of federal grants for demolition of public housing, and some say it has resulted in a 'dramatic loss of housing.' Some critics have said that local authorities use the programme as a legal means to evict poor residents in favour of more affluent residents in a process of gentrification. They have said that less than 12% of those displaced from old housing eventually move into the replacement housing. One writer asserted that in the case of a section of Cabrini–Green in Chicago, residents were forced out for HOPE VI redevelopment by armed police. Federal auditors in the United States found that HUD was awarding grants based on the ability of the area to generate income for the city rather than the actual state of the housing project in question. Only seven of the first 34 grants went towards the development of high-rise housing.

5.2.5 Problems and Challenges Associated With American Housing Policies

When examining the problems with these policies a central issue that these programmes do not produce their hypothesized results and there is little evidence that the expected benefits will be realized (DeFillipis and Fraser, 2008:9). According to these scholars, poor people do not seem to benefit much from mixed-income. The issue of moving people around urban areas and promoting mixes of income distributions is viewed as commensurate with opening opportunity structures to people in poverty. Arguably, these policies often leave poor people in places without the social networks and informal social support of prior neighbourhoods (Ibid:10). Despite assumptions to the contrary, poor urban neighbourhood have dense networks of social support that have been created largely out of necessity because services that are commodities in wealthy neighbourhoods (childcare, watching after each other house and helping out one another) must be negotiated as non-commodity when the participants do not have money. Fraser and Kick (2007), in their study of Hope VI project in Durham, North Carolina, found that those residents relocated into other public housing developments not only face the challenge of building social networks, but did so in the context of harsh environment of crime and violence. Mixed-income policies have failed to create social mixing, networks and interaction – that is, social capital. This is because the mixed-income leave the larger social cleavage unaltered (DeFillipis and Fraser, 2008:11). Such policies are self-defeating as poor people (especially those with vouchers) often re-concentrate in new places. Mixed-income housing development/neighbourhoods are comprised of residents who have pre-existing and differentiated sets of economic, cultural and social capital (Bourdieu, 1986), hence, the existence of power differentials in a mixed-income locality. While segregation is a barrier to social justice, it does not necessarily follow that integration is a solution. Space, it seems, can more easily be part of the problem than part of the solution. Being in close proximity need not engender interaction, and when it does, that interaction may mean conflict as much as anything else (DeFillipis and Fraser, 2008:14). The physical criticisms of HOPE VI also include with destructive urban renewal of the past-including the potential conflict of interest created by the involvement of private developers (Johnson and Talen, 2008:302).

5.3 Mixed-Income Housing Development in United Kingdom

The concept of 'social mix' was first introduced in the United Kingdom in the 1800s in the 'old style liberalism of utopian experiments' seeking to reverse the class-based spatial segregation produced by capitalist urbanization (Melis et al., 2013). The creation of socially mixed housing has been a policy aspiration sought by many governments of different politically persuasion and can be traced back at least as far as the post war New Towns programme. The policy in the United Kingdom, as compared to other nations, including the United States, is argued to aim at delivering significant number of housing in the South East and addressing market failure and poor condition in the Housing Market Renewal Pathfinder areas in Midlands and North of England. It is also aimed at addressing a range of problems, including deteriorating housing stock, lack of services and amenities, crime, and resident population with high rates of unemployment, dropping out of school and single parenthood (Levy et al., 2010:3). The objectives are also to provide 'well-designed housing in pleasant environment, designed to meet the needs of the whole community now and in future which the residents will call home' (Ibid:16). According to Sarkissian (1976) the common belief was that the better off would take more of an interest in the problems of the poor, while the poor would be encouraged to emulate 'respectable working class' behaviours. While government policy favours the creation of mixed communities in order to increase social cohesion, there is little detailed guidance on what constitute 'mix' and 'affordability' and how these can sustain in the longer term? The primary objective in most new developments and in diversification of existing estates is to engage experienced developers and Registered Social Landlords (RSLs) in a collaborative effort to deliver a high-quality residential environment and appropriate infrastructure, services and facilities. Linked to this is the setting up of an effective management system which will sustain the area in the longer term. The government is seeking to avoid creating the kinds of racial and economic isolation seen in the United States and has developed a model similar to HOPE VI that will transform its assisted housing into mixed-income, mixed-tenure communities (Levy et al., 2010).

5.3.1 The Growing Economic Segregation and Concentrated Deprivation

Poverty has an important spatial dimension, and Britain's performance is more lacklustre (Barube, 2005). Its households continue to experience significant levels of economic segregation. This segregation is visible at several geographical levels and regionally between the North and South. Notable features of this include:

- Gross Value Added (GVA), a measure of economic productivity is about 70% higher for London residents than for residents of the North East and grew 60% faster per annum in London from 1989 to 2000 (Robinson, 2005).
- After taking housing costs into account, 29% of households in London and South East have incomes in the top quantile nationally, compared to just 13%–15% in the northern regions.
- Even among demographically similar groups, regional differences are stark. The employment rate for young men with no qualification living in council housing in the South-East increased from 58% in 1983 to 85% in 2002. By contrast, employment among the same group in the northern conurbation fell from 32% to 25% over the same period (Faggio and Nickell, 2003).

Economic segregation apart from the North-South divide, some London boroughs and northern cities and towns share high levels of deprivation associated with limited local jobs opportunities, and low employability and income among the local population (Barube, 2005:7). On key measures such as age, ethnicity, wealth and employment, the country became more divided at the local authority level in both the 1980s and 1990s (Dorling and Rees, 2003). Analysis of deprived neighbourhoods suggests that poor children tend to be more spatially concentrated than poor adults (Lupton and Tunstall, 2003). In view of this, policymakers in England acknowledge that concentrated deprivation is a problem worth addressing. According to Barube (2005) some of the factors that contribute to the rising economic segregation includes: Rising income inequality, residential choices and housing policies. With respect to concentrated deprivation, notable consequences include:

- *Concentration of deprivation reduces private sector activity and raise prices for the poor*
  Large numbers of low-income and low skilled households living in the same place make a community less attractive to private sector investors and employers. There is lack of competition among retailers in these communities, and the lack of accurate consumer information needed to set prices, also result to low-income families paying more than families in middle-income neighbourhoods for basic goods and services (Fellowes, 2005; Wrigley, 2002).
- *High levels of worklessness limit job networks and employment ambitions*
  The high levels of labour force inactivity among the working age-population in these neighbourhoods are fuelled by low skills or limited work experience, long-term illness and weak local labour demand. According to Social

Exclusion Unit (2004) evidence from the United Kingdom and elsewhere suggests that individuals living in the most deprived are 5%–15% more likely to be out of work than similar individuals elsewhere

- *Schools struggle to educate overwhelming poor population*
  Concentration of low-income pupils at the school levels present several potential obstacles to students' achievements, some acting through individual students' background and others through environmental influences. The probability of pupil success at the primary school level it is argued is strongly related to intake characteristics and neighbourhood wealth, more so than teachers qualification and expenditures per pupil (Gibbons, 2002). Parents and teachers may have lower expectations for children from disadvantaged backgrounds and this can lower aspirations and performance (Barube, 2005).
- *Area-based deprivation exacerbates health inequality*
  Residents of poor and deprived neighbourhoods are most likely to experience inferior health outcomes even after holding their individual circumstance constant (Joshi et al., 2000 cited in Barube, 2005). The physical characteristics of poor neighbourhoods it is argued may contribute to these health deficiencies.

5.3.2 Changes in the Policy Context

Government policy in England and other parts of United Kingdom has strongly endorsed the principle that new housing developments and existing social rented estates should become mixed-income communities. In the Housing Green Paper, *Quality and Choice: A Decent Home for ALL* (DERT, 2000), the government states clearly its objectives to promote an 'urban renaissance' by encouraging better use of existing buildings and previously developed land to meet the projected housing requirements. It is expected that there will be a need to accommodate about 3.8 million new households between 1996 and 2021, and to do this the government supports the implementation of the idea of the 'compact city', that is higher density, mixed-use development (Burton, 2003). This principle is now being embedded in a wide range of housing, planning and development policies. The direction of housing policies in the United Kingdom in recent times has also been geared towards encouraging local authorities to require the provision of affordable housing through Section 106 agreement and to embed the need for mixed communities in planning policy. The desire to achieve mixed communities should not be seen as an end in itself but as one important precondition for achieving successful and sustainable place to live. The location of affordable housing largely defines households 'geography of opportunities' whether these households will have access to schools, to safe and clean streets, to local shops and employment options (Barube, 2005). These residential environments should not only be well designed and well managed, but also provide access to the full range of high quality services including leisure and employment opportunities (Ibid:22). At the national level in England, Planning Policy Guidance Note 3 on housing is constantly being amended so as to enable Local Development Documents (LDD) to set out 'the broad balance between the numbers of different household types to be provided across the plan area over plan period'. The document also contains policies on affordable housing, reflecting different housing market conditions, proportion of affordable housing on the development is also negotiated by local authorities so that it should not be more than 15 dwelling or sites of more than 0.5 hectares. Government does not consider that different types of housing and tenure make bad neighbours. Planning plays an important role by ensuring that appropriate mix of housing that addresses the needs of households, including in terms of what they can afford. In the draft version of Planning Policy Statement 3, published in December 2005, the creation of 'sustainable, inclusive, mixed communities in all areas' is one of the three primary objectives of housing policies. The policy further argues the need to ensure that:

(1) Communities are mixed in terms of tenure, income and ethnicity,
(2) Set target to transform all social housing estates into mixed tenure communities by 2012,
(3) Use the many small unused sites within already built-up areas to increase the supply of affordable housing close to local amenities and open spaces by using public funds to lever in a variety of housing types of different scales, costs and sizes that responds to the needs, aspirations and budget of ordinary households,
(4) Improve city conditions through better schools, greater policing and more neighbourhood management,
(5) Renovate, modernize and build in-fill housing within the existing framework by reshaping units and adding new high-quality units to older neighbourhoods.

5.3.3 Mixed-Income Housing Development as Policy Goal and Policy

The broad goals of mixed communities in the United King cover both broad policy goal and a specific policy approach. Tunstall and Lupton (2010) argue that the aims of the mixed-income housing development policy include:

- Mixed communities are a general social good, reflecting an integrated and egalitarian society in which people of all social classes and income share same space, services and facilities, creating conditions in which mutual understanding and/or shared norms can potentially develop;
- Mixed communities as spaces to encourage racial, ethnic or religious cohesion, or which prevents increasing segregation;
- Mixed communities as workable or sustainable communities, following a notion that a combination of different land uses, building types and people is more sustainable, more mutually supportive, easier to manage and more capable to support a varied range of activities, facilities and services.

The underlying assumption is that these kinds of communities are likely to be better for individuals as well as society as whole, promoting better life chances. Broad mixed communities in the United Kingdom as compared to other countries are relevant to the policy goal 1 and 2, but this is not the principal motivation for intervention. In a review of Castle Vale Housing Estate, Levy et al. (2010) note that 'Diversity and relations among residents are concerns for staff and board members of the estate because increasing equality and diversity is a goal for the community'. The regeneration of this neighbourhood is noted to have enabled a reduction in crime of 30% between 2003 and 2006 (Ibid). The primary objective of mixed communities as can be seen, including the Section 106 provisions is to address the problems of disadvantaged areas. Mixed communities policies are seen as solutions for disadvantaged areas, not just as a broad social goal worth pursuing (Tunstall and Lupton, 2010). They are proposed to restore conditions of integration, cohesion, workability and sustainability, or to create them.

The British approach to urban planning and regeneration is distinct from the emphasis on dispersal that is found in many other parts of European urban policies, as it seeks to improve the life chances of the poor urban households in situ (Brooks, 2005; Busch-Geertsema, 2007; Imbroscio, 2008 cited in Melis et al., 2013:16). The emphasis is mainly to increase social diversity within deprived neighbourhoods, without any major displacement of poor households. Policy is posited on the assumption that, if spatial concentration of poverty can be avoided, the area effects associated with deprived neighbourhoods should not arise to the same extent. Unemployment, substance misuse, crime, and other social problems will still exist, but once they are not spatially concentrated, the strain on public services, risks to public order and other negative effects should be less (Melis et al., 2013).

5.4 Mixed-Income Housing Development in Australia

Australia associates the term social mixture of tenure to denote Mixed-income housing development. The strategy as used is almost the same way as other cases reviewed so far to tackle the problem of concentrated poverty in public housing as well as issues of criminal activities, bad social behaviours, bad impression of these neighbourhoods and low education level. These problems are addressed by urban revitalization and rejuvenation aimed at creating a social mix of the neighbourhoods (Arthurson, 2012; Atkinson and Jacobs, 2008; August, 2008; Bond et al., 2011; Wood, 2003). In this chapter of this book, we will examine social mixture of tenure, interaction, unemployment, the well-being of concerned society, the physical environment quality and social amenities, and anti-social behaviour. The research will also review some important policies and plans that guide housing.

5.4.1 The Meaning of Social Mix

Social mix can be considered as a very complex phenomenon which cut across other issues that characterizes the era of public housing as it relates to marginalization, poverty, vulnerability and seclusion (Patulny and Morris, 2012). In an attempt to explain this concept further, this researcher reviewed 266 referenced articles and found that what constitute a neighbourhood that is socially integrated and mix of social class is not easy. The definition of social mix go beyond an explanation merely based on tenure mixture as it is the case in most countries, rather it considers issues of level of income, race, attainment of education, customs and age (Atkinson, 2008; Kleit and Carnegie, 2011). It is also argued in the literature that social mix also considers how the subsidy beneficiaries relate to the private owner (Darcy, 2009; Randolph and Wood, 2004). As compared with other developed countries, social mix in Australia as a housing policy framework and strategy is seen as a fight to tackle the social marginalization as manifested in public housing with the aim of addressing localized disadvantaged and social marginalization by promoting proper way of life, good behaviour and values to low income earners as practiced by middle income earners. According to (Ruming, 2011:2) the benefits of social mix include: increase the propensity of tenants in public housing to be able to network with middle to high income earners and this increases their chances to get job and social associations, copying of the appropriate behaviours, mannerism and platform for owners to act as good examples and pace setters thereby reducing discriminations experienced by the concentration and location of social housing. As a policy initiative social mix feature at most prominently in housing regeneration that is aimed at addressing local circumstances in marginalized and socially discriminated areas (Jacobs et al., 2011).

5.4.2 Housing Policy and Social Mix

When the Commonwealth Housing Commission was set up in 1943, one of its initial tasks was to conduct an inquiry into the condition of Australian housing. The inquiry found that housing demand was far more than housing supply in the whole states of Australian, and that the majority of the housing that is existing were of poor quality (Arthurson, 2012:27). Housing shortages as reported was due to the reduction and slow down in construction industry during the Great Depression of the 1930s and the World War II. This commission argued that to address these problems, at least 700,000 houses needed to be built over the following decades (Sandercock, 1977: 103–105 cited in Arthurson, 2012:27). Based on the recommendations of the inquiry, the Commonwealth – State Housing Agreement (CSHA) was enacted in 1945 and then renegotiated every few years by the government with both the federal and state governments until end of 2008, when it was replaced by the (NAHA). This new agency resulted to considerable change in the way the financial and policy framework for Australia social housing is structured, by offering tax and other funding incentives to encourage institutional investment in affordable housing (Ibid, 2012). The aim of this is principally to avoid what are perceived as the current problems with social housing, including concentration of housing in particular neighbourhoods, issues of stigma, lack of access to services and employment, and highly disadvantaged residents experiencing social exclusion (Arthurson, 2012). The findings show that due to how busy the homeowners were there was limited interaction and social relations with the public housing residents. Social contacts only take place in the local schools. Due to the fact that these children are coming from different tenures system and structures it also triggered and facilitated some contacts between parents who come from different tenure system, especially during school activities. In the absence of proper planning framework and public participation, government efforts to facilitate social mixture of housing can negate the existing social networks and results to unnecessary stress, rather than promoting social cohesive environment with a feeling of community lifestyle. Stubbs et al. (2005:99 cited in Patulny and Morris, 2012), in a case study of an estate built and resided by the public in Sydney, found that the social relations and interaction of residents were hampered by the re-development as many felt loss of sense of community, friends, neighbours and networks.

5.4.3 The Goals of Social Mix

For several years in the past, the notion of social mix in housing is attributed to strategy to accomplishing a set of housing objectives and goals. These set goals are listed as follows:

5.4.3.1 Social Acceptance and Well-Being

Researchers argues that social mix of residents and their social well-being in a public housing tenants in an integrated residential neighbourhood is far more deplorable and of low standard than that of tenants in socially mixed areas. Patulny and Morris (2012), in exploring this, used two criteria of socially acceptable well-being outcomes: access to jobs and health facilities. In reviewing the work of Randolph and Wood (2004 cited in Patulny and Morris, 2012), it is noted that in the Australia that four selected public housing estates that had passed through urban renewal exercise together with (another set of public housing estates of about four that had not experienced social mix) both show dissimilarities in terms of residents behaviour and attributes. In analyzing the census data collected from the period 1996 up to 2001 in order to find out the emerging social relations and tenure changes, it emerged that there was no scientific proof on how social mix has contributed in changing the access to jobs and employment.

5.4.3.2 Raising the Living Standard Through Emulation

The attempt to improve and raise the living standard of most neighbourhoods has been the principal goal of Australia housing programme since the 19th century. According to Sarkissian et al. (1990), the poor and marginalized are compelled to copy through observations how to keep neighbourhood neat, clean and very attractive as practised by higher income residents. Their curiosity and interest are expected to be heightened through emulation, mingling with and indulgence with the middle-class residents.

5.4.3.3 Attributes of the Physical Environment and Amenities

Social mix policies results to tangible improvement in the physical environment, especially the quality of the housing units/stocks and overall appearance of the entire neighbourhood. Van Beckhoven and Van Kempen (2003:869), in one of their research, noted that residents were very optimistic and confident about the changes that are taking place in their neighbourhood, especially living quality, spatial design features, green spaces and the general appearance of the entire neighbourhood. This point is also supported by Randolph and Wood (2004), who noted that the visual aesthetic of the area was improved significantly. The varieties and mix of residential buildings/apartments in areas occupied by different social groups could add beauty and enhance the residents' appreciation to keep their houses up to date and of standard (Sarkissian et al., 1990). The findings shows the success of renewal and how social mix has improved the desirability and property value of the areas and can also contribute to economic growth.

5.4.3.4 To Increase Opportunities

Residential mix is seen by many social theorists as one of the strategies to bring back the lost glory, aspirations and hope of previous disadvantaged communities. It is argued that mixed housing can provide needed platform to climb political ladder and enhance participation as well as give voice to the voiceless in terms of governance (Sarkissian et al., 1990:5).

5.4.4 Key Priority on Government Housing Policy Agenda

In view of a shortfall in private dwellings in Australia resulting from the inability of private dwellings constructed to keep pace with swelling population, together with increase difficulties, the young generations are facing in breaking into the homeownership, the government has now set key policy agenda. According to a report by the Asian Pacific Network for Housing Research (APNHR) of 2014: Firstly, it is noted that regulatory reforms in land release and planning need to be implemented to streamline development processes; Secondly, there is proposal to make changes to the reporting requirements of the National Affordable Housing Agreement (an agreement between the Federal, State and Territorial governments that is aimed to tackle the problems of access to housing and affordability issues through a whole-of-government approach).

5.4.5 Comparing Mixed-Income Housing in the United States and Australia

In America, the mixed-income housing development through HOPE VI is aimed at decreasing site density, whereas in Australia it is aimed at increasing densities. With tenure, according to Guenther (2015:14) the distribution is different as seen in other areas, with mixed-income developments in the United States guided by the 'rules of 3rd, with one in three units as public housing, one in three set aside for affordable rentals, and the remaining one in three market rental for-sale units'. Whereas communities that are redeveloped and revamped in Australia are in the ratio of market rate and public housing respectively with 70% and 30% each. Australia has no alternative housing option, unlike the United States with Housing Choice Vouchers. In terms of design, majority of the estates in Australia, especially New South Wales, are of Radburn-style suburban developments and Garden City concepts; whereas in United States, the buildings are classified as 'severely distressed' by HUD (Guenther, 2015:15).

5.4.6 Critique of Social Mix

Several studies have criticized the kind of interactions of households of varying tenure rights and income group in a mix residential areas (Atkinson and Kintrea, 2000; Ruming et al., 2004 cited in Arthurson, 2012). Others have critiqued on the ground of reduction in the housing units built, as this is expected to lead to increase in the waiting times of prospective applicants (Arthurson, 2010). Another radical argument against social mix housing initiatives is provided by Gans (1961 cited in Arthurson, 2012:33). Gans raised several questions about the desirability of creating heterogeneous communities together with the efficacy of social mix policies and robustness of the underlying ideas used to implement it. According to this theorist, if the underlying economic and social inequalities attached to class were addressed, then the increased opportunities may naturally lead to greater heterogeneity within neighbourhoods. Forced heterogeneity or varying social mix of the different classes within particular neighbourhoods could in some instances threaten resident security and cause conflicts or dispute between neighbours (Ibid). Other scholars also argue that the desegregation weakens working class communities, in effect rubbing them of their collective power. In view of the contentious nature of social mix as a housing policy, Willmott and Young (1960 cited in Arthurson, 2012) called for more empirical studies to be conducted to test the propositions associated with it.

5.5 Mixed-Income Housing Development in Netherland

In Netherland mixed-income housing provide the platform for affordable housing schemes and inform to a great extent the countries urban development policies. This section looks at the countries housing affordability and urban development strategies through mixed-income housing development.

5.5.1 Housing Affordability in Europe

The affordability question in terms of access to housing is considered an effective and strong political weapon for most countries in Europe both in the East and Centre, including Netherlands, though each might have quite different housing programmes (Liias, 1998). The result of this shows that, housing burden and expenditures in most of the East and Central European countries are very severe and stressful. The aspiration for homeownership as a nation has resulted in more than 90% of the housing stock to be owner-occupier, thereby creating additional problems some of which have grown from bad to worse in recent years. Notable primary objectives and goals of national housing policies strategies in the European countries are geared towards making housing affordable (Joseph Rowntree Foundation, 1990). Housing policy of the welfare states typically has the aim to provide good and affordable housing to all, rather than being responsible only for people with special needs. Affordability as it relates to housing has been narrowly defined by various scholars and the interpretations in policy document are questionable (Liias, 1998). Sometimes it is used in a meaningless manner that denotes other social issues (Joseph Rowntree Foundation, 1990). Observers view it as an aspect of political slogan which every dick and harry uses, but on a serious note nobody is held accountable or responsible. The term can be considered as meaningless and stand for nothing if proper definition is not well spelt out. Consideration is given to the fact that 'affordable should be attributed to the households'. Basically model of interpreting 'affordable housing' and affordability is by calculating the ratio between the housing expenditure and income available for the household in question. This is:

$$\frac{\text{Housing } \textbf{EXPENDITURE} \text{ of the occupier}}{\textbf{INCOME} \text{ of the occupier}}$$

5.5.2 Affordable Housing Programme in Netherlands

The Netherlands has one of the most unique affordable housing programmes in Europe to be emulated and studied. Affordable housing in the real sense of it is considered a right rather than a privilege. The idea of mixed neighbourhood in Netherlands which form part of the affordable housing dates back to the World War II. During this period the district as part of neighbourhood was consider as an appropriate entity for its residents. The principal aim is geared not to mix groups of people but rather to ensure that functions are mixing and coexist with each other (Van Kempen and Bolt, 2009 cited in Melis et al., 2013). The Dutch urban policy give priority to the issue of social classes and mixing in order to reduce the inequality and segregation that unfolds (Goodchild and Cole, 2001 cited in Melis et al., 2013:18). The new housing policy that came into effect in the 1980s reinforced this by noting that the social housing segment to ensure provision of living space for the middle income group, thus thereby creating homogenous housing market (Melis et al., 2013). The idea was focus on those that has excess disposable income: those in the higher-income bracket could afford to move, leaving behind the low-income households to less expensive dwellings. During the 1990s this idea about the similar patterns of the urban districts occupied by the poor households and neighbourhoods in terms of low socio-economic cluster of the population was reviewed further. Hence the call for the poor inhabitants to be dispassed and the creation of mixed-income housing with more separated neighbourhoods that came into effect in 1996 (Bolt et al., 1998; Musterd, 2008). The assumption behind this was that an expansive social mix would lead to an increase and growth of social contacts between the old and the new inhabitants, thereby resulting to more prosperity and the improvement of the impoverished areas (Beckhoven and Van Kempen, 2003:854). Also, there were desire that the new arrival inhabitants would bring a boost to the neighbourhood that they moved into by buying from local cafes, food cot and shopping centre. Mixed-income housing development is looked upon and expected to bring about with it the replacement of the same category of low-income households by a neighbourhood that is very active, thriving and full of lively social contacts between separate groups of residents and fresh opportunities for local amenities such as shops and schools.

5.5.3 New Urban Housing Policy

Dating back to 2001 the debate on social mix changed drastically with the diversification of the housing supply in 'Unbalanced Areas' with the demolition of part of the social-rented units and replacement with more expensive dwellings. The present Dutch urban policy aims to reduce the spatial concentration of low-income households in urban neighbourhoods and to combat the negative effects of the concentration of minority ethnic groups on their integration (Melis et al., 2013:19). The idea is to encourage households notwithstanding social or cultural orientation to live together. Policies in the Netherlands that regulates the migration and movement of low-income people into the cities of the South is seen as one of the most contested debate on anti-segregation issues. Using as an example the laws of the city of Rotterdam, a country wide law was promulgated that empowers and give them authority to implement a separate allocation policy for some marginalized areas. Persons from outside given cities who do not have a steady job (except students and retired persons) are refused to be given a permanent residence in these identified neighbourhoods (Bolt, 2004 cited in Melis et al., 2013). This law has been criticized on several grounds: people without a job (of which majority of them are from the minority) are held accountable for the problems in high density residential neighbourhoods. Rather than the creation of opportunities to accommodate diversity and inclusivity for everyone, urban policy tend to ignore those without a job. In addition, questions and social debate have been resonated severally if these earmarked neighbourhoods will benefit from these enacted policies by the government. The mere fact that a certain neighbourhood is singled out and recognized or painted as a 'hot spot' is most probably to damage and affect adversely its image and name (Bolt et al., 2008).

Resulting from increased level of liberalization that is seen now in the housing sectors has intensified and given rise to inequalities and segregation in most residential areas. There is phenomenal difference between the social rental stock stand with 36% as compared to 52% owner occupiers. In spite of this rental stock that is currently being administered and coordinated by housing corporations are still by far the most important element of Netherlands housing market in recent times as proven by several research.

5.6 Lessons Learnt From Mixed-Income Housing Development in Developed Nations

- One of the important lessons that cut across all spheres of the housing authorities in the UK, the United States and Australia is the move towards increase in urban renewal and regeneration specifically aimed at tackling the issues associated with social exclusion through the replacement of areas of concentrated public housing with 'mixed-income' development.
- To reverse the social injustice and the years of hostile and segregation based on race and divisions in granting access to housing to certain groups of people, there is need for the revision and reconsideration of the implementation

strategies of mixed-income housing projects in the United States. Here, it is seen as an instrument to transform and change failed housing projects for the public with the aim of addressing the problem of living in areas of concentrated poverty, with associated social problems such as crime, violence, substance abuse and juvenile delinquency. Mixed-income housing development also failed in some areas in an attempt to creating social mixing and interactions.

- In the United Kingdom, mixed-income housing is also aimed at addressing more of market failures and poor conditions in some neighbourhood. Unlike in the United States, it is meant to mitigate social cohesion, but with unanswered question on what constitute 'mix' and 'affordability'. The government drives to advance the development of urban areas through renaissance by supporting any programme that betters the use of already existing and available building and the idea of compact city. Mixed-income, as compared to what is obtainable in other countries, is not seen as an end to itself, but rather as an attempt to promote 'geography of opportunities' that increases access to schools, to safe place to live, clean streets and employment opportunities. The government, in order to accomplish all this living conditions, set clear goal to tackle and change all social housing estates into mixed-income community.
- In Australia, the emphasis is on the use of mixed-income housing as a renewal strategy that focuses specifically on creating social mix. Social mix as used here in relation to mix-income housing development and is interpreted not only to include mix tenure as seen in so many countries, including the United States, but also incorporates other social indicators level of earning, schooling, race background, type and composition of household and sex. As compared to other nations, social mix in Australia is considered a housing policy framework that responds to marginalization through skills transfer and the promotion of values in society from middle income owners to low income public renters. Experience here shows if care is not taking as it relates to adequate planning framework and transparent public participation, all the efforts by the government to foster and promote a conducive environment for social integration and cohesive society can end up impacting negatively on the already existing social network and reciprocities.
- For the Netherlands, affordable housing is considered a right rather than a privilege. The idea of mixed neighbourhood in the Netherland forms part of the affordable housing strategies. Hence, the idea was not mix per se of group of people, but rather a mix by functions. The Dutch urban policy gives priority to the issue of mixing social classes to reduce the problem of inequality and segregation. Mixed-income was implemented with unique feature as it has to do with 'diversified neighbourhood' and with added objective to replace 'monoculture' of low-income household by a lively social contact and opportunity. Mixed-income is implemented as a first step to get needed planning approval and funding.

5.7 Conclusion

In conclusion, the net effect of the United Sates tax law is to reduce the price of homeownership relative to renting by a sizeable amount as compared to other countries. As a result of these policies, the relative price of homeownership varies by income level and the level of inflation. The central goal of mixed-income housing is to build community, and this is a new wave in low-income housing development strategy. The percentage of Americans living in government assisted housing provision is lower as compared to in France, United Kingdom and Netherlands. The Hope VI projects assisted in addressing the problems associated with public housing, but other issues of concern have been noted by scholars, such as lack of social network and social support are lacking. Residents are provided with high quality materials and houses thereby forcing them to appreciate quality living space and good ethical values as well as proper behaviours in living with others and maintenance of the built environment. The reluctance of the Department of HUD to furnish detailed and proper record about the operation and programme of HOPE VI has resulted to a situation whereby people create unnecessary impression about the achievements of the programme and its basic purposes. The goal of the redevelopment and the mixed-income housing opportunity provided in the United Kingdom is aimed at improving the housing stock and infrastructure as well as safety, increase in residents' economic and racial diversity, and increase the well-being of the disadvantaged households. One important challenge is how to foster a healthy community in the area. The manner that UK addresses urban planning issues and rejuvenation programmes is unique and different from others as they focus more on the dispersal strategies which tend to improve the life opportunities and privilege of the poor households living in cities. Social diversity within deprived neighbourhoods as shown in some case studies in this case study are noted to increase and improved upon. Mixed-income housing strategies are generally seen as social mix that brings life and upliftment to areas considered as disadvantaged, without only geared towards only broader social goal as noted in other countries worth pursuing. The review of social mix in Australia points out that renewal alone in the real sense of it and tenure security mixing are not just the only strategy to provide the kind of social integration that can lead to sustainable living conditions. The studies show that the idea of building social networks may not occur with the realities of contemporary social life. Nevertheless, the campaign for policies that support social mixing is based on the understanding that the underprivileged are left out most of the time and at risk of being excluded due to living in neighbourhoods with concentration of similar individuals, such as social housing estates. The major expectation from these findings is that any strategy that promotes social mixing of housing will assist in enhancing a community that is sustainable. The current debate is not about planning for social mix, but rather in the diversifying housing options and tenure rights and socio-economic mix. Finally, in the Netherlands, it is now a requirement that for any residential development to be supported by the government, it must set aside as a certain percentage of the site for the development of some components of social housing.

Chapter 6

Mixed-Income Housing Development Model in Developing Nations

6.1 Introduction

Due to the increased rate of urbanization throughout the world, housing provision and implementation is facilitated by the government (UN-Habitat, 2012). The concept housing has witnessed a number of paradigm shifts and innovative approaches in an effort to addressing the challenges of informal settlements upgrade, local economic development and climate change. The housing policies and strategies as it is formulated and implemented in developing world are guided by social, cultural and political considerations (Arku, 2006). In this section, we shall look at housing development in Brazil, Malaysia, Singapore, Nigeria, Botswana and Ghana.

6.2 Mixed-Income Housing Development in Brazil

This chapter provides a guide and insight to the literature on housing and implementation in Brazil, especially in the region of Sao Paulo and Rio de Janeiro, the two biggest cities in the country. In recent past there has been a lot of work written about the low-income housing in Brazil (Heather, 2005; Huchzermeyer and Karam, 2006; Maricato, 2005; Palmer et al., 2017; Moreira, 2009; Selvanayagam, 2012). The study of Brazil reflects the investigation of a country with a lot of differences. The country has a large extent of land mass of about 8,515,767 km^2, and it is larger than the 48 states of the United States combined. In South America, Brazil with 208 million people is one of the largest countries and ranked the fifth largest country in the whole world. According to current estimate it shows that 85% of the population of Brazil resides in urban areas (UN-Habitat, 2013:5). The highest population growth rate was between the periods of 1950s and 1960s with 3% annual growth rate. Furthermore, from the year 2000 to the year 2010, the population of the country grew at an average annual rate of 1.17% and this is noted to be the lowest ever witnessed in the country. The housing challenge and problems are among the most serious social issues in Brazil (Moreira, 2009).

Mixed-Income Housing Development Planning Strategies and Frameworks in the Global South, 71–86
Copyright © 2024 George Okechukwu Onatu, Wellington Didibhuku Thwala and Clinton Ohis Aigbavboa
Published under exclusive licence by Emerald Publishing Limited
doi:10.1108/978-1-83753-814-020231006

To add to this is complicated rapid growth in urban areas that grow faster than the development of infrastructure, basic social services and housing provisions in major cities (UN-Habitat, 2013:18). Any attempt to redress and find solutions to the Brazilian housing problem requires a new paradigm shift and equation in public policies. To do this, the current investigation looks at the historical background of Brazil housing situation, with the focus been on favelas (squatter settlement), the housing policies of National Housing Bank, and more recently the housing in the peripheral areas.

6.2.1 Favelas

Out of all the alternative housing options identified for the urban poor in Brazil, the squatter settlement, best known as favela (or mocambo, invasao or baixada) is the most common and most important (Valladares, 2005 cited in van Vliet et al., 2005:224). Housing research and investigations on housing started in Brazil in the 1960s, at a time when the favela was viewed as the residence for the poor people living in urban areas, also during the era when social marginality theory was widely acclaimed throughout the South America. This is in the beginning attributed to the fragile and sleepy housing conditions, to this extent the marginality population came to be identified with traits, such as low wages and education levels, underemployment, unemployment, disorganization of families, anomie and lack of social participation (Ibid, 2005). The first time that Favelas appeared in the urban landscape was in the 1890s. Until the 1950s favelas was housing 6.7% of the total population of Rio de Janeiro; 9.3% in 1960 and 13% in 1970 (Valladares, cited in van Vliet et al., 2005:224). Municipal estimates in recent times point to the existence in 1981 of 377 favelas with population of 1.5 million, which is 25% of Rio de Janeiro's population. In Sao Paulo favelas are more recent than in Rio, and housed fewer residents, especially when compared to percentage of the population living in older low-income housing (Ibid, 2005:225). In 1958, no more than 1.5% of the city of Sao Paulo lived in favelas a figure that grew to 1.6% in 1975, when 117,000 people lived in favelas, as compared to 615,000 in tenements and 1.8 million inhabitants in 'precarious' housing on the periphery. In 1978 the figure reached 4.1%. Given the socio-spatial makeup of favelas, its geographical limit and the fact that it houses a significant portion of low-income population Brazil have given tendencies to so many researches. According to UN-Habitat report of 2013, the period between year 2000 and 2010 Brazil recorded a number of achievement in tackling both economic growth and creating better opportunities for more people.

6.2.2 The Process of Land Occupation

The process of land occupation is of particular interest in Brazil that it requires attention. The interesting thing about this phenomenon as far as favelas is concerned is the way in which the land is occupied. By invading and occupying the empty urban spaces, the favelas come to be recognized as an illegitimate form of land tenure (Leeds, 1969:151–152 cited in Valladares et al., 2015:225). Statistics data concerning ownership of lands occupied by favelas in Rio shows that 23% belonged to federal government, 27% belong to state government, 44% belonged to private proprietors and 6% was unknown ownership (Valladares, 1978:31 cited in Valladares, 2005). It is argued that until the period of 1974, 55.9% of favelas in Sao Paulo were located on private property and 37.1% on city government and 6.6% on state or federal land. One question that always comes up in urban studies concerns the origin of favelas, whether they were occupied through organized invasion. The question of how the land was taken over in different cities by the invaders has been addressed by scholars. In this respect, studies in different cities suggest that in Brazil the occupation takes various forms. In Rio de Janeiro, for example, the pattern has been one of gradual takeover, in some cases, occupation has been encouraged by the proprietor themselves or by the canvassers and politicians (Valladares, 1978:14). In Salvador the occupation is based on collective movement; whereas in Sao Paulo there is direct takeover, without the participation of a third parties and purchasers or rent of a shack that already exists.

6.2.3 Housing Policies in Brazil

The Brazilian government has not been able to adopt a widely accepted housing policy and legislation ever since the 1970s (Ramos Coelho, cited in Palmer et al., 2017 :21). The only time that the housing and urban issues gained prominence and popularity was in the year 2000 with the creation of the Ministry of Cities (UN-Habitat, 2013). Many city dwellers are still living in poverty and over-crowded area known as 'favelas', which are plagued by crime and drug problems. Brazil is not different from other emerging economies and also experiences an explosion the growth of informal settlements dating back to the period 1950s–1970s. This is as a result of industrialization and the attraction provided by cities to rural dwellers who migrate in volumes to metropolitan life. The Brazilian government's mass affordable housing programme, Minha Casa, Minha Vida or My Home, My Life, which started in 2009 as part of social policies, is being seen as a model for developing countries and a way to address the housing needs of an estimated 1 billion squatters and slum dwellers worldwide. Brazil's $15.5 billion (more than R150 billion) housing programme is focused on poor and lower income families as part of its efforts to respond to the world economic problems that is aimed at simultaneously boosting job creation and expanding housing. According to Palmer et al. (2017), the housing units are constructed by the private sector companies that act and stand as middlemen with the banks on behalf of the end users or beneficiaries. These approved housing schemes are given or allocated by the private developers working together with the municipalities, provincial governments together with some stakeholders as well as interested parties. Land are at times provided, made available or donated by either the state government or other interested and stakeholders. According to this scholar as part and parcel of these plans an estimated amount of 1 million housing units are being delivered and provided to families at much reduced prices and subsidized level that is affordable. The amount of subsidies available and accessible to the households varies depending on the income level of these end users. Using federal, state and municipal funds, the housing programme covers the whole amount of the total cost of a complete home for families earning between zero and 10 times minimum wage (in 2015, m.w. is $253 per month) (Furtado and Freitas, 2015:3). The amount funded by the state diminishes as the beneficiary's income rises. These loans and subsidies are readily available to lower and middle-income families. To safeguard the recipients and families who participate in these schemes a guarantee fund is provided by the government to those who lose their income and cannot repay back. A deed of transfer certificate is issued whenever these houses are handed over to a female member of the family. Other benefits include reduced legal fees and low-cost insurance. My Home, My Life programme as can be seen from this case study aims at changing these areas into more acceptable and good living areas with secure tenure, facilities for recreation and social amenities.

This unique programme is not without problems as some of the targeted beneficiaries complain about the slow pace in which the houses are being handed over. Moreover, some of the large cities like Belo Horizonte and Sao Paulo are not having enough space of land for future development of any kind.

6.2.4 Good Lessons of My House, My Life (MHML)

The implementation and adoption of My House, My Life (MHML) employed a system of a decentralized structure of government powers, responsibilities and relies heavily on the strengthened cooperation among the national, state and municipal tiers (UN-Habitat, 2013). The scheme also enjoys smooth operation and adoption due to the nature of Brazilian municipalities that are constitutionally designed to implement urban development as well as housing projects at the local level. The coordination between the tiers of government is a challenge and affects the project implementation. MHML is also notable for priding itself with a well-defined and properly structured subsidy policy as well as increased access to credits, which is possible because of consistent growth in the economy, low rate of inflation, gradual increase in minimum wages and over 10 years of consistent good social development programme (UN-Habitat, 2013). Due to a number of fiscal incentives (for example tax exemptions on inputs on building projects) together with set arrangements by various institutions/ministries to speed up the purchasing and contract awarding processes as well as to reducing the risks of any default of any kind have gone a long way to making the programme very interesting to so many sectors. Moreover, the amount of the investment by the public sector to these two programmes – the Growth Acceleration and MHML programmes – both provided an enabling environment and sustained confidence that stimulated other sectors to provide needed technical and financial support (UN-Habitat, 2013). Although this scheme yielded some evidence on good result, the long-term increase in providing accessibility and opportunities to the ownership of houses and other social amenities will not overnight provide safe net to socio-economic inclusion. MHML as it relates to environmental sustainability has a double standard and incoherent approach in terms of the design element of housing and the urban land use strategy. For the sake of clear monitoring and evaluation, some academic institutions were opted into the scheme to embark on comprehensive research programme to evaluate and carry out additional studies on various aspects of the MHML Life Programme and the Growth Acceleration Slum Upgrading efforts (UN-Habitat, 2013).

6.3 An Overview of Africa's Mixed-Income Housing Development

Housing project development and research initiatives in Africa are built on legacy of colonization and the liberation with independence in the 1960s that follows. This section will discuss some of the countries that are considered best case examples as it relates to mixed-income housing development. The countries are Botswana, Nigeria and Ghana.

6.3.1 The Case of Botswana Housing Programme

Botswana became independent in 1966, after 80 years of British protectorate administration (Ministry Local Government and Housing, 1997:32). Constitution adopted in 1965 established a non-racial democracy and provided for a uni-cameral legislature within a National Assembly representing 38 constituencies. The country is divided into 10 districts for the purpose of administration (although there are nine district councils). A Department of Housing, responsible for housing functions (including policy formulation, planning, research, development and estate management), was established in the country in 1994 (MLGH, 1997). The country has a population of 2,038,228 million with a land mass of 581,000 sq.km. It has a population density of 3.5 persons per square kilometre. Annual growth rate of the population from 2001 to 2011 is estimated to be 1.9% and this shows an increase at diminishing rate (Census, 2011). The economy as compared to other economies of the world is one of the fastest growing, from $70 per year in 1960s to nearly $16,400 as of 2013 per year estimate (CIA, 2014). The country has a Gross National Income of $7,316,880 thereby affording the country a modest standard of living with a relatively very high Human Development Index (HDI) of 0.684, as compared to Egypt 0.682, South Africa 0.658 and Nigeria 0.504, respectively (UNDP, 2014). In terms of Urbanization, 52% of the entire population resides in urban centres, and this classification is based on 1981 census that classified settlements of 5,000 or more as urban area (MLGH, 1997: 35). Botswana in a period less than 40 years as compared to other countries has turned out to be a predominantly urban society with majority of the population living in urban centres and the trend continue to increase from 4% before independence in 1966 to about 52% by the year 2002 (Adams et al., 2003). The government played an important critical role in the provision of housing and policies implementation as it relates to financing, housing project providers and owners (Mosha, 2010). However, some of these roles are gradually changing in line with change in circumstances as it relates to Policy on Housing by the Government.

6.3.1.1 The Policy on Social Mix

Another urban policy is of 'social integration'. According to Mosha (2010:5), the aim of this policy is to see to it that the planning of the urban areas is not such that they result to social class's differentiation and polarized society. In this regard any planning scheme should make provision for all income groups irrespective of social status. This approach to housing provision is highly regarded all over the continent and beyond as it provides the low-income people equal opportunities and privileges as well as benefits as it relates to access to social facilities and amenities as compared to other income earners. Access to land is cross subsidized as the low-income earners are subsidized by the high income group (Mosha, 2001 cited in Mosha, 2010:5).

6.3.1.2 Services on Land

In Botswana urban land for development is available in two categories: land that is fully serviced normally allocated to parastatal and those for the private companies for their own development (Mosha, 2010). The advantage of this approach is that no entity can embark on any development of any kind without first ensuring that services are readily available. This strategy has gone a long way to reduce the proliferation of informal settlements or squatter areas as development planning controls are very strict and any violations are met with an iron fist. The allocation in the rural areas is different in that land is allocated on unserviced stands.

6.3.2 Botswana Land Tenure Policy

Tenure reforms as it relates to land access is form of changes in the planning for the development of the parcel of land in terms of how people use it, occupy it and make livelihood from it in a sustainable manner (Adams et al., 2003:2). The primary objective of any given tenure reforms exercise is to bring about and facilitate equal and fair distribution of land resources to the people or community concerned so as to secure their future control over the land rights and to provide needed sustainable livelihood. Customary rules and procedures govern land rights in Botswana. FinMark Trust study of 2007 categorized and isolated three different land tenure systems that are in coexistence in Botswana:

(1) Land for the State that constitutes 23% of the total covers wildlife and forest reserves and most urban areas. Urban land tenure is through Certificate of Rights (COR) – discontinued in 1992 – or Fixed Period State Grant (FPSG), usually 50–99 years lease.
(2) The Tribal land of 71% is granted under Customary Land Grant (for citizens) or Common Law lease (for foreigners or commercial properties). Tribal

land Customary Land Grant can be converted to Common Law Leasehold (CLL), subjected to the necessary cadastral survey (and sometimes not inconsiderable cost) and used as collateral.

(3) The Freehold or lease land of 6% of the total is generally farming land, but some peri-urban developments fall under this regime, particularly new townships on the outskirts of the major centres.

One of the remarkable features of the tenure land reform system as well as administration is the reluctance to land registration and how this hinders development. In so many instances, research shows that tribal or traditional land held for generations is lost because of the owners' inability to obtain or provide the correct certificates or documentation (FinMark Trust, 2007). Transfer to Common Law Leasehood (CLL) is not considered as important since only 27% of the people do register their title deeds due to lack of understanding about inherent benefits and also as a result of the cost involved. Perception is also high and scepticisms around the idea that land resource is an inheritance to the family and sacred to the family thereby should not be put up for mortgage as it can backfire.

6.3.3 Botswana National Housing Programme

Botswana adopted a system of both legislative and customary security of tenure immediately it got independence similar to other countries in Africa (Adams et al., 2003). The policy on land as it relates to tenure security is known to be very unique and innovative as it addresses the country's specific needs (Adams et al., 2003). Botswana vision 2016 envisages that 'the entire citizens of Botswana are entitled to gain access to land and quality shelter as far as the county is concerned' (Mosha, 2010:8). A lot of emphasis is on home ownership and citizenship right as far as access to housing is concerned. Recent studies point out that though a lot of strides have been made in the housing programmes, there is still a lot to be achieved before these goals can be fully achieved. The countries housing programme and implementation strategies (as adopted in 1999) have in it milestones that are aimed at realizing these objectives, as it indicates that its goal is to 'speed up housing provision that are of good quality and liveable for all in a secure and safe conditions'. To achieve these objectives, FinMark Trust (2007) noted that the government set down four thrusts in the National Policy on Housing of 2000 and these includes: (1) government adoption of an enablement approach instead of home provision to facilitate the development of various settlements together and jointly with other role players, (2) the drive for more resources to the development of low- and middle-income housing in the whole country, (3) the use of housing as an instrument and key factor for local development and economic empowerment as well as poverty alleviation and (4) the encouragement of public–private partnership. As can be seen the policy is very clear and sound as it pays attention to major areas of need, though, questions abound on the extent this set objectives are being implemented. According to Mosha (2010), the housing development and implementation in Botswana is faced with so many challenges: affordability of the housing units due to increasing innovation and new building standards, increase in population and urbanization, scarcity of strategic land for housing purposes, problem of housing finance and bank loans for low-income households, inappropriate housing programmes and delivery strategies and difficulties in bringing in the private sectors.

6.3.4 Self-help Housing Agency

In Botswana the Self-help Housing Agency (SHHA) has been in operation and existence since the 1970s in both the urban areas and some villages. This programme assists and supports the low-income earners and other households to access urban land and housing finance. The allocation of land by SHHA follows certain procedure that is close to the tribal land allocation process for tribal land areas; this is formerly carried out by the chiefs or headman and later by the Land Boards (FinMark Trust, 2007). It is specifically only for the citizens of Botswana and the concerned candidate must be previously in employment or legally self-employed in the town or city where the application is submitted. Whereby the application is successful and he or she qualifies for a housing loan of R20 000 once off. It caters for only both the low income and middle income. The major criticism against the SHHA is that it provides a maximum loan of P20 000 that has remained unchanged for some time now, whereas the housing cost has soared every year due to inflation. The shortages of land available for allocation, especially in major cities such as Gaborone, result in long waiting list periods of 10–15 years. It is also noted that large expanses of land are left underdeveloped for a long period of time for several reasons. Finally, there is a delay in the manner the loan is repayed due to poor administration, accountability and management (FinMark Trust, 2007). Hence, the scheme is very good but people are taking advantage.

6.4 Housing Delivery Efforts in Nigeria

Nigeria is one of the countries in Africa where the majority of the people are living and residing under precarious situation due to problem of housing to cater for the teaming population that has continued to grow. The housing challenge is complicated and complex due to the rapid rates of urban development, poor infrastructure upgrade and slow economic growth (Olayiwola et al., 2005). Access to housing is even made more difficult and worse for the majority of low-income groups due to high cost of land, speculation in the real estate industry and migration and problem of physical planning. To address these problem of accessing housing and the built environment in Nigeria, a recent study shows the implementation of a number of innovative measures and policies. In this chapter, the research explores the challenges and relevant measures adopted by the government to address the issues as well as the shift to mixed-income housing development.

6.4.1 Nigerian Housing Problems

Inadequate housing and poor living condition has been a persistent problem in Nigeria's urban history for some time now. There has been tremendous and rapid increase in the percentage of the Nigerian population that is living in urban centres (Kabir and Bustani, 2009). A recent report by the United Nations as contained in the Business Report of 2015 indicated that Nigerian population is ranked among the highest in the world but still growing more (Pretoria News, 2015). The Nigerian Institute for Social and Economic Research in one of the research conducted in the rural areas of Nigeria found out that between 2000 and the year 2010 the population has grown from 7.0 million to 9.5 million in 2010 (Onibokun, 1985).

6.4.2 Nigeria Public Housing

The construction of public housing in Nigeria has its root and genesis right from the colonial British rule in Nigeria and this period is marked with special reserved areas for the white (Olayiwola et al., 2005). The provision of housing was specifically for the white colonial population who are residing in a protected and developed areas, referred to as Government Reserved Areas (GRAs) (Ibid). These areas are 'forbidden' to the indigenous population, the design of the housing and alignment patterns of the GRAs portray the type of English city planning style known as 'Garden City' (Olayiwola et al., 2005). The period from 1962 to 1968 that marked the first National Development Plan was a turning point as attention was directed at policies and programmes of the government to ensure that people of low- and middle-income group should benefit from public housing. Not much was done in respect of public housing provision within the first 10 years of independence in 1960. Housing provision, implementation and development are all considered as part of industrial estates, land acquisition and town planning. Government's aim at that time was for the roll out and delivery of 24,000 housing units during the plan period, but only 500 housing units were built by the Federal Government before the outbreak of the civil war in 1967 (Olayinka et al., 2005). According to Olayinka et al. (2005) the period for second National Development Plan that span from 1970 to 1974 was quite unique because government accepted housing as a part of its social and political responsibilities. Housing provision as it was noted was targeted at all social groups, whether displaced or not, from competitive housing market.

6.4.3 The National Housing Programme (1994–1995)

The period 1994–1995 saw the implementation and adoption of the National Housing Programme (NHP) for Nigerians with purpose to provide 121,000 different housing units throughout the whole country to serve varying income band (Kabir and Bustani, 2009). According to (Olayiwola et al., 2005:7) the NHP, target was to ensure that all Nigerians who are eligible have access to quality housing and place to live at affordable cost by the year 2000. The main objective and target of the programme was to ensure that the number of housing units are increased; increase the number of the teaming population who can own houses; implementation of a national housing development policy and to ensure that adequate resources are made available (Olayiwole et al., 2005).

6.4.4 Current Housing Delivery Approach

In 2003, the Federal Ministry of Housing and Urban Development was established with the main objective to restructure the housing situation in Nigeria (Kabir and Bustani, 2009). The private sectors were called to the party increasingly from the period 2003–2004 to Forster more cooperation and good working relation with the government. Principal focus during this period was the need to place the private sector in a good position where they can deliver sustainable and affordable housing that can be sustainable; support to the government as enabler; and the revision of the applicable Town Planning legislations to speed up land allocation and release.

6.4.5 Lesson to Be Learnt With Housing Development in Nigeria

The approach by the government to continue to intervene through direct housing construction and delivery should be done away with. The Ministry of Housing and Urban Development was noted to be faced with a number of challenges and obstacles that impede its efforts in carrying out its mandate. There are a number of mega housing projects that are carried out without adequate capacity and systems in place to execute it successfully. Proper planning mechanisms are required to ensure that proper coordination and alignment are in place for housing delivery.

In conclusion, proper resourcing and increased skill capacity of civil servant are needed to ensure the planning for housing work hand in hand with the implementation. There is also need for the government to embrace innovative building solutions. There is a need to ensure adequate monitoring and evaluation of housing units delivered so as to keep track of backlog and waiting list of low income that deserve attention.

6.5 Housing Delivery Efforts in Ghana

Ghana is one of the countries whose housing institutions has undergone fundamental changes since the 1990s with previous policy that focuses on state provision shifting towards active private sector participation in the housing production, financing and production of building materials. It is noted that this is as a result of the failure of the public housing programme, dwindling state resources, unimpressive performance of state-owned enterprises and liberalization and increasing recognition that government alone cannot solve the housing problems. Housing 'inadequacy' in Ghana is usually interpreted in two ways: One interpretation emphasizes inadequate quantity; the gap between housing supply and housing demand and the other slum housing (Obeng-Odoom and Amedzro, 2011:128). A recent United Nations Human Settlements Programme (UN-HABITAT) reports on improving housing conditions in Ghana suggested that inadequate housing implies slum housing when it noted that '[e]ven though housing is a basic necessity of life, more than half of the population in Ghana live in poor houses where they have no access to adequate sanitary facilities, water and warmth to meet their daily physical needs' (UN-HABITAT, 2010:4). In this chapter emphasis will be on causes of inadequate housing in Ghana, housing policies and programme and shift to integrated human settlements.

6.5.1 What Are Causes of Inadequate Housing in Ghana?

Seven factors are specifically responsible and attributed for the inadequate housing provision in Ghana as depicted by previous researchers, and these includes: a poor attitude towards maintenance, skills shortages in estate management professionals, policy inconsistency, unclear tenure security, defaults in rental payments, rigid and unflexible rent control system and high cost of building materials, urban growth and poverty (Obeng-Odoom and Amedzro, 2011:129). This is also related to the fact that the maintenance culture is poor and unregulated. According to UNESCO, 1997 (cited in Obeng-Odoom and Amedzro, 2011), it is noted that maintenance is a huge problem in Africa as a whole and can be related to or ascribed to very poor and unethical maintenance culture. On issue of lack of credible estate agency management professionals, this manifest in the poor services that these professionals render maintenance, cleaning, security, marketing and financial management. Insecure tenure is another problem because many transactions or sale of land are not backed up or covered with necessary documentations (Ab dulai, 2006, 2010). Lack of rental payment is evident based on the principle of 'Filtering Model' which stipulates that buildings depreciate with age and this is related to the level and frequency maintenance that it undergoes. The efforts by homeowners or landlords spent on maintenance are noted and argued to depend on (1) the amount of returns they expect to receive from rent and (2) what the homeowners expect to recoup from the sale of their homes (Obeng-Odoom and Amedzro, 2011). Rent control is noted to discourage maintenance by the landlords as they focus more on the capital return on their investment. Though there have been several calls for the Rent Act to be abolished, this has not been done thereby resulting to systematic noncompliance. The result of this is that landlords can charge whatever amount of rent they desire, even demanding 2–3 years rental payment upfront (Obeng-Odoom and Amedzro, 2011). Expensive building materials are another factor that contributes to inadequate housing in Ghana. The price of home in Accra the capital of Ghana in comparison to income ratio at 14.0 is one of the highest in African cities of comparative figure of 12.5 (UN-HABITAT, 1998). The level of poverty in a given society can be measured and assessed based on the housing conditions available (Barton, 1977 cited in Obeng-Odoom and Amedzro, 2011:132). With 28.5% of the population trapped below poverty line bracket and majority working in informal sector this go a long way to impact negatively on the quality of housing unit they occupy.

6.5.2 Urbanization and Settlements

The situation in Ghana is consistent with, the trend of the world and Africa, albeit slightly higher. According to Obeng-Odoom (2009b), with Ghana's 47.8% of urban population, this is higher than the percentage of urban population for West Africa at 41.7, sub- Sahara Africa 35.0 and the whole of Africa at 37.9. The estimated rate of urbanization in Ghana between the period 2005 and 2010 is around 3.54%; this is lower than the figure for West Africa (3.77) and sub-Saharan Africa but higher than Africa (3.31) and the world (1.91) (Adarkwa, 2014). Until year 2010, 51.5% of the people lived in urban Ghana and this figure is more than the number living in rural Ghana (48.5%) (Ghana Statistical Services, 2012), and by the year 2050, it is estimated that the population living in urban areas will be 75.5% and this is expected to be about three times the share of the population living in rural areas (24.4%). The direct consequence of this is that the number of large- and medium-sized human settlements (those with more than 5,000 people) in Ghana will likely increase marginally because settlements with less than 5,000 population will grow beyond this benchmark to become urban centres. In addition, the medium and large settlements will continue to experience increase in their population (Adarkwa, 2012 cited in Adarkwa, 2014:7). This trend has huge implications and impact on housing provision and implementation of policies in this regard. There is also evidence that the size of the aggregate population who live in urban areas in Ghana, which was 13.9% in 1948, increased to 51% in 2010, representing 266% increment over the period. On the other hand, the number of urban settlements in the country rose from 41 in 1948 to 366 in 2000 accounting for 788% increment over 52 years. Population trends suggest that by the year 2030, an estimate of 65% of the population of Ghana will be residing in urban areas (Farvacque-Vitkovic et al., 2008). According to Akiyode (2011), and as shown above, the trends in urbanization present severe challenges to ecosystems and human lives as human settlements are increasingly becoming inefficient and unliveable. A typical catalogue of problems that characterizes human settlements in this urban century include traffic congestion, limited supply of mass transport vehicles, environmental degradation, poor air quality, inadequate shelter, poor housing conditions, energy challenges, limited access to essential services, water shortages, rapid areal expansion of cities, pollution, long journey-to-work and uncontrolled development (Adarkwa, 2014:7). In light of the above challenges, the UN-HABITAT (2003), argues that understanding and managing the dynamics of urbanization and more importantly tackling challenges in relation to addressing the needs of new population is critical for human survival. In view of this, academia, governments, international development agencies, non-governmental organizations, city authorities, as well as other concerned institutions, have developed policies and programmes to address these challenges. To be able to overcome these challenges listed above requires long-term sustainable solutions. Studies suggest that these environmental problems cannot be tackled in isolation as they are very complex together with their causes that are interrelated at the human settlements level.

6.5.3 Ghana Housing Deficit Statistics

In view of this deficit, there is now a shift from high-end only to a diversified offering of mixed-income housing. The move is to ensure that every income bracket within the Ghanaian economy needs to be able to afford housing of good quality standard. Kwame-Bediako (2014) notes that for players within the industry to thrive within the current economy, they need to offer a product – mix of high-end, middle-income and low-end housing to satisfy all segments of the market. The emphasis is to build mixed-income housing that draws inspiration from high-end.

6.5.4 Ghana Housing Policy

In an effort to evaluate Ghana housing performance over the years, several draft housing policies have been drawn up including: the Draft National Housing Policy (2009), which is still in the offing, the National Shelter Strategy Volumes 1 and 2 (1993), the Istanbul Declaration and The Habitat Agenda (June 1996), the National Shelter Strategy part two (revised in June 2000) and the report on 'Housing Programmes and Action Plan to Implement the National Shelter Strategy' (2003). According to Addo (2014), the aim and goal of these policies was to provide adequate decent and affordable housing that is accessible and sustainable with infrastructural facilities to satisfy the needs of the Ghanaians. With respect to the Draft National Housing Policy of 2009 that is currently guiding the production of housing in Ghana, the policy tends to address: (1) institutional coordination; (2) governance for housing provision; (3) environment and housing; and (4) energy and housing.

Addo (2014), based on the above, noted that the aim for the housing policy include, first, to facilitate access to land for the low-income population to pave the way for an increased stock through their own efforts and also assemble and allocate land so as to reduce overcrowding in slums and informal settlements, and provide for new household formation.

6.5.5 The Challenges Faced in Low-Income Housing Delivery in Ghana

6.5.5.1 Access to Land

Litigations are very common and rampant in Ghana on issue of land and housing. As a result of Litigation that is very common and likely there are several houses being destroyed, filing of court cases over who is the owner of the land and fake documentation, which in most cases the financial institutions have rejected as collaterals in sourcing for housing loans (Gough and

Yankson, 2000; Karley, 2008 cited in Addo, 2014:16; Payne, 1997; Tipple and Korboe, 1998). The issue of land litigations and the lengthy processes it takes for the court to make ruling dissuades most private sectors to effectively take active part and contribute to housing investment. Another problem that is frequently encountered is related to customary rights and equipments. This frustrates and creates bottlenecks in people accessing land since the need to satisfy customary requirements as well as approved legislations that is in operation can be very cumbersome. On previous occasions, land registration process in Ghana requires several departments to endorse the document until recently when the Land Administration Project (LAP) was established to coordinate and facilitate the various institutions involved in the registration of land (Addo, 2014:17). The primary goal and objective of the project is to speed up and coordinate properly land policies and regulations in a bid to bring about institutional changes, capacity building and establish an efficient, fair and transparent system of land titling, registration and valuation (LAP Coordinating Unit, 2007 cited in Addo, 2014:17). In general, the acquisition of land in Ghana and the line of processes to be engaged have been described as laborious involving several complex arrangements. The issue of red tape in land registration, corruption and the lack of institutional transparency resulting in duplication of registrations of lands in Ghana thereby inhibiting access to land for human settlements. According to Addo (2014), some officials who are working in the Lands Department, as a result of corrupt practices, delete the names of original land owners and introduce new owners in the land records. It is also noted that the buyer who have more money or access to funding and who can quickly develop the land thereby asserting that 'the one who builds on the land is the first to occupy the land'. Bearing this in mind and as a widespread knowledge, a number of households tend to commence buildings as a sign of occupying the land before registering the land at the Lands Commission, and this is contrary to the requirements of building regulations (Addo, 2014:17).

6.5.5.2 Housing and Mortgage

Uncoordinated planning of human settlements in Accra, with cheap and unsustainable materials affects the financing options available to urban low-income households, including mixed-income housing (Addo, 2014). The draft Housing Policy of 2009 identified and pointed out difficulties associated with urban housing provision with respect to low capital base and serious absence of long-term borrowing options. The high bank interest lending rates, low household incomes and poor savings attitude all compound the problem. A newspaper financial report in the *Ghana Business News* of 2009 cited in Addo (2014:18), macroeconomic instability, reflected by high and intractable inflation, high interest rates with huge volatile economy, has characterized Ghanaian economy over the past two decades, thus creating disincentives for investment in long-term instruments, such as mortgage for sustainable housing development. The macroeconomic environment defeats government private sector involvement in affordable urban housing supply.

6.5.5.3 Regulations Guiding Building Standards

The regulation also states that any house that is in excess of 120 square metres or a two or more-storey building in the urban or metropolitan areas shall be designed by an architect in consultation with a qualified engineer. It also stipulates that a minimum of 2.4 metres is left at the sides and back of building. The building regulation also stipulates that a minimum of 3 months is required for an applicant to get a building permit before construction. This period can often extend to over 1 year even after much lobbying (Addo, 2014). However, according to Addo (2014:21), a considerable number of households especially in lower income groups overlook these requirements because they cannot afford the services of professionals. No building on any plot of land should exceed 60%.

6.5.6 Lessons Learnt From Ghana Housing Studies

Key lessons that are noted with the Ghana housing programme and implementation strategies include:

- There is haphazard planning of low-income housing in Accra with less durable materials and this affects the financing options available to urban low-income households, including mixed-income housing.
- For players within the industry to thrive within the current economy they need to offer a product – mix of high-end, middle-income and low-end housing to satisfy all segments of the market. The emphasis is now to build mixed-income housing that draws inspiration from high-end.
- The policy, which tends to focus on state provision, has shifted drastically that private sector participation is now highly encouraged and promoted in the production, mortgage financing and manufacturing of building materials.
- Inadequacy housing supply in Ghana is usually categorized in two. At one end is inadequate quantity, the gap between housing supply and housing demand, and the other slum housing.
- The issue of land litigations constitutes a major setback that discourages private sector effective participation and a favourable environment for housing investment.
- Lower income households tend to overlook the National Building Regulations that set standard for the design, approval of plans and construction as they cannot afford the services of professionals.
- The bureaucracy in land registration and the lack of transparency have resulted in multiple registrations of lands in Ghana and inhibit access to land for human settlements.

6.6 Conclusion

Moving forward therefore, MHML based on the experience of the Programme, has shown how the longitudinal gap between housing demand and supply can be addressed and have laid the foundation for a continued reduction in the housing deficit in Brazil. In design, the programme has evolved towards a smoother flow of resources and more reasonable division of responsibilities among the tiers of government with positive implementation and speed of project execution. The programme is faced with a number of challenges with respect to the capacities of local administration, technical/institutional, and the unavailability of well-located land. Learning from the challenges, the programme has had many achievements and emerged in a better position to make positive contributions to improve the provision of housing in Brazil. The major criticisms against the SHHA as implemented in Botswana is that it provides a maximum loan of P20,000 (Botswana Pula) that has remained unchanged for some time now, whereas the cost of standard 'two-and-a-half' house has risen to between P35,000 and P47,500 (Botswana Pula). There is also severe shortage of available plots of land, particularly in the key urban areas such as Gaborone, resulting in waiting list periods of as long as 10–15 years from the date of application. A large track of plots tends to remain underdeveloped years after allocation for various reasons. Finally, the repayment rate on the service levy and construction loans is low and inadequately managed, resulting in the loan scheme not being self-sustaining. Hence, the SHHA remains a very great idea, but it is being fully exploited. Apart from the fact that the Ministry of Housing and Urban Development was faced by many constraints which affected its performance level, the houses built were usually very expensive which put them beyond the reach of the low-income group. Many government housing projects were embarked upon without effective programme of action and appropriate institutional arrangement for their execution. This means that the project lacked adequate and sound planning, which led to their failure. In conclusion, lack of financial prudence, public probity and accountability, inefficiency and ineffective administrative machinery, as well as mass importation of foreign technology, material, personnel and inflation caused the low performance of the public housing programmes in Nigeria. Finally, the aim and goal of these policies for the Ghanaian was to ensure that adequate as well as decent housing that is affordable, accessible and with sustainable infrastructural facilities to satisfy the needs of the Ghanaians are made available.

Chapter 7

South African Housing Policy and Legislative Framework

7.1 Introduction

South African housing policy and legislation as it evolve over the years form an important component of this research as it unpack the journey travelled so far. It is shaped and informed not only by global treaties, accord and issues and developments but also with the unique nature of South African history. Other challenges emanate from segregated apartheid planning and settlements pattern that define the fragmented nature of the urban landscape together with high-level income inequality and polarlization of the society that add up to shape the South African housing policies and legislation overtime. This chapter will look at South African Housing programme and strategies in view of these challenges.

7.2 Explanation of the Term Adequate Housing

These includes all measures and mechanisms that are put in place to ensure that people are not unduly subjected to deplorable living conditions of homelessness, eviction without court order and total discrimination of any kind as it relates to housing. South Africa is guided by the Constitution. This document is highly respected all over the world due to the fact that it enshrines the right to have access to adequate housing. The definition of the term adequate housing is not an easy one. It is noted in the literature that it encompasses the tenure right, affordability, habitability and the availability of essential services (www.ohchr.org). The right to housing is also associated to a list of other social and economic rights such as the right to take part in a public participation, to have access to information, fair and equal opportunities, the right to privacy and human dignity and to express one self. The right to housing as can be related and expanded further in relation to the above: tenure security; social services availability; affordability; and cultural adequacy in any human settlements (SERI, 2011:25). Adequate shelter, according to UNCHS (1997), is very broad and comprises of, in addition to roof over one's head, more than this.

Mixed-Income Housing Development Planning Strategies and Frameworks in the Global South, 87–99
Copyright © 2024 George Okechukwu Onatu, Wellington Didibhuku Thwala and Clinton Ohis Aigbavboa
Published under exclusive licence by Emerald Publishing Limited
doi:10.1108/978-1-83753-814-020231007

7.3 Negotiating South African Housing Policy Pre-1994

South African housing policy resulted from series of debate and negotiations as reported in the National Housing Forum from 1992 to 1994 as cited in the literature (Huchzermeyer, 2001:304). The forum composed of a multiparty non-governmental negotiating body made up of 19 members from private sector and businesses, community organization, government sector, the labour unions, development organizations and other alliances. The vision of the African National Congress (ANC) and other stakeholders as listed above all support the supremacy of democracy, human right and fair distribution, as it relates to large scale roll out of mass housing (Ibid, 2001). The main goals of this approach are to alleviate poverty and address the segregated apartheid planning and housing provision based on racial composition. The private sector supports the move to stabilize the increasing labour unrest sweeping across the country against the ruling government policies. Their focus was for land and housing to be commodified as this is vital and necessary for economic advancement and sustainable growth of the country. At the negotiation held at Botshabelo, each party presented their broad interest and need to the forum and this form the basis for new Housing policy. According to the report by SACN (2014), the National Housing Summit at Botshabelo accorded stakeholders' opportunity to proceed with two approaches: (1) State would facilitate housing delivery process and (2) Private Sector would identify land and construct housing by assessing subsidies on behalf of shelter seekers. The above agreement saw the establishment of what came to be known as the Housing Accord that culminated in the White Paper on housing policy of 1994. The National Unity Government of 1994 accepted these negotiations as well as investigations when it finally formulated South Africa's National Housing Policy (Huchzermeyer, 2001). All this led to National Housing Accord signed by all the parties involved, in October 1994. The beginning of the collective and unified vision that guides South Africa's National Housing Policy was born. The aim is a working document committing that all must work together and cooperate to achieve the vision signed in the Accord.

7.4 South African Housing Policy of 1994

The White Paper policy document places emphasis on the need to speed up delivery processes. During this period the housing White Paper gave additional clarity for the need for the housing implementation strategy to now focus on social and spatial differentiations in South African human settlements landscape.

7.4.1 Navigating the South African Housing Policy

South African housing policy has its bedrock and genesis from 1994 White Paper approved by the government in December. The Housing Code 2000, now revised, looked at housing policy in a broader context. A review of this policy document is relevant in South African housing debate because it defines the guidelines and implementation strategies. It includes but is not limited to an analysis of the national set target and point of departure.

7.4.2 South Africa's Vision for Housing

With the outset of democratic government in 1994, the approaches to housing delivery were very unique in that it considers current constraints and the expression of key important values that underpin the rest of other strategies. The national housing vision is meant to remain as a key focus area to all stakeholders and sectors and requires broad thinking by linking housing development strategies to broader economic and spatial development.

This vision also underpins urban and rural development. The emphasis here will be on urban vision as this is of significance to mixed-income housing development, which the Housing Code recognize as the need for integrated human settlements that can assist in social transformation and spatial justice.

7.4.3 National Housing Subsidy Programme

The Housing Code is the policy document that spells out the norms and standard to be followed in accessing various housing opportunities. It contains various categories of subsidies that are available, and this includes: individual subsidy, Integrated Rural Development Programme (IRDP), consolidated subsidy, institutional subsidy, rural subsidy and relocation assistance.

7.4.4 The Constitution of South Africa, Act 108 of 1996

The Constitution of South Africa is among the legislative documents which guides and informs key government decisions in the Republic. It also defines all aspect of social, economic and political environment as well as cultural aspects of the fundamental human rights of every citizen in the country (Constitution, 1996). Chapter 2 of the Bill of Rights section 26 outlines: Housing as a basic Human Right:

(1) Everyone, including all South African should have the right and access to adequate housing in South Africa;
(2) The state is obliged to take all reasonable legislative and other necessary measures, within its available resources, to achieve the progressive realization of this right;
(3) On no account should anyone be evicted from their home, or have their home demolished, without an order of court made after considering all relevant circumstances. No legislation may permit arbitrary eviction.

Constitution Court was established in 1995 to deal with any one whose right to adequate housing is negatively infringed on or cases of eviction. This right is now recognized as one of the significant socio-economic right in South Africa. Access to housing and the right of people residing in informal settlements are hereby not neglected. The Government is obliged to enact and enforce relevant laws, develop appropriate programmes as well as implementation strategies to speed up housing delivery and take people out of informal settlements for more suitable accommodation.

7.4.5 Prevention of Illegal Eviction Act (1988) (PIE)

The Prevention of Illegal Eviction (PIE) Act is argued is an important piece of legislation that was enacted to give effect and backing to section 26 (3) of the Constitution: No one may be evicted from their home, or have their home demolished, without an order of court made after considering all the relevant circumstances. No legislation may permit arbitrary evictions. The PIE Act provides a sort of safeguard against the eviction of unlawful occupiers living on both private and public-owned land. There have been several confrontations and people challenge this piece of legislation on several grounds including: The Grootboom Case in Western Cape; Olivia Road case; Joe Slovo case with the City of Johannesburg that compel the City Council to provide alternative accommodation to the residents and other socio-economic rights due to their eviction. For the PIE Act to be considered in any court of law, the concerned community must prove beyond reasonable ground that they have been residing on the land/property for at least 6 months and are relatively settled. The Act always acts in good faith by seeking options on whether there is readily available land to which the affected communities may be relocated or whether the land can be made reasonably available by the owner or the local authority concerned. If there is no alternative land available then the eviction order must be reconsidered and weighed more properly in terms of the merit of the lay. This legislation went further to highlight that:

- The affected community must be notified of an eviction order by the land owner in writing.
- The land owner must apply to the court to have a written notice served on the occupiers/explaining the owner's intention to evict the occupier/s.
- No eviction may take place without a court of law declaring it and after taking several issues into consideration as it affects the community.

7.4.6 The Housing Act (Act 107 of 1997)

The Housing Act as enacted also outlines and expounded the general principles applicable to housing development and set the tone for all spheres of government on what is expected from the National, Provincial and Local Municipalities. The Housing Act is the primary piece of housing legislation recognized in South Africa (SERI, 2011). It legally entrenched policy principles outlined in the 1994 White Paper on Housing as explained in section 6.4. The Act provides guidance for a sustainable housing development process thereby laying down general principles for housing development in all three spheres of government; it also defines the functions of national, provincial and local governments in respect of housing development; and it lays the basis for financing national housing programmes (Housing Act, 1997). Section 2(1) the Act states that all spheres of government must give priority to the needs of the poor in respect of housing development, and consult meaningfully with individuals and communities affected by housing development (SERI, 2011). Housing development should also aim at providing a wide range of choices for people irrespective of race or background together with tenure options as is reasonably possible. Further, in section 2(1) (e) the Act states that all spheres of government must promote, inter alia, the following: a process of racial, social, economic and physical integration in urban and rural areas; measures to prohibit unfair discrimination on the ground of gender and other forms of unfair discrimination by all actors in the housing development process; higher density in respect of housing development to ensure the economical utilization of land and services; the meeting of special housing needs including the needs of the disabled; the provision of community and recreational facilities in residential areas; the housing needs of marginalized women and other groups disadvantaged by unfair discrimination (SERI, 2011). Housing Development is noted by the Act as:

> The establishment and maintenance of habitable, stable and sustainable public and private residential environments to ensure viable households and communities in areas allowing convenient access to economic opportunities, and to health, educational and social amenities in which all citizens and permanent residents of the Republic will, on a progressive basis, have access to a permanent residential structures with secure tenure, ensuring internal and external privacy and providing adequate protection against the elements; and b. potable water, adequate sanitary facilities and domestic energy supply.
>
> (Housing Act, 1997)

The Act has been severally amended in 1999 and 2000 to incorporate and take into consideration new development and establishment that need review, e.g. the abolishment of South African and Provincial Housing Board.

7.4.7 National Norms and Standard 1999

This was introduced in 1999 to serve for the purposes of construction of stand-alone residential dwellings by the Minister of Housing in terms of section 3 (2) of the Housing Act. It is argued that it provided technical specifications and services that are required in any RDP housing units. These specifications were further revised in the Housing Act and listed below are the norms and standard for any stand-alone government housing provisions.

- Minimum gross floor area of 40 m^2;
- Two bedrooms;
- Separate bathroom with toilet, a shower and wash hand basin;
- Combined living area and kitchen with wash hand basin;
- Ready-board electrical installation or solar connection depending on what is available in the area;
- Water – single stand pipe per stand (metred);
- Sanitation – ventilated improved pit (VIP) latrine or alternative system that is agreed;
- Roads-graded or gravelled paved road access to each stand;
- Storm water-lined open channels;
- Street lights – high mast security lighting for residential purposes where this is feasible and practical.

7.4.8 Breaking New Ground 2004

The Break New Ground (BNG) is a comprehensive and detailed plan for the development of sustainable human settlements and was approved by the cabinet and presented to the Ministers' Council for Social Development (MINMEC) in September 2004 (NUSP, 2015). This is a radical and paradigm shift in policy that outlines the provision of housing as an asset and for the sustainable development/revitilization of neighbourhood with more access to social, economic and environmental facilities. This is the first policy document to recognize informal settlements and the need to upgrade them. Prior to this, housing policy focused primarily on providing a formal subsidized house (stand-alone) for ownership without any attachment so far. The beneficiary meets up set down criteria and not too much emphasis was placed on informal settlements not to talk about upgrade. With BNG, the upgrading of informal settlements and the intensification of property market as well as more encouragement for the private sector to come forward served as an important impetus for poverty eradication and alleviation in South Africa. The plan aligns to international best approach and prefers *in situ* upgrade as compared to eviction/relocation. According to the Department of Housing (2004), BNG brought into focus the progressive and consistent phased approaches to informal settlements upgrade that led to the establishment of the Housing Development Agency.

7.4.9 National Housing Code of 2009

The revised National Housing Code 2009 provides a detailed outline of the national housing policy of South Africa as well as the guidelines surrounding the national subsidy programme and the various types of subsidies that is available. The National Housing Code, first published in 2000 in accordance with the Housing Act, set out the underlying policy principles, guidelines and norms and standards which apply to the National Housing Programmes (SERI, 2011). Some of these programmes have been updated or removed, and new programmes included, after the adoption of Breaking New Ground in 2004. The Code is binding on provincial and local spheres of government. Chapter 6.6 of this book outlines the National Housing Code in more detail. The revised National Housing Code outlines a general framework applicable to certain National Housing Programmes which form part of the National Housing Subsidy System (NHSS), i.e. Individual Subsidies, IRDP, Consolidation Subsidies, Institutional Subsidies and Rural Subsidies. These programmes are administered through an operational and administrative tool called the Housing Subsidy System (HSS) and all beneficiaries who have applied for or received housing subsidies are recorded on the National Housing Subsidy Database (NHSDB), which is managed by the Department of Human Settlements (DHS) and used by provincial departments and accredited municipalities to administer housing projects and subsidy applications (SERI, 2011). These systems have been developed in line with section 6 of the Housing Act, which obliges the national department to 'establish and maintain a national housing data bank and a national housing information system'.

7.4.10 National Development Plan of 2012

The National Development Plan (NDP) offers a long-term perspective. It defines a desired destination and identifies the role that the different sectors of society need to play in reaching that goal. The NDP aims to eradicate poverty and decrease disparity by 2030. South Africa seeks to achieve these objectives by drawing on the energies of its kin, growing a comprehensive economy, building capabilities, improving the limit of the state, and advancing partnership throughout the general public. One of the NDP's aims is to have the spatial pattern of apartheid broken down through retrofitting of existing settlements in order to enable South African citizens to have access to affordable housing and services in living environments that are improved. The National Planning Commission (NPC) (2012) lists the following goals of the NDP:

By 2030:

a. Achieve a spatial planning system that is efficient, strong and integrated among all tiers of government,
b. Upgrade all informal settlements and ensure they are located on suitable land that is located well,
c. Ensure that majority of the people reside nearby their work place,
d. Provide quality public transport and
e. Ensure there are more employment opportunities closer to urban townships that are dense.

This vision is broken down into provincial and local municipalities' frameworks such as the Integrated Development Plan (IDP) and Spatial Development Frameworks (SDFs) for implementation. The actions required to achieve the vision and goals stated above includes:

a. The present system of planning needs to be modified for improved coordination,
b. There is a need to establish a densification of cities' strategy that will ensure the realization of well-located human settlements,
c. Affordable and reliable public transport needs to be attainted,
d. Introduce SDFs and norms, and strike a balance between jobs and the location of people,
e. Review the grant and subsidy regime for housing,
f. Establish a national spatial restructuring fund, and integrate currently defused funding,
g. Establish a national observatory for spatial data and analysis,
h. Incentivize the activity of citizens for local planning and the development of spatial compacts and
i. Ensure effective functioning of land markets by introducing methods that would support livelihoods for rural and urban areas and make land markets work more effectively for the poor.

The NDP is a 17 year plan starting from the year 2013 until the year 2030. The long-term plans of government departments are aligned with the NDP and areas are identified where policy change is required to ensure consistency and coherence. It is the Government's responsibility to engage with all sectors, including National Home Builders Registration Council (NHBRC) to understand how they are contributing to implementation, and particularly to identify any obstacles to them in fulfiling their role effectively. The Plan plays a pivotal role in shaping the budget allocation over the years until 2030. The Plan identifies the enhancement of the quality of public services as critical to achieving transformation. Hence, the NHBRC should, at some stage, propose and argue its budget vote to the Parliament in view of the realization of the NDP's vision. This requires concerted approach, including Provinces to focus on identifying and overcoming the obstacles to achieving improved outcomes, including the need to strengthen the ability of local government to fulfil its developmental role. Planning and implementation should be informed by evidence-based monitoring and evaluation. The President and Deputy President are leading champions of the Plan within the Cabinet, in government and throughout the country. Premiers and Mayors are required to be visible and active champions of the Plan, with their offices being the catalytic agencies to drive implementation at provincial and municipal levels bringing in all sectors including NHBRC.

7.4.11 Spatial Planning and Land Use Management Act (2013)

According to the United Nations Economic Commission for Europe (UNECE, 2005) report for countries in transition, spatial planning is defined as methods used by the public sector to influence the future distribution of activities in space. To balance the demand for development with the need to protect the environment and to achieve social and economic development objectives, rational use of space is the common goal. It is an interdisciplinary activity involving all sectors (Cullingworth and Nadin, 2006:91). Why is spatial planning important to be considered and requiring Legislation in South Africa? It is good for delivering economic, social and environmental benefits. It is good for the creation of more stable and predictable conditions for investment and development. It is the prudent use of land and natural resources for development. It has economic benefit (E.g. More stability and confidence in investment). It has social benefits (E.g. considers the need of local community in policy development). It has environmental benefits (E.g. promote the use of land, building and infrastructure). Addresses environmental risks and it helps to avoid duplications.

Spatial planning and Land Use Management Act 16 of 2013 (SPLUMA) provides a system for spatial planning and land use management in the Republic. This act provides for comprehensive, advanced, impartial and effective spatial planning at the various spheres of government. Requires National, Provincial and Municipal spheres of government to prepare SDF's that establishes clear vision which must be developed as it relates to environmental, social and economic objectives. SPLUMA addresses the past spatial planning and land use management practices in the Republic of South Africa which depended on the racial disparity, segregation and unsustainable settlement patterns. The act tries to change the irregular characteristics of the past and to ensure that there's equity in the application of the spatial planning and land use management frameworks seeks to create and promote *consistency* and *uniformity* in procedures and decision-making as it relates to spatial planning and land use management.

SPLUMA (2013) provides five principles related to spatial transformation, which are as follows:

a. *Spatial justice:* aims to redress the spatial imbalances of the past by ensuring that access to land and the use of land is improved.
b. *Spatial sustainability:* is concerned with promoting the development of land that is within fiscal, institutional and administrative means of the Republic and ensuring that land that is prime and agriculture is protected.
c. *Efficiency:* whereby the development of land makes use of already existing infrastructure and resources.
d. *Spatial resilience:* is concerned with ensuring sustainable livelihoods in societies who are at risk to bear the negative effects of economic and environmental shocks, by ensuring that spatial plans, policies and the systems of managing land use are flexible and accommodative.
e. *Good administration:* whereby all tiers of government ensure an integrated approach to land use and development, guided by the SPLUMA system.

SPLUMA applies to the whole of South Africa and is an enactment sanctioned in terms of the Constitution of the Republic. SPLUMA regulates both the municipal and provincial government planning. The Minister of Rural development and Land Reform after consultations with the organs in the provincial and local spheres of government prescribes the standards and guidelines and measures for the land use management and land development that are uniform with the Act. NHBRC should explore how and where to part of this conversation. The Minister within the available resources must offer the support and assistance in the performance of the land use management functions and related obligations. The National government and Intergovernmental Relations Framework Act in accordance with this act develops the mechanisms to support and strengthens the capacity of the provincial and municipalities to adopt and implement an effective spatial planning and land use management framework (Department of Rural Development and Land Reforms, 2013). Spatial planning is critical for the development of *informal settlements* strategies as it focuses on delivering economic, social and environmental benefits. This is through the creation of more stable and predictable conditions for investments and development, by securing community benefits from development and by promoting prudent use of land and natural resources for development (UN, 2008).

7.4.12 The City of Johannesburg Inclusionary Housing Policy

The City of Johannesburg adopted the inclusionary housing policy with the aim of increasing mixed-income housing development based on Council approval of 21st February 2019. The policy is in line with already existing legislation and policies including the IDP; NDP, 2030; SDF, 2040; Housing Act of 1997; and the SPLUMA of 2013. This policy was borne out of the need to address the historical apartheid spatial geography of marginalization and segregation as well as inequality that is still inherent in the City of Johannesburg Metropolitan Municipality. Due to the increasing housing, backlog is estimated at about 460,000–500,000 households according to *Daily Maverick* of June 2022 and the remark by the former Mayor in July 2022. Most affected by this are the low-income earners and many poor residents of the City who are still living in areas at the edge of the city (townships) with very limited social amenities or access to jobs (CoJ, 2019). The need for this policy was informed by the post 1994 democratic era that has seen and witnessed limited interactions and mixing of households in settlements across the city both in terms of race and income. The Inclusionary Housing Policy is aimed at assisting and support for land capture value to support the city rates and taxes as well as facilitate partnership with private developers and investors. It is also aimed at reconciling spatial transformation and leveraging infrastructure investment in all areas (CoJ, 2019). The requirements are that this inclusion of low-income housing units is compulsory to all development application above 20 dwelling units or more. The policy does not apply or affect approved townships or building rights. It is now included as one of the conditions of the development of any Township Establishment of Rezoning. It is for only dwelling units and not residential units based on the City of Johannesburg Land Use Scheme of 2018 and relevant by-laws of 2016. It is applicable to the entire City of the seven regions (see Appendix 2). Developers are required to disclose all development controls as it relates to height density, coverage, Floor Area Ratio (FAR) as well as bonuses as stipulated. This policy comprises of four options; option 1, 2, 3 and 4. For option 1, developers are to set aside 30% of the total units in the development must be for inclusionary housing (Social Housing, FLISP or for households with rental capped at R2100 as per 2018 price value). All the units must be of the same outward appearance like the market units on the same property. For Option 2, 10% of the residential floor area for units averaging 24 m^2 for areas where 60 du/per hectare is supported. As for Option 3, 20% of residential floor area for smaller units and for Option 4, to the satisfaction of the City Council. This policy, on adoption, attracted wide cry but has been commended as a welcome development in view of the Not in My Back Yard (NIMBY) factors and segregation tendencies as seen in some housing projects at strategic sites.

7.4.13 South African Housing Goals in Relation to Sustainable Development Goals (SDGs)

South Africa is one of the countries that aligns itself properly to global affairs and development agendas. One of this is the United Nations Sustainable Development Goals (SDGs). This is also referred to as one of the Global Goals and was adopted by the United Nations in 2015 as one of the fundamental calls and outreach strategy to bring poverty to an end, protection of the environment and to ensure that by 2030 all people enjoy peace and prosperity. Of great significance is the SDG 11 that touches on sustainable cities and communities and the desire to be able to make cities and human settlements inclusive, safe, resilient and sustainable. This goal came as a result of the tremendous increase in the number of people who are now living in cities and attended problems that came as a result of this. According to the UN Department of Economic and Social Affairs report, it is noted that in 2008 the global urban population of people living in cities outnumbered the rural population. As a follow up to this trend, the Habitat III of the UN held in Quito adopted a New Urban Agenda of 2016 and with other several commissions there was a universal call for the need to promote and champion 'Sustainable Human Settlements Development' and this was also reflected in Chapter 7 of Agenda 21. Among the highlight of this agenda is the need to promote adequate shelter for all and the improvement of human settlement management and planning together with capacity development as well as integrated services provisions. Mixed-income housing development is one of the housing options that is pioneering and taking this global vision and goals forward.

7.4.14 Lessons Learnt From the Review of Literature

Below are the lessons learnt from the review of South African Housing Literature.

- Housing is seen as one of the key and principal interventions to create an urban environment that are liveable, integrated and multifunctional.
- There has been several reforms in the housing delivery systems, particularly demarcation of the local government boundaries with the Municipal Structural Act of 1998, financial support programmes, legislative framework all forming important landmarks to housing delivery and processes post 1994.

- Policies to fill in brownfields and peri-urban zones as well as density increase at all scales of housing development and implementation are all in line with International trends (UN-Habitat, Sustainable Development Goals, Global Housing Network and the New Urban Agenda).
- In view of the capacity challenge that has been experienced by Municipalities, emphasize is now directed at the mechanisms for delivery in the form of bringing in the private sector to work closely with the public sectors. There is now shift from 'quantity' to 'quality'.
- Institutional capacity challenges for the development of social housing component was identified as one of the weakness in the system and led to setting up of a regulatory body known as Social Housing Regulatory Authority (SHRA) with mandate to provide capacity, skills and needed technical assistance systems to non-governmental organizations (NGOs), community-based organizations (CBOs), Local Authorities, Corporative and Private sectors who wish to invest in rental properties.
- The switch over to integrated human settlements from housing and increase in capacity to Informal Settlement Upgrade Programme strategy.
- Due to the legacy of apartheid and the attendant segregation, debate is increasingly shifting to mixed-income residential development and aided self-help housing. Though, the debate on aided self-help housing has not been fully resolved.
- The need to encourage and promote more inter-sectoral and intergovernmental collaboration in the delivery of human settlement programmes is noted, especially Planning Department, Social Development, Education, Health, Safety and Security and key stakeholders, NGOs, CBOs and other informal groups.
- Constant shift in housing policies and legislations and implication on delivery/implementation. Since 2004, emphasis is on incremental informal settlement upgrading and more on mixed-income housing development.
- Support for human settlement within the fiscus/budget has risen against the backdrop of backlog. Since 2015, there has been a shift to integrated human settlement and human settlement is strongly linked to National Development Plan.
- Paradigm shift that makes Peoples Housing Process (PHP) to be different from the other housing delivery strategies that are targeted at the poorest of the poor is now seen as part of empowerment and nation building.
- Focus is also shifting to innovative building technology and the creation of sustainable livelihood through human settlement delivery aimed at poverty alleviation as well as to create integrated settlements that can enable household to live, work and play.

7.4.15 Gaps Identified in the Literature and Contributions of This Study

Considering the reviewed literature so far and the highlighted lessons learnt, the following knowledge gaps have been identified, which this study attempts to address.

- There is relatively a policy vacuum as it relates to mixed-income housing development programmes and initiatives.
- No alignment of housing project, especially mega projects, with both Policy and Development objectives of successive government resulting in confusion on and around allocation/disbursement of funds.
- Another gap is that, in spite of the huge resources pumped into housing development initiatives, the state has not been able to put together a property market that combine subsidized and affordable housing for the low-income earners.
- The increasing Private Sector participation and engagement and their interest to getting involved in a more practical manner in human settlement development and Planning.
- There is lack of proper mechanisms to identify key features that inform beneficiary satisfaction of residents of low-income housing units.
- Lack of, and in some instance absence of, inter-sectoral and inter-governmental collaborations in housing projects and planning. Complex intergovernmental relations and institutional structures.

7.5 Conclusion

The legislative and policy framework guiding housing development was reviewed in this chapter. Shifts in policy since 1994 were also highlighted, particularly the way in which it shaped the human settlements programme and implementation strategies. The intention of using housing development projects, as one of the principal instruments to confront the socio-economic, political, moral, cultural and environmental, was confronted with serious problems. Breaking new ground and shift from 'quantity' to 'quality' in housing implementation plan is noted. The 12 national outcomes as portrayed by the National Development Plan were discussed. The research also discussed the focus of outcome 8. The impact of the two urban development legislations, SPLUMA and Urban Development Framework (as it relates to human settlement roll out) was reviewed. Provision of houses should not be just about shelter but also about growing the housing asset in order to erase generational poverty is also important. Hence, the reason for the shift to sustainable human settlement in South Africa has been driven by all stakeholders. Also discussed is the City of Johannesburg Inclusionary Housing Policy and various options. The roll out National Upgrading Support Programme (NUSP) across all Provinces in South Africa is informed by the need to tackle asset poverty in housing as municipalities lack the requisite skills, capacity and competencies or even the resources to roll out informal settlements upgrading. This is seen as one of the South Africans challenges that need urgent attention at all levels of authority.

Chapter 8

The Use of Delphi Study in Mixed-Income Housing Development

8.1 Introduction

The methods used in this study comprise of three rounds of iterative processes solely aimed at obtaining general agreement among the members of the panel. Socio-spatial issues relating to mixed-income housing development were also included as questionnaire. The rounds of Delphi questionnaire used in this study are attached as Appendix 1–3. Questionnaires were prepared based on the literature review with aimed to ascertain study objectives as stated in the introductory chapter. The questionnaire took an average of 4 months from October 2014 up to January 2015. Based on the analysis of the responses from the panel, some of the issues identified inform the conceptual framework for the broader study. In this chapter, we shall deal with the result of the Delphi and answers to the questions raised in Chapter 1.

8.1.1 A Theoretical Overview of the Delphi Technique

Research methods are derived from a theoretical position about how reality operates (Johnson, 2006:268). A researcher selects a given method because it resonates with their ontological perspective and because there are theoretical reasons to expect that the method will be appropriate for the research question and data to be pursued (Altheide, 1996 cited in Johnson, 2006:268). For several reasons, Delphi method is the best research method suited to this book. This is because, according to Turoff (1970), there are four possible objectives or secondary goals, for any Delphi exercise, namely:

(1) To explore or expose underlying assumptions or information leading to differing judgements;
(2) To seek out information which may generate a consensus of judgement on the part of the respondent group;

Mixed-Income Housing Development Planning Strategies and Frameworks in the Global South, 101–129
Copyright © 2024 George Okechukwu Onatu, Wellington Didibhuku Thwala and Clinton Ohis Aigbavboa
Published under exclusive licence by Emerald Publishing Limited
doi:10.1108/978-1-83753-814-020231008

(3) To correlate informed judgement on a topic spanning a wide range of disciplines;
(4) To educate the respondents group as to the diverse and interrelated aspects of the topic.

The Delphi method as will be used in this book will encompass a combination of these objectives as the essence is based on (Strauss and Zeigler, 1975) work that highlighted that Delphi techniques can also be used to solicit interpretation, predictions or recommendations. Adler and Ziglio (1996) also argue that Delphi method is a good communication method and process, especially to produce a detailed examination of a topic/problem and discussion from the participating group, but not one that forces a quick compromise. Thus, the structuring of the group communication is an essential component of the Delphi. The contribution of individuals via this tool produces a group perspective not otherwise obtainable. In selecting the most appropriate research tool, however (Linstone and Turoff, 1975 cited in Stitt-Gohdes and Crews, 2004:56) cautioned the researcher to consider the circumstances surrounding the 'necessarily associated group communication process'. They suggested this guiding question: 'who is it that should communicate about the problem, what alternative mechanisms are available for that communication, and what can we expect to obtain with this alternative'. Depending on the answers to these questions, one may then choose the Delphi as the most effective research tool for the study at hand. The reason being that the problem at hand in this research is controlled by:

(1) The problem does not lead itself to precise analytical technique but can benefit from subjective judgements on a collective basis.
(2) More individuals are needed than can effectively interact in a face-to-face exchange.
(3) Time and cost make frequent group meetings infeasible.
(4) Disagreement among individuals and experts in this field are so severe or politically unpalatable that the communication process must be refereed and/or anonymity assured.

The heterogeneity of the participants must be preserved to assure validity of the results, i.e. avoidance of domination by quantity or my strength of personality (Linstone and Turoff, 1975 cited in Stitt-Gohdes and Crews, 2004:57). The Delphi technique is a qualitative research method, and therefore many scholars argue and criticize it as not being empirically verifiable. To understand better the Delphi technique as research methods, and its applicability to this research, a literature review was done on the technique. The objective of the literature study was (1) to confirm the suitability of the Delphi methods to test the validity of several mixed-income related propositions, and (2) to assess the various aspects of the Delphi process. After evaluation of the process, it was applied as prescribed by Delbecq et al. (1975 cited in Botha and Steyn, 2008:139) in the following manner:

(1) The content of the questionnaire was based on the proposition developed from the literature review,
(2) The panel of experts consisted of experts in the field,
(3) There were first, second and third round of questionnaire,
(4) The second and third round incorporated feedback from the first round,
(5) Both consensus and disagreement on the various propositions were valuable to the formulation of a mixed-income framework, and
(6) From the data analysis a mixed-income housing development model was formulated.

Delphi approach is employed for problems that are difficult to solve with conventional technique (Banks, 2011). It helps structure communication in a way that allows a group of individuals to deal with complex problem by identifying consensus. In supporting this argument about the adequacy of Delphi, Laakso et al. (2012:3) have noted that 'Delphi method is well suited to setting up a communication structure among members who possess the same general core of knowledge and who are already well informed'. This method is particularly useful for topics on which there are strong differences of opinion or when high levels of uncertainty are present which is much broader in scope than the knowledge that any single individual can possess (Bank et al., 2011; Hussler et al., 2011; Kuusi, 1999). It is for these reasons that this study uses the Delphi method.

8.1.2 Delphi Study Objectives for the Case Study

A review of the literature highlighted key important factors that characterize mixed-income housing development projects. Notable among this are description based on the characteristics of the tenants, employment, families with children and income mix. Levy et al. (2010)'s focus has also, at some stage, shifted on the housing tenure and physical design as well as the nature of the project and sustainability. More arguably, HUD (2003), in supporting the above definition and characteristics of mixed-income, identified the need to include income diversity. Joseph (2006) elaborates on this further by noting that there is need to include the middle income, tier between the poorest and wealthy residents. Mixed-income housing as can be seen is broad term that 'carries different meaning for different audience' (Smith, 2002). Authors disagree about the range of incomes, the grain of the mix (e.g. unit-by-unit mix, income-segregated floors within a single building, or income-segregated buildings on a single site), and the demographical make up, tenure mix, unit mix, and scale required for a development to be considered 'mixed'. What was not clear from the literature was how this housing typology can provide the needed solution to access to housing in South Africa in view of multiplicity of housing programmes, legislation and implementation strategies. Previous models/framework as indicated have not been able to provide a detailed linkage of all the role players in a given project and the associated theories together with the housing product. Hence there is need for a broad conceptual framework that can guide and inform policies on the implementation of mixed-income housing development projects. The Delphi method was chosen in this section to examine this and come up with conceptual framework and answer to the research questions.

8.2 Response Rate

Response rate for round one was 75% as 15 participants out of 20 identified completed and returned the questionnaire. As Jillson (1975:132) notes, this is an acceptable response that all initial response rate of more than two-thirds was considered high for a Delphi study and showed significant interest on the part of panel experts. In view of the tight busy schedule of the senior executives and researchers who agreed to take part in this study, it is common knowledge that not all participants would complete all rounds, and this was the case in this study. The response rate for round two was 80% as 12 out of the 15 who agreed to participate actually completed round two. The response for round three was 83% as 10 out of the 12 panel members returned the questionnaire after completing it. The aggregate rate of response of 79% for the three rounds was acceptable considering that Round Three sample size was 12. Ziglo (1966:14) noted that 'even with small panels of 10–15 individuals good and acceptable results can be obtained'. This argument is further supported by scholars who revealed in their investigation that reduction in response rates from the first to the final, particularly those involving voluntary participation should be expected (Jillson, 1975: 132). Table 8.1 and Appendix 1–3 shows all the various rounds of the Delphi as used.

8.3 Analysis of the Result

Data analysis results and reporting are known to be directly related to the type of questions used in the Delphi instrument. According to the work of (Skulmoski et al., 2007) researchers are advised and compelled to make sure that they do apply accurate analytical techniques. Interpretations, explanations and presentation of Delphi instruments are noted to have been discussed extensively in order works (Dalkey and Helmer, 1963; Delbecq et al., 1975; Dietz, 1987; Linstone and Turoff, 1975; Schmidt, 1997). A number of researchers are found to include not

Table 8.1. Response Rate to the Questionnaire.

No of Questionnaire	Participants	Returned Questionnaire	Response Rate
Delphi Round one	20	15	75%
Delphi Round two	15	12	80%
Delphi Round three	12	10	83%
Average Total			79%

Source: Authors Note (2016).

only the analysis of the results as sorted out according to the areas of agreement and disagreement but also where no opinions are expressed (Keil et al., 2002). This approach is adopted in this study. One area of serious debate and where no general agreement is forthcoming in Delphi technique application is on how to measure the consensus (Giannatou and Zervas, 2014:73). The analysis of the Delphi results will assist in providing answers to the following research questions and sub questions:

- *RQ1.* How can mixed-income approaches enhance affordability and integrated human settlement strategies?
- *SRQ2.* What other housing development framework could be adopted or promoted in South Africa?
- *SRQ3.* Could a selected group of housing experts and professional developers reach a common consensus, using a Delphi technique, on the key principles and components of mixed-income housing development?
- *SRQ6.* Why is there lack of capacity within Government and Municipalities?

8.3.1 Round One

Once interest was confirmed by the voluntary participants, the consent letter was e-mailed to all of them seeking their participation and informing them that the round one questionnaire will be sent to them on receipt of their signed consent. Round one question was sent to 20 participants and they were required to read the rationale behind the research, follow the instructions carefully, and attempt to complete the questions. The questionnaire is comprised of open-ended questions and Likert Scale. This approach is adopted because it has added benefit of ensuring 'richer responses' (Nworie, 2011:26). The Likert scale is self-explanatory. Likert scales usage can be known to get disrupted for a number of reasons, according to Botha and Steyn (2008), which includes: The people responding may (1) decide not to use extreme response categories (central tendency bias); (2) accept and tend to agree on statements as prepared (acquiescence bias); or (3) pretend that all is well with them or their organization in an acceptable manner only (social desirability bias). These factors were mitigated using a 5-point forced Likert scale on questions covering social, spatial and economic features of mixed-income housing development. These include intergovernmental relations, developers' concerns/issues, planning and design forms, housing typologies, finance and access to land and neighbourhood effects.

The questions are prepared not to be a leading one or to direct respondents or participants straight to the answers and participants also completed the questionnaire in isolation from others. This approach is very important to avoid bias and to improve the rigour of the outcome. The initial questions are typically broad as the researcher is expected to cover all the areas that are necessary without leaving anything behind (Adler and Ziglio, 1996; Delbecq et al., 1975; Linstone and Turoff, 1975). See Appendix 1 (Page 293) for the round one questionnaire. Participants were requested to rate each statement on whether they agree with it or not. The scale rating shows that for 'Strongly Disagree,' it is lower in anchor, whereas for 'Strongly Agree' it is referred and rated as higher in anchor. As for in round one, the experts' panel members were encouraged to provide both qualitative feedback and their ratings. While several issues were listed and mentioned by more than one respondent, this is welcomed as diversity of opinion and responses in this round is necessary (Cowan, 2009:62). The responses assisted to enable the development of 48 and 40 Likert scale items in both round two and three. See Table 8.2 for the qualitative data received from round one. These qualitative data are essential, as noted by Nworie (2011), because provision could be made on the instrument for the panellists to include written comments or questions that they deem pertinent. See Table 8.2 for the round one qualitative data information and responses.

Table 8.2. Round One Qualitative Data.

Questions	Responses
22. Please identify any critical issues that affects housing provision for low income group in South Africa through mixed-income housing strategies that is currently implemented in different municipalities	– The current subsidy model does not allow for diversity in tenure options. – Green building procurement policy (lack of it) – Alternative construction materials/ Up scaling challenge – Lack of critical mass of mixed-income housing asset development and sustainability – The cost to provide serviced land – Unaffordability – Process of authorization (Town Planning) – Access to land and problem of finance – Affordability of the product – Land availability – Access to finance – No opinion
24. Which of the following conditions do you consider to be extreme important in attracting people of higher income households in mixed-income housing development to reduce vacancy rate? – Location of the development	– Location of the development – All categories listed above are important – Cost of the units – Conditions of the neighbourhood – Social amenities – Design and aesthetics

Table 8.2. *(Continued)*

Questions	Responses
– Cost of units – Design and aesthetics – Size of house – Social amenities – Conditions of the neighbourhood	
25. Which of the following housing delivery models will best respond to the needs of the low-income, middle-income and high-income groups in South Africa? – Public housing (Free Subsidy) – Self-help housing – Enabling the market to work – Mixed-income housing – Provision of social housing – Hostel upgrade – National upgrade support programme	– Mixed-income housing – Self-help housing – Provision of social housing – All except hostel upgrade – Public housing (Free Subsidy) – Hostel upgrade – Enabling market work
29. Why is the demand for market rate units in mixed-income housing lower than affordable units?	– Perception of affordable lifestyle and quality of environment – Housing consumer perception of mixed-income housing as inferior – Poor branding, marketing and lack of a sustainable and viable mixed-income housing steering mechanism and system – It is the other way round. The affordable market has the greater demand – If people have a choice, they would rather not live in a mixed-income neighbourhood – Country Economy – It is about cost of capital, borrowers' credit worthiness, credit extension system etc. – In truth, it is easier to obtain affordable, subsidized units than go for market rates units. In all likelihood, the said units are further in close proximity to each other

Table 8.2. *(Continued)*

Questions	Responses
30. What do you envisage will be the turnaround strategies of the South Africa Housing Policy in the next 10–15 years?	– New subsidy schemes + site and services options – Shift from subsidy housing towards self-help/assisted housing programmes – To eradicate informal settlements as soon as possible – Speculation – Less emphasize on RDP and reserve it only for poorest of the poor and disabled – Movement to low-income rental – Move to Financed Linked Individual Subsidy Programme (FLISP) – Possible relaxation of the full subsidy, migration to semi-subsidized housing – Less reliance on subsidy – Mobilization of private sector participation – There will be a shift from provision of free housing stock to affordable rental and gap-market solutions, with financing more accessible than currently
34 & 35. If you strongly disagree to the previous statement that the problem of unemployment and side effects of concentrated poverty in urban areas can be addressed with proper planned mixed-income housing development, what do you think?	– It varies among projects and dependent on a host of other factors. Capacity building etc. – Will take a lot more than this – The problem is a question of skill and where do you start them into the project. The equity employee get to demand so much that developers can't afford to pay them – Employment opportunities can be created through housing projects – Build robust economy through industrial policy. Invest in capital & labour-intensive programme

Table 8.2. *(Continued)*

Questions	**Responses**
36 & 37. Mixed-income housing development impact negatively to the surrounding neighbourhood in terms of decrease in property value. If you disagree to the previous statement, what do you think?	– Dependent on the quality and design of the project. Well designed and planned projects can increase property value – Properly developed townships increase property value – Depend entirely on the project – Property value is always a function of good living environment. Mixed-income areas tend to generally be safer environment, and therefore maintain good value, the danger of resisting mixed-income housing is having quasi-apartheid enclaves based on class
39 & 40. Access to housing and a place to live is on top of the priorities of the poor and low-income groups in South Africa. If you disagree to the previous statement, what do you think should be the paramount needs of the poor and low-income groups in South Africa that the government should give priority?	– Some communities require basic needs, but housing is a top priority – Jobs – Employment and supply of daily supplements
44 & 45. Access to reliable finance is a very big obstacle to the developers for rapid roll out of mixed-income housing units. If you disagree to the previous statement, what other factors hinder the development?	– This depends on who the developer is. The construction industry is one of the most lacked transformed sectors in South Africa. This leads to an inevitable monopoly by established developers with a track record and access to funds – On the other hand, emerging developers have vast challenges in accessing financing from financial institution

Source: Authors Note (2016).

8.3.2 Round Two

Experts' answers to the questions posed during the time of circulating round one questions were copied from the questionnaire and inserted into a five-point Likert scale statement for round two. The essence of first round was to come up with listed item of interest, and according to Schmidt (1997), it is acceptable commonly to write down these lists in the second round. These experts are expected to give their recommended opinion and answers just in the same manner as in round one to 48 statements regarding mixed-income housing development. A 16.0 SPSS version tool was employed in order to calculate the standard deviation and mean of each Likert scale statements, whereas 5 was for Strongly; Agree was 4; No Opinion was 3; Disagree was 2; and Strongly Disagree was 1. If the standard deviation happens to be low, and the mean records high ratings, it shows that the majority of those who took part in the survey collectively agree with the statement. Moreover, whenever the standard deviation and the mean were found to be of low result, it signals that the majority of experts disagree with the statement and that there was high nature; so consensus in that decision. Response of 'No Opinion' is considered as no commitment in, in a situation where the majority of the respondents have no opinion at all or the majority are one side of agreement or disagreement (other than neutral), the question was not identified as an area of dissensus. Complete consensus results when the standard deviation score was equal to 0.00 and deemed high when the standard deviation score was less than 1.00. During round two exercise, a high consensus was recorded. Out of the total number of 40 Likert scale questionnaires administered to the experts, excluding eight items from which general comments were expected, 27 of the statements had a high level of consensus and 13 items of dissensus. This represents 68% of the statements and 32% of dissensus. Refer to Table 8.3 for the responses received from round two.

8.3.3 The Delphi Study: Round Two Items of Consensus

The major goal of the Delphi in any research is to obtain consensus (Armstrong, 1989; Murray and Hammons, 1995; Zemke and Kramlinger, 1982), and in this study, consensus will be used to mean 'a general agreement' (Thompson, 1995). Consensus is noted to be influenced by three factors: groups that are of low bearing members might be swayed to join or collaborate with the opinion of group members with a higher order; a possibility of a group to pressure on its members to do like others and a possibility of a more powerful group member to weigh heavily on the opinion of the group (Fein et al., 1997; Gupta and Clarke, 1996; Zolingen and Klaassen, 2003). In this study, these undue influences are guided by anonymity and this is aimed at guaranteeing and encouraging opinions that are free from any influence from others. Experts were encouraged to make statements and respond to the questionnaire in an objective manner based on their personal knowledge of the subject and experiences. The identified experts all reported general agreement and consensus in round two on items with ($X = 4$) on the following items in the Likert scale items.

The experts all agreed and responded 'Agreed' with (X = 4.00) on the following statement:

- Mixed-income housing development in South Africa is designed to improve and promote integrated human settlements to accommodate households with disparate income band.
- Mixed-income housing development can lead to strong community building and correct previous apartheid segregated settlement and planning.
- It is necessary for there to be strong and good intergovernmental relationship and coordination for the delivery of mixed-income housing development.
- An important issue that is lacking in the development of mixed-income housing development is level of cooperation between the public and private sectors.
- Strong leadership from government is of high importance in any human settlement project development and planning including mixed-income housing.
- Access to integrated Public Transport system and provision of social amenities are important elements to be considered in a mixed-income housing development project.
- Concern with the cost that delays and long process in getting Town Planning approvals and adhering to the land-use regulations is having on mixed-income housing development.
- Nearness to upmarket housing units might slow the approval and implementation of mixed-income housing development as a result of objections and resistance from neighbours.
- Mixed-income housing development is believed to enhance as well as broaden the affordability of housing in South Africa.
- High cost of prime land is of great concern to the roll out of mixed-income housing project.
- Expected return on capital invested is good for any completed mixed-income housing project.
- Government support for integrated human settlements is shifting towards mixed-income housing development.
- The informal settlements challenges and social ills of concentrated poverty can be addressed with mixed-income housing development.
- Capacity within Government and other municipal structure to drive mixed-income housing development.
- How the economy performs has a negative impact on the development of mixed-income housing development.

8.3.4 The Delphi Study: Round Two Items of Dissensus

The order of disagreement among the members of the panel selected is noted by the type of dissensus. According to Hanafin (2004:39), with high standard deviation, the panel members are noted to disagree. See Table 8.3. The dissensus is depicted with (X-3.5) and Standard Deviation (1.5). Items that the panel fail to agree are as follows:

Table 8.3. Round Two Mean and Standard Deviation.

	Q1	Q2	Q3	Q4	Q5	Q6	Q7	Q8	Q9
N Valid	40	40	40	40	40	40	40	40	40
Missing	0	0	0	0	0	0	0	0	0
Mean	4.4	4.5	4.3	2.4	4.25	3	4.39	3.4	4.4
Std. Deviation	0.41	0.73	0.5	4.33	0.5	1.28	0.55	0.34	0.94
	Q10	Q11	Q12	Q13	Q14	Q15	Q16	Q17	Q18
N Valid	40	40	40	40	40	40	40	40	40
Missing	0	0	0	0	0	0	0	0	0
Mean	4.4	3.4	1.4	3.42	4.43	4.4	1.5	4.55	2.4
Std. Deviation	0.97	1.2	3.7	0.99	0.36	0.5	3.0	0.5	0.79
	Q19	Q20	Q21	Q22	Q23	Q24	Q25	Q26	Q27
N Valid	40	40	40	40	40	40	40	40	40
Missing	0	0	0	0	0	0	0	0	0
Mean	4.4	2.4	3.4	3.45	4.5	4.45	4.00	4.0	3.4
Std. Deviation	0.56	1.23	1.39	1.5	1.38	0.86	0.15	0.38	0.86
	Q28	Q29	Q30	Q31	Q32	Q33	Q34	Q35	Q36
N Valid	40	40	40	40	40	40	40	40	40
Missing	0	0	0	0	0	0	0	0	0
Mean	3.4	2.5	4.4	3.7	2.4	2.56	3.8	4.15	3.4
Std. Deviation	0.25	1.72	0.55	1.87	1.39	0.15	0.55	0.5	1.57
	Q37	Q38	Q39	Q40					
N Valid	40	40	40	40					
Missing	0	0	0	0					
Mean	2.46	2.4	4.0	3.0					
Std. Deviation	0.15	0.15	1.5	1.00					

Source: Author Primary Data Reporting (2016).

- An important issue that is lacking where mixed-income housing development is taking place is the kind of working relationship between the public sector and private sectors.
- Accessing finance is not a major obstacle or impediment to the owner in the roll out of mixed-income housing development.
- Concerns are raised on the percentage of low cost housing units (RDP) that is permissible in a given mixed-income housing development project and its impact on the viability of the project.
- Nearness to upmarket housing units can slow the approval and implementation of mixed-income housing development due to objections and resistance from neighbours.
- The occupancy rate in any completed mixed-income housing development is very slow and unsustainable.

- Backyard shacks are not major issues for consideration in the implementation of mixed-income housing development.
- Compliance to National Homebuilders Registration Council and other statutory regulations is a major obstacle to the increase in delivery of mixed-income housing development.
- Mixed-income is considered to bring along with it local economic development to the surrounding areas.

8.3.5 Round Three

In round three, the questionnaire included those items that met with dissensus. Results of the feedback and answers from all the experts who have been participating in the research survey were listed against each Likert scale. The participants were requested to either change or stick to their previous answers. They were also requested to consider giving comments on items where their responses were not in agreement from the rest of the participants. They were notified that this round is the close out round, that they have the right to change their opinion and that they could also provide written responses. The software SPSS version 16.0 was used to analyze and sum up the mean and standard deviation of each of the Likert scale statement, where Strongly Agree = 5; Agree = 4; No Opinion = 3; Disagree = 2; and Strongly Disagree = 1. See Table 8.4 for the mean and standard deviation scores.

8.3.6 Delphi Study: Round Three Items

Currently there is no one size that fits all as it concerns the measurement and how consensus is arrived at among the participants. There is no one common practice to measure it (Giannatou and Zervas, 2014:67). Hence, some research studies use and measure agreement through frequency distributions and whereas others use the standard deviation or the interquartile range. In case one, percentages of respondents to a given question is defined, which according to McKenna (1989), is capped at 51%? Studies employing the standard deviation method or interquartile range to evaluate the level of consensus, the standard deviation should be lower than 1.5 (Christie and Barela, 2005) and the interquartile range less than 2.5 (Kittell-Limerick, 2005) or 1 (Raskin, 1994; Rayens and Hahn, 2000:311). The percentile is the tipping point value of a variable below, at which point certain percentages of observation falls. The first quartile (Q1) is defines as 25th percentile, while the 50th percentile is known as the median or second quartile (Q2), and the third quartile is 75th percentile. Both standard deviation and the mean range are adopted for the present study. Consensus can also be determined by measuring the central tendency of the various responses on all questions (Aigbavboa and Thwala, 2013:317).

Table 8.4. The Mean and Standard Deviation of Round Three.

	Q1	Q2	Q3	Q4	Q5	Q6	Q7	Q8	Q9
N Valid	40	40	40	40	40	40	40	40	40
Missing	0	0	0	0	0	0	0	0	0
Mean	4.58	4.25	5	4.16	4.83	1.5	3.91	3.75	4.75
Std. Deviation	0.094	0.11	0.0	0.47	0.37	0.288	0.11	1.73	0.28
	Q10	Q11	Q12	Q13	Q14	Q15	Q16	Q17	Q18
N Valid	40	40	40	40	40	40	40	40	40
Missing	0	0	0	0	0	0	0	0	0
Mean	4.75	3	1.91	2.33	2.92	4.33	2.67	4.83	4.83
Std. Deviation	0.28	0.53	0.77	1.73	0.24	0.18	0.79	0.76	0.09
	Q19	Q20	Q21	Q22	Q23	Q24	Q25	Q26	Q27
N Valid	40	40	40	40	40	40	40	40	40
Missing	0	0	0	0	0	0	0	0	0
Mean	4.33	4.33	4.58	4.08	2.5	4.25	3	4.67	4.58
Std. Deviation	0.18	0.18	0.094	0.11	0.23	0.115	0	0.18	1.7
	Q28	Q29	Q30	Q31	Q32	Q33	Q34	Q35	Q36
N Valid	40	40	40	40	40	40	40	40	40
Missing	0		0	0	0	0	0	0	0
Mean	2.0	1.83	3.75	3.83	2.33	4.68	2.75	2.75	4.25
Std. Deviation	1.9	0.11	0.1	0.18	0.23	0.188	0.09	0.09	0.11
	Q37	Q38	Q39	Q40					
N Valid	40	40	40	40					
Missing	0	0	0	0					
Mean	4.33	2.5	4.66	3.0					
Std. Deviation	0.23	0	0.66	1.0					

Source: Author Note (2016).

Identified and contributed experts in unison responded that they 'strongly agree' ($X = 5.00$) with one item. The item is:

- It is necessary for there to be strong and good intergovernmental relationship and coordination for the delivery of Mixed-income housing development.

Identified experts also reported complete dissensus ($s = 00$) in round three on only one item in the Likert scale item. They unanimously responded that they have 'No Opinion'

- Factors at the National, Provincial and Local levels all impact on mixed-income housing development as the projects involves complex level of coordination.

8.4 Items That Experts Achieved Consensus

8.4.1 Promotion of Integrated Human Settlements

The analysis of the third round of the Delphi shows significant evidence to achieving the objective of this research together with answering the research questions. The first question is on whether mixed-income housing development in South Africa was designed to enhance and promote integrated human settlements to accommodate households with disparate income band.

In Fig. 8.1, 42% of the respondents of the final round of the Delphi round three agree that mixed-income housing development in South Africa was designed to improve and promote integrated human settlements to accommodate households with disparate income bands. Also 58% responded that they strongly agree to this statement. However, no respondents strongly disagree, disagree or express no opinion at all. This shows that a greater percentage of the respondents are of the view that mixed-income housing development are designed to enhance and promote integrated human settlements to accommodate households with disparate incomes band, thereby answering the first question of this research (*RQ1*). The findings are supported by the other literature as (Hackett et al., 2006) noted that consensus is achieved if 51% of the experts responds to the category 'strongly agree' and this response is between four and five on a 5-Likert scale. The case study of Cosmo City according to Onatu (2010) also agrees to these findings.

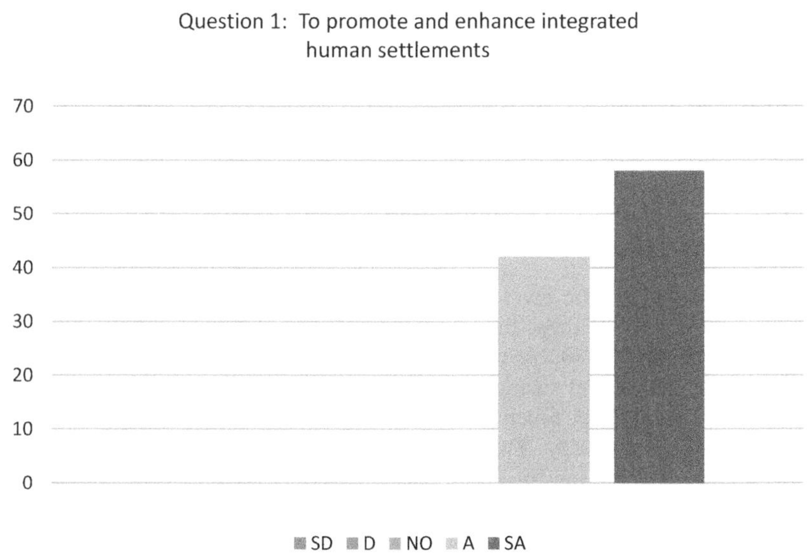

Fig. 8.1. Mixed-income Housing Development to Enhance and Promote Integrated Human Settlements. *Source:* Author Primary Data Reporting (2016).

Inclusionary Housing Policy as initiated by South Africa in 2007, as shown in the literature reviewed, was aimed at catering for the low-income households in any given mixed-use project and to give added opportunities to this category of people (Tissington, 2011:7 cited in Lategan, 2017). The policy was crafted to drive initiatives such as to develop middle- and higher income empowerment to housing to the benefit of the entire socio-economic spectrum and to leverage affordability in housing development. This is done by providing adequate incentives or subsidies in the form of tax exemptions so as to motivate and compel the private sector to develop housing for low-income and middle-income groups in previous areas of high risks (Onatu, 2010).

8.4.2 Intergovernmental Relations and Coordination

When asked if it is necessary for there to be strong and good intergovernmental relations and coordination in the delivery of mixed-income housing development, 100% responded that they strongly agree that it is imperative for there to be strong and good intergovernmental relationship and coordination. The survey result is also supported by the evidence from the case study as the entire relevant government department played a major role in the delivery of housing. This includes various government departments such as Transport, Education, Development Planning, Human Settlement, Health and Safety and Security Services as well as Disaster Management together with Department of Social Development. Comments from the respondents suggest that this is necessary to address the housing challenge such as inclusion, integration and construction as well as good governance. These act as preconditions for sustainable mixed-income housing development and replication. Fig. 8.2 shows the need for intergovernmental coordination and relation in the implementation of mixed-income housing development.

8.4.3 Collaboration Between Public and Private Partnership

Questions related to the level of cooperation between the Public sectors and Private sectors, 83% of those that took part responded and agreed that there is a need for a strong and reliable cooperation between the private sector and public sector. Seventeen percent strongly agree to this statement. Literature review from developed world did not touch on this but evidence from developing world suggests that this is necessary. The problem with South Africa human settlements strategies and interventions has been compounded by the lack of sustainable and coherent cooperation between the private sectors and public sectors. This result is also supported by the work of Johnson in (2009) which found that mixed-income can be a way to bring energy to the private sector resources by creatively providing seed finance through government incentive programmes. Property developers and investors might benefit more by offering varieties of housing products at a range of price that can go a long way to reduce the overall risk of the project and help increase absorption rates by widening the scope of the target

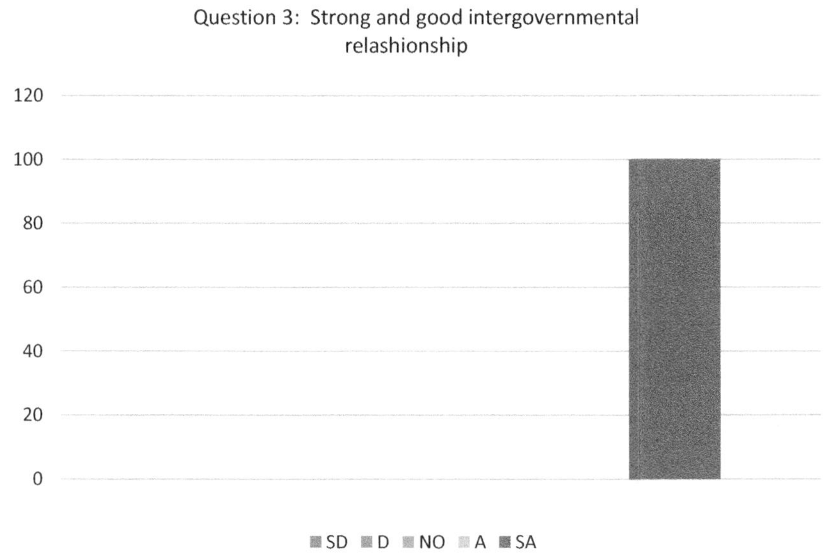

Fig. 8.2. The Need for Strong and Good Intergovernmental Relationship and Coordination. *Source:* Author Note (2016).

market. Density bonus, as offered to a private developer in United States, can enable the provision of affordable units in their project (Ibid, 2009). Khadduri and Martin (1997) and Schwartz and Tajbakhsh (1997) have noted that the lower income households can be subsidized by the market-rate units rents with support from the government. Payne (1997) also found out that formal partnership improved the way the low-income have access to housing in India, Pakistan, Egypt and United Kingdom. Another study comparing two mixed-income developments by Fraser and Kick (2007) proposed for mixed-income housing to achieve desired goals and succeed that four key groups of stakeholders play very important role, namely, financiers, the local authority and community associations.

This result shows that PPP in South African human settlements draw rich experiences from other countries. All these findings point to the need for public-private partnership in any human settlement development in South Africa for sustainability. In Fig. 8.3, 82% of the respondents are in support and agree for strong collaboration and relation between the private sector and the public sector, whereas only 16% Strongly Agree.

8.4.4 Strong Leadership From Government

In the Delphi third round, a question to determine whether strong leadership from government is of high importance in any human settlement project development

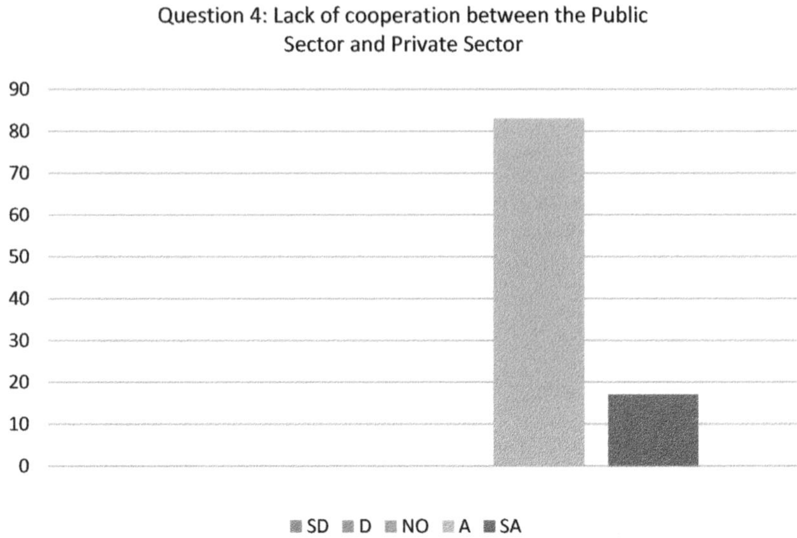

Fig. 8.3. Public–Private Partnership. *Source:* Author Primary Data Reporting (2016).

and planning, including mixed-income housing development was posed. The result suggests that 17 Agree and 83% Strongly Agree that strong leadership from government is needed for the development and planning of human settlement including mixed-income housing development. None of the participants expressed any view with disagree, strongly disagree or no opinion at all. The Hope VI housing programme as implemented in the United States in early 1990s provides a radical shift from previous Public Housing provision and still stand out clearly and emerged as a strong leadership position of government to address concerns of people living in deprived neighbourhoods and having low-life expectancies. South African government National Development Plan (NDP) is benchmarking on this international best practice, as according to the Presidency (2010:2), refer to Chapter 7 the intention of the government is to provide these households with improved shelter that has adequate basic services. The target set to address this from 2010 to 2014 is that at least 400,000 households will be upgraded in well located informal settlements with tenure, services and good access road. The National Upgrading Support Programme (NUSP) was meant to address this via the Upgrading Informal Settlements Programme (UISP). The strategy is meant to transform the living conditions of these households into sustainable human settlements, thus incorporating integrated development planning, coordinated municipal and provincial service delivery and good urban management (NDP, 2012). See Fig. 8.4 showing the results of leadership from government.

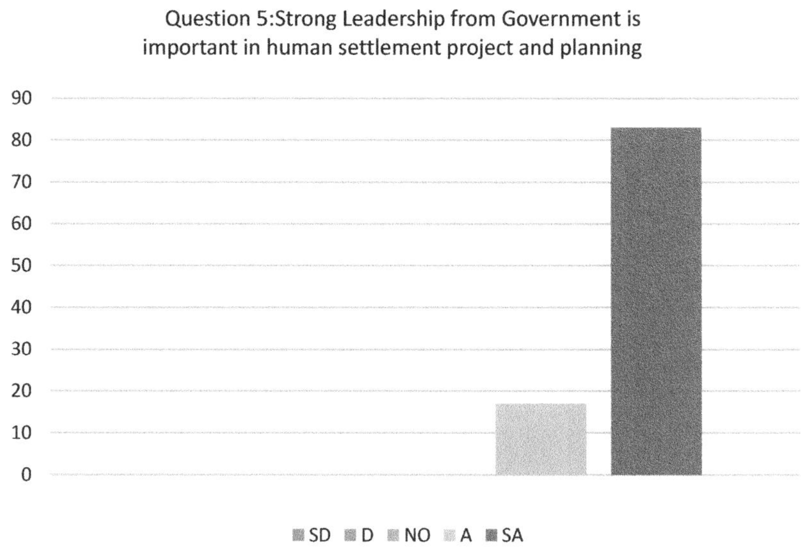

Fig. 8.4. Provide the Frequency of the Impact of Leadership From Government on Mixed-income Housing. *Source:* Author Primary Data Reporting (2016).

8.4.5 Access to Finance

When asked whether access to finance is not a major obstacle or impediment to the developer in implementing mixed-income housing development, 66% of the respondents strongly disagree to this statement, 17% of the respondents disagree and 17% have no opinion. This point to the fact that access to finance is very crucial for the sustenance of mixed-income housing development as it is a problem for developer to access loan and tax incentives for the development of mixed-income housing in South Africa. The Financial Charter Agreement between the private sector and the government is meant to address this but more still need to be done. These findings is also supported by the National Human Settlements Indaba outcome in 2014 at which point a Social Contract meant for the advancement and development of Sustainable Human Settlements which was supported by all role players including, banking associations, housing developers and government agencies with the commitment to provide funding of R250 billion ($15,812,776,723) by 2019 (Housing in South Africa, 2016:8). Density bonuses as practised in the United States is a good attempt to support the private sector financially since it cushions the huge financial outlays they suffer in the provision and implementation of mixed-income housing units. Fig. 8.5 shows the results of access to Finance as it affects the development of mixed-income housing development.

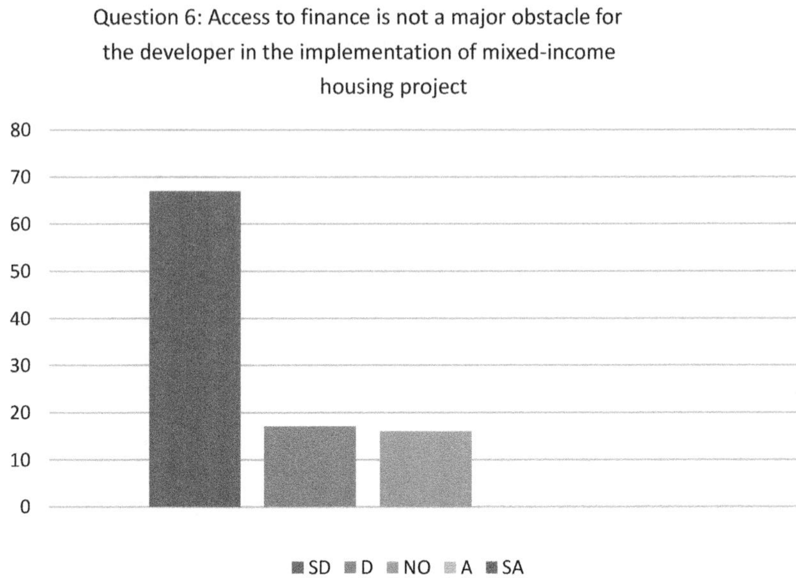

Fig. 8.5. Present the Result of This Finding of Access to Finance.
Source: Author Primary Data Reporting (2016).

8.4.6 Delays and Long Process in Getting Town Planning Approval

When asked to comment on the concern that delay and long process in getting Town Planning approvals and adhering to the land use regulations is having on mixed-income housing development projects. About 75% Strongly Agree to this statement and only 25% Agree. No response was received from the other items in the questionnaire. Comments received from one of the respondents show that the landscape will change with the introduction of Spatial Planning Land Use Management Act (SPLUMA). This finding is one of the contributions of this research, as the literature reviewed from both developed and developing countries did not dwell on this phenomenon. Fig. 8.6 shows the results of Town Planning regulations as it affects the development of mixed-income housing development.

8.4.7 Enhancement of Affordable Housing

To enhance and broaden affordability of housing in South Africa, 67% of the respondents agree to this statement, 8% strongly agree and 25% of the respondents disagree that this is the case. To provide housing with dignity and respect to fundamental human privileges is considered as one of the major challenges facing South Africa. Despite that, access to housing is a right in the Constitutional; the realization of this obligation and right is still far-fetched according to Landman

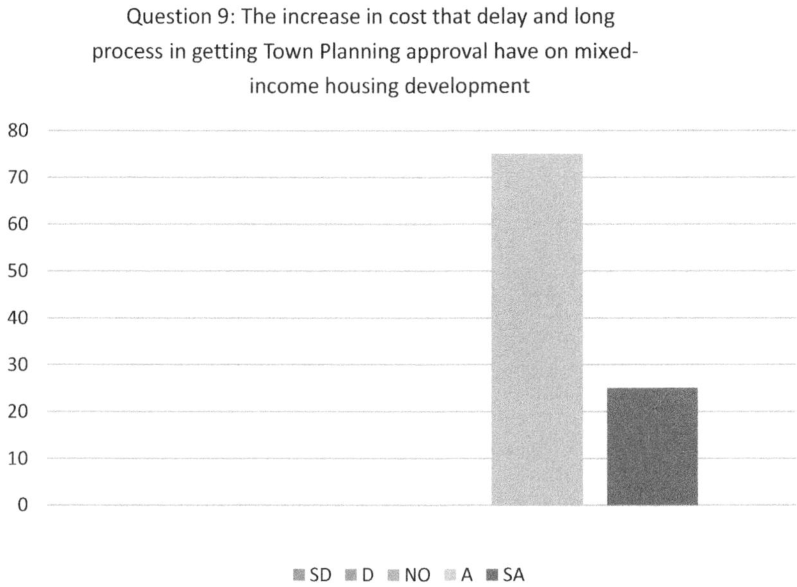

Fig. 8.6. Town Planning Approvals and Processing. *Source:* Author Primary Data Reporting (2016).

and Napier (2010), who noted that the South Africa constitution guarantees the right to 'adequate shelter' for all citizens with state available resources. How these state resources are to be made available and accessible to the households that are poor and marginalized has continued to remain a neglected area in policy discussions. Huchzermeyer (2001) points out that shifts in housing finance have tendered to overlook the plights of the poor in society in terms of affordability. This is also aggravated by a slow economy, problem of unemployment and inflationary hike. Fig. 8.7 shows the results of affordability as it affects the development of mixed-income housing development.

8.4.8 The View That Factors at All Spheres of Government Impact on Mixed-Income Housing

All the experts express no opinion on whether factors at three spheres of government impact on mixed-income housing development as the projects involves complicated multilevel coordination. There was not enough evidence to support this statement, and all the experts expressed no opinion.

Fig. 8.8 shows the results of all spheres of government as it affects the development of mixed-income housing development.

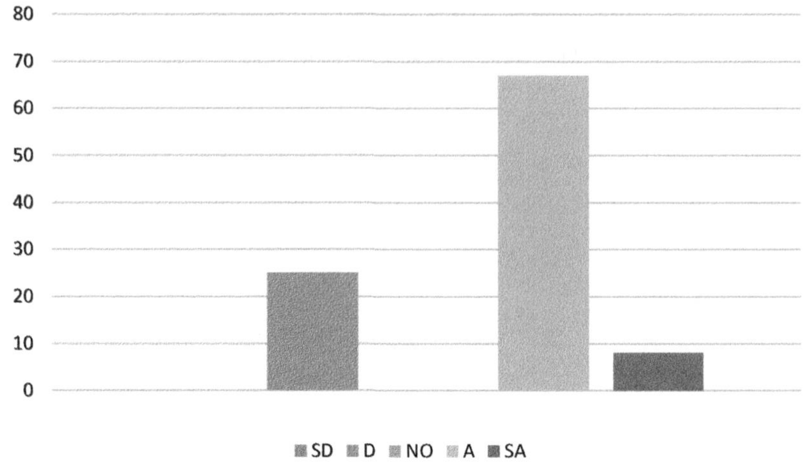

Fig. 8.7. Mixed-income to Broaden Affordability in Housing. *Source:* Author Primary Data Reporting (2016).

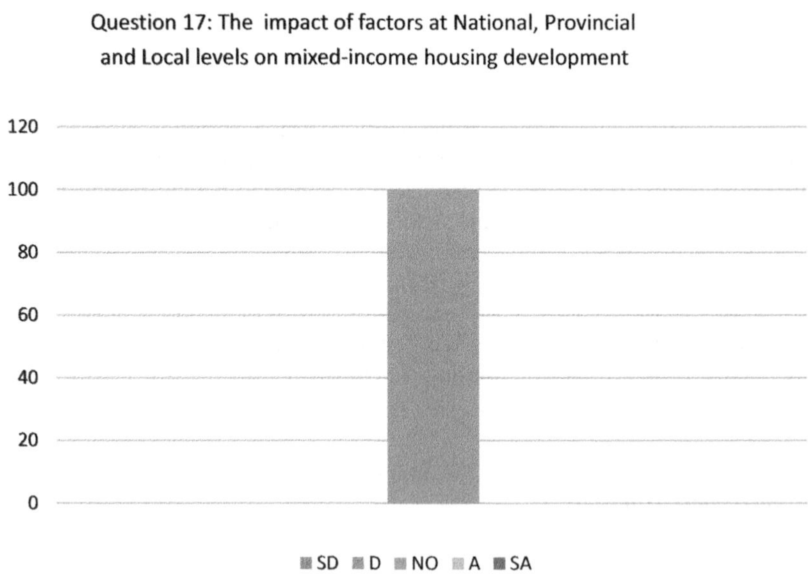

Fig. 8.8. Factors at Three Spheres of Government. *Source:* Author Primary Data Reporting (2016).

8.4.9 The Problem of Informal Settlements and Concentrated Poverty

The question was posed to the experts on whether the problem of informal settlements and concentrated poverty can be addressed with mixed-income housing development strategy, 67% of the responses strongly agree that it does, while 33% also agree. Fig. 8.9 shows the results of how the problem of informal settlements as it affects the development of mixed-income housing development.

8.4.10 Mixed-Income Housing Development Eradication of Informal Settlements

On whether mixed-income housing development will eradicate informal settlements in future, 66% of the respondents disagree that this will ever happen and 17% strongly disagree and strongly agree on this statement. This response should be able to send strong signal and requires more robust discussions on the rationale of the several mega housing projects that are aimed at uplifting the living conditions of people in informal settlements. The word 'eradicate' as used by professionals on matters pertaining to informal settlements challenges and how solutions can be found need to be treaded carefully with as studies suggests otherwise on the proliferation of the phenomenon in spite of the several initiatives by Government to find a lasting solution to this. Fig. 8.10 shows the results of the

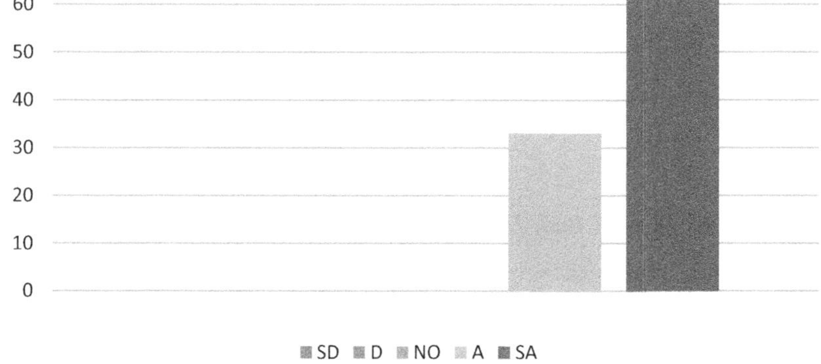

Fig. 8.9. The Problem of Informal Settlements. *Source:* Author Primary Data Reporting (2016).

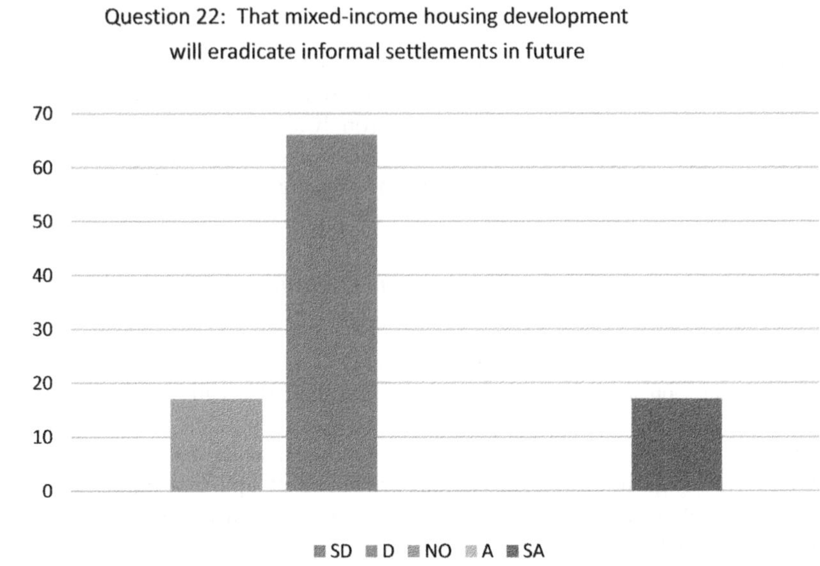

Fig. 8.10. Eradication of Informal Settlements. *Source:* Author Primary Data Reporting (2016).

eradication of informal settlements as it affects the development of mixed-income housing development.

8.4.11 Mixed-income Housing Development as Good and Safe Place to Live/Work and Play

The 66% of the experts indicated that mixed-income housing development initiatives are good place to live, work and play, and only 33% agree to this view. Fig. 8.11 shows the results as it affects the development of mixed-income housing development.

8.4.12 The Problem of Bulk Infrastructure

When asked whether bulk infrastructure is seen as one of the impediments and obstacles to the development of mixed-income housing development, 58% of the respondents strongly agree on this and 42% agree. Fig. 8.12 shows the results of bulk infrastructure as it affects the development of mixed-income housing development.

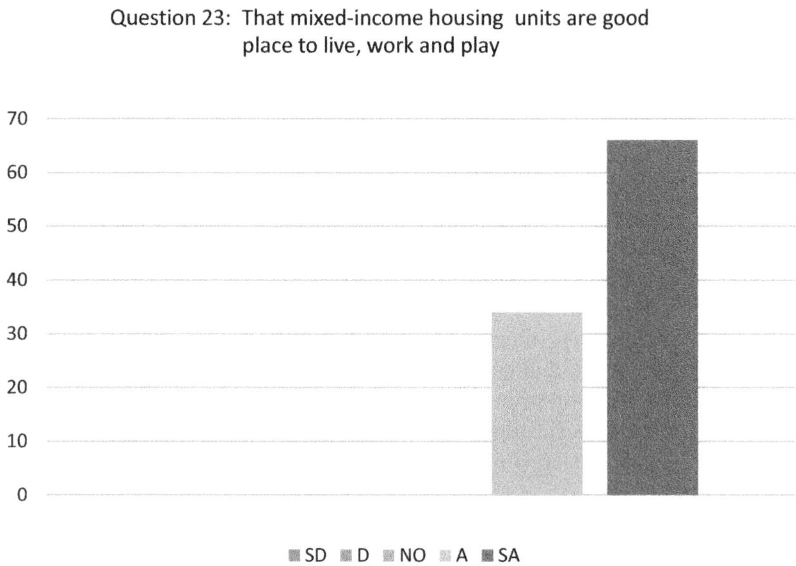

Fig. 8.11. Good Place to Live, Work and Play. *Source:* Author Primary Data Reporting (2016).

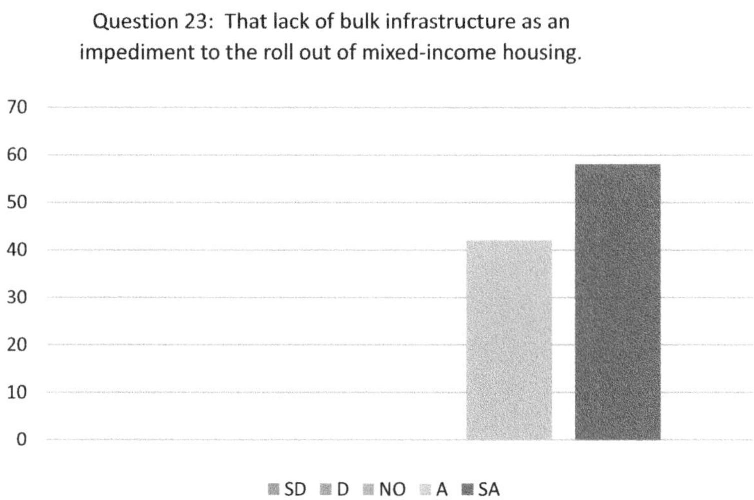

Fig. 8.12. Lack of Bulk Infrastructure. *Source:* Author Primary Data Reporting (2016).

8.4.13 Capacity Within Government and Municipality

A question was posed to the respondents whether lack of capacity exists in government and other local authorities to drive mixed-income housing development. In response to this, 42% agree that there is a lack of capacity at these two levels, and 58% strongly support this view on capacity challenges. This result is in line and agreement with the United Nations Agenda 2030 Global Goal of Sustainable Development Goals (SDGs) that built on the progress made by the Millennium Development Goals (MDGs) between 2000 and 2015 that was agreed by 193 member states on the 25th of September 2015 which South Africa is signatory to. Goal 11, item 11.3 states that by 2030, calls for the need 'to enhance inclusive and sustainable urbanization and capacity for participatory, integrated and sustainable human settlements planning and management in all countries' (UN General Assembly, 2015). There is now increasing call for the professionalisation of civil service and upskilling of staff to be able to tackle these global challenges more effectively. Fig. 8.13 shows the results of capacity at the municipal levels as it affects the development of mixed-income housing development.

8.4.14 Shift of Human Settlements From Subsidy Housing to Self-help

In view of the current challenges facing the housing subsidy programme, the experts were asked to consider a turnaround time and a shift towards self-help or

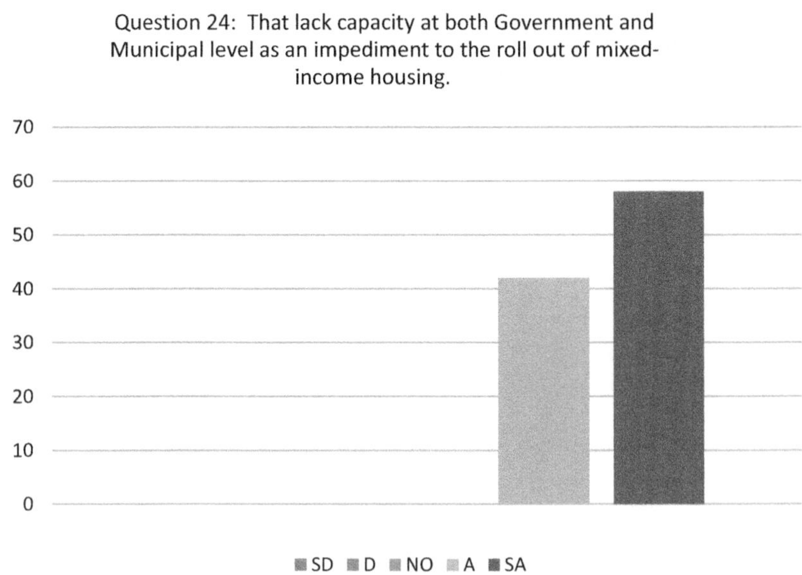

Fig. 8.13. Capacity Challenges at Government and Municipal Levels.
Source: Author Primary Data Reporting (2016).

assisted housing programme. On this note, 17% disagree and another 17% agree on this, whereas 66% are in strong agreement on this as a future consideration. Fig. 8.14 shows the results of a shift from subsidy housing as it affects the development of mixed-income housing development.

8.5 Items of Dissensus

8.5.1 Community-Building Strategy and Corrections of Apartheid Settlement Planning

When asked whether mixed-income housing can influence strong community building as well as correct previous apartheid segregated settlements and planning, only 42% agree to this statement. About 42% also strongly agree that mixed-income housing development gives rise to strong community building and correct previous apartheid segregated settlements and planning. Sixteen percent of them indicated that they do not have any opinion, while none of the respondents strongly disagree or disagree to the statement. We conclude that 84% of the respondents suggest that mixed-income housing can propel community building as well as correct previous apartheid segregated areas and planning. Analysis of the comments from the respondents suggests that while this can be achieved theoretically and rhetorically, the reality is that on its own mixed-income developments cannot achieve this in South Africa given South African history.

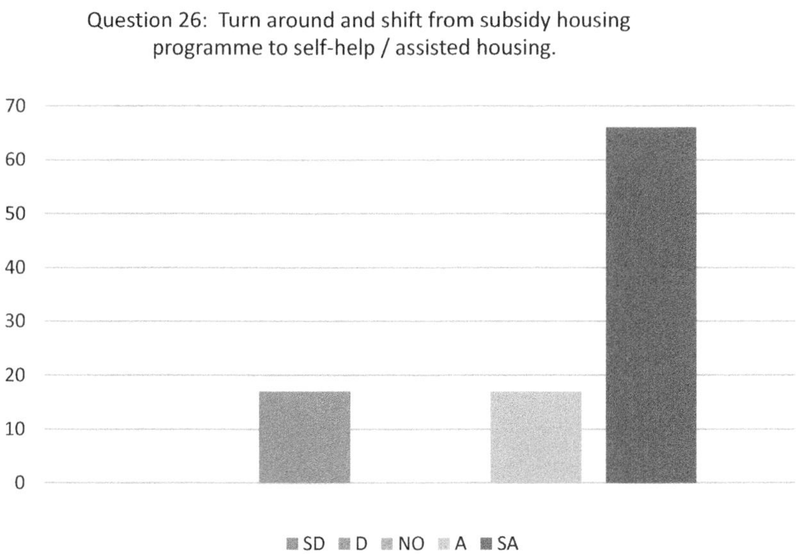

Fig. 8.14. Shift From Subsidy Housing Programme. *Source:* Author Primary Data Reporting (2016).

However, supplemented by other supportive programmes and activities such as adequate communal hall, newsletters and sporting facilities, parks, food festivals, campaigns against any form of social and political exclusions and violence, etc. then the goals can be approached. Fig. 8.15 shows the results of a strong community as it affects the development of mixed-income housing development.

8.5.2 The Shift of Government Towards Mixed-Income Housing in 9–10 Years From Now

In predicting on whether government will shift in 9–10 years from now to mixed-income housing development, 42% agree on this and 42% strongly agree, whereas only 16% still feel that this might not be the case in view of certain challenges. This result is very important and significant as some of the local authorities in South Africa are now for the first time developing Inclusionary Housing Policy, thereby encouraging developers to include or set aside 20%–30% component of affordable housing in a given mixed-income housing project. An example of this is the City of Johannesburg that has now implemented this policy to guide developers and Town Planning approvals of housing projects. This is an example of where policy is seen informing planning. Fig. 8.16 shows the results of

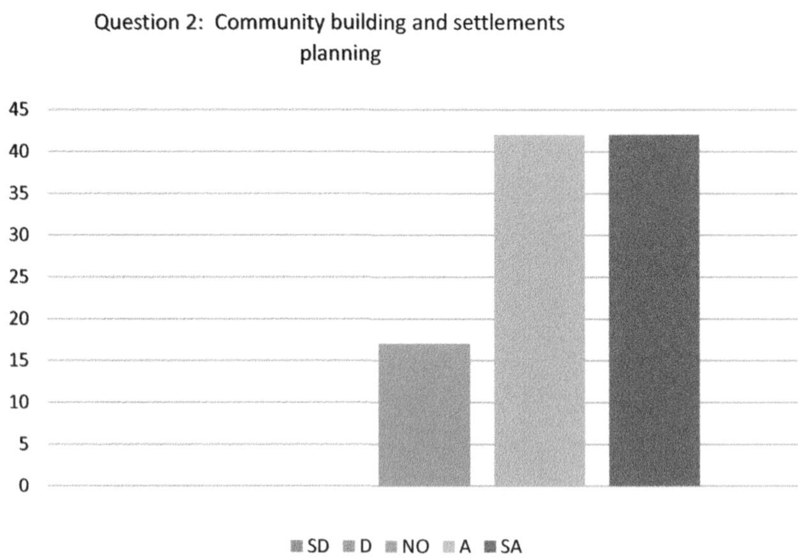

Fig. 8.15. Mixed-income Housing Result to Strong Community as well as Correct Previous Apartheid Spatial Planning and Settlement Pattern. *Source:* Author Primary Data Reporting (2016).

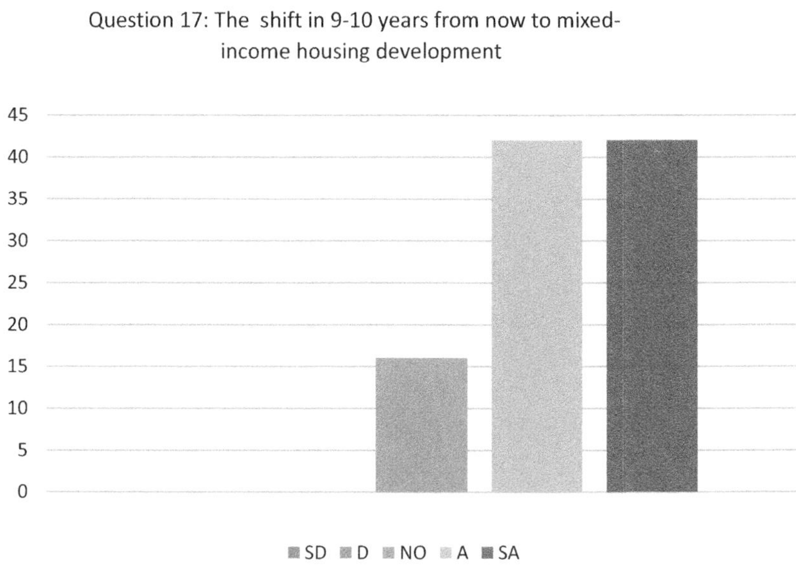

Fig. 8.16. Shift to Mixed-income Housing in 9–10 Years. *Source:* Author Primary Data Reporting (2016).

shift to mixed-income housing in 9–10 years from now as it affects the development of mixed-income housing development in general.

8.6 Conclusion

This chapter explains the gains in the use of Delphi technique in housing research and both the advantages and disadvantages. Responses from the three rounds showed significant interest on the part of the panel members that took part with 79% aggregate which is considered acceptable. The need for intergovernmental relations and coordination in the implementation of mixed-income housing development scored full consensus among the panel as all of them supported this idea. There was a shift in opinion as all express no opinion on whether factors at three levels of government impact on mixed-income housing development. A significant number of the participants of 66% disagree that mixed-income housing development and implementation strategies will eradicate an informal settlement.

Chapter 9

Case Study Area, Cosmo City Johannesburg

9.1 Introduction

The purpose of this chapter is to present the case study of Cosmo City. Before we do this, we need to explain the meaning of case study research and features. The literature review revealed that a gap exists for a mixed-income housing development case project in South Africa. To arrive at or realize the aims and objectives of this book together with data collected from the literature review, the case study design was used to find out the extent of intergovernmental support, public–private partnership, Town Planning regulations and collaboration in a given mixed-income housing development project. Also, this chapter will look into and interrogate the efforts to building a well-functioning community and how to create a cohesive society within and around the new mixed-income developments and to also evaluate the linkages between urban land use planning and housing policy on mixed-income housing. This chapter will look at the location and history, the logic system that guided the planning of the human settlements around Cosmo City. There will also be an evaluation of the design principles guiding the development, the typologies of settlements, social amenities and infrastructures and key challenges encountered in the project. The essence of this is to present the story and shared experiences that will guide such projects in both developing and developed countries together with Global South in future.

9.2 What Is Case Study Research?

Case study is an inquiry that focuses on describing, understanding, predicting, and/or controlling the individual (process, animal, person, households, area, organization, group, industry, culture, or nationality) (Woodside, 2010). This definition is internationally broader than the definition put forward by Yin (1994: 13). Yin (2011) in subsequent research sees the case study research as 'an empirical inquiry that investigates a contemporary phenomenon within its real-life context, especially when the boundaries between phenomenon and

Mixed-Income Housing Development Planning Strategies and Frameworks in the Global South, 131–140
Copyright © 2024 George Okechukwu Onatu, Wellington Didibhuku Thwala and Clinton Ohis Aigbavboa
Published under exclusive licence by Emerald Publishing Limited
doi:10.1108/978-1-83753-814-020231009

context are not clearly evident'. Anderson (1993) sees case study as being concerned with how and why things happen, allowing the investigation of contextual realities, and the difference between what was planned and what happened. Case study is not intended as a study of an entire organization or entity, rather it focuses on a particular issue, feature or unit of analysis. It is a good research method when attempting to measure on-going thinking (e.g. Van Someren et al., 1994). This point is also supported by (Cyert et al., 1956; Witte, 1972; Woodside and Wilson, 2003), as they considered the case study as a good method when measuring thinking by the same person using multiple interviews over several weeks. Case study also enables an investigator to get deep understanding of an issue or phenomenon using triangulation or multiple method of analysis. To achieve this, case study research relies on many of the same technique as historical research. However, according to Botha and Steyn (2008:138), this requires two sources of evidence: direct observation and systematic interviewing. Several interviewing methods exist, one of which is the Delphi method. The use of Delphi method in this research investigation is because, according to Skulmoski et al. (2007:3), the Delphi method may be only one component of the research project; for example, the Delphi outputs may be verified and generalized with a survey. The case study, as will be used to verify the Delphi method, also enables an investigator to gain a holistic view of phenomena or series of events and, as such, provides a round picture (Noor, 2008).

9.3 How to Conduct Case Study Research

There are three conditions that are necessary for carrying out case study research: (a) the type of research question posed, (b) the extent of the control an investigator has over actual behavioural events, and (c) the degree of focus on contemporary as opposed to historical events. Defining the research question is probably the most important step to be taken in a research study. The research question that focuses on 'how' and 'why' favours the use of case studies, histories, and experiments as the preferred research methods. This is because esuch questions deal with operational links that needs to be traced over time, rather than mere frequencies or incidence. They deal with phenomenal issues with real life context (Yin, 1994). By focusing on the 'how' and 'what' question, we tend to benefit from the descriptive powers of the social sciences methods and thus obtain stories which can be used to find out about the 'why' question. Foucault (1984:76) emphasises a point of departure for social and political research in his works in what he calls 'the little question . . . flat and empirical'. On the question of 'How' Foucault stressed that our understanding will suffer if we do not start our analyses with this question, because we will not understand the dynamics of practice. According to Yin (2009:10) the case study is preferred in examining the contemporary events when the relevant behaviour cannot be manipulated. The case study tends to suffer and, hence, relies on many of the same technique as a history, but it adds two sources of evidence, which includes, direct observation of the events being studies and interviews of the person involved in the event. The unit of analysis defines what the case is. This could be groups, organisations or countries, but it is the primary unit of analysis. Linking the data to propositions and the criteria for interpreting the findings are the least developed aspects in case studies (Yin, 1994). Case studies can be either be single or multiple-case designs. Single cases are used to confirm or challenge a theory, or to represent a unique or extreme case (Yin, 1994 cited in Tellis, 1997:12). Single-case studies are ideal for revelatory cases where an observer may have access to phenomenon that was previously inaccessible. Single-case design requires careful investigation to avoid misrepresentation, and to maximise the investigator's access to the evidence (Tellis, 1997). According to these findings, the studies can be holistic or embedded, the latter occurring when the same case study involves more than one unit of analysis. Multiple-case follows replication logic and the examples used in this study are based on it.

9.4 Application of Case Studies as a Research Strategy

The application and use of case study research method has been viewed from many angles, directions and standpoints by researchers. The case study method is seen in some quarters as lacking in rigour and objectivity to be considered as a research strategy, as compared to other method. This point has been a very hot potato, not easy to digest for pure science students and social science advocates. Rowley (2002:16) cautioned strongly that one has to be extremely careful in the articulation of the research design and implementation. Case studies have also been viewed as a useful tool for the preliminary, exploratory stage of a research project, as a basis for the development of the 'more structured' tools that are necessary in surveys and experiments. Eisenhardt (1989 cited in Rowley, 2002:16) notes that the case study is useful in circumstances: 'Particularly in circumstance where existing theory seems inadequate and serve as a complimentary to incremental theory building from normal science research'.

Conventional thinking in the Management Information System (MIS) literature indicates also that case study approaches are highly appropriate for the exploration and hypothesis-generation phases but are generally ill suited for the hypothesis-testing phase (Benbasat, 1984; Bonoma, 1985; Roethlisberger, 1977). A recent article by Lee (1989 cited in Onsrud et al., 1992) challenged the conventional wisdom about the use of case studies in the hypothesising stage. He argues that the data or results generated from case studies need not be quantities, statistical or mathematical to be analytically rigorous or scientific. This is because a single case study meets the requirement of scientific method if it adequately addresses four methodological problems: making controlled observation, logical deductions, allowing for replicability, and allowing for generalizability (Lee, 1989:120).

9.5 The Suitability of the Case Study Research Design

The case study is also effective for generalization using the type of test that Karl Popper called falsification, which forms part of critical reflexivity. Falsification is one of the most rigorous tests to which a scientific proposition can be subjected to:

if just one observation does not fit with the proposition, it is considered not valid generally and must therefore be either revised or rejected. Popper himself used the now famous example of, 'All swans are white,' and proposed that just one observation of a single black swan would falsify this proposition. This has general significance and can stimulate further investigations and theory-building. The case study is well suited for identifying 'black swans' because of its in-depth approach: what appears to be 'white' often turns out on closer examination to be 'black' (Flyvbjerg, 2004).

A case study should incorporate an element of protocol and strategies that contains more than the survey instruments; it should also contain procedures guided by ethical controls and general rules that should be followed in using the instrument. Yin (1994:64) listed this necessary protocol to include:

- An overview of the case study project (objectives, issues, topics being investigated),
- Field procedures (credentials and access to sites, sources of information),
- Case study questions (specific questions that the investigator must keep in mind during data collection),
- A guide for case study report (outline, format for the narrative).

To achieve deep understanding in case study research requires a multiple research method across multiple time periods (i.e. *triangulation*). According to Woodside (2010), triangulation includes (1) direct observation by the researcher within the environments of the case, (2) probing by asking case participants for explanations and interpretations of 'operational data', and (3) analysis of written documents and natural sites occurring in case environment. The use of mixed or multiple methods in case study usually contributes to increasing accuracy, robustness and complexities/coverage in a study more so than generality according to Woodside (2010:33).

9.6 Strengths, Weaknesses and Opportunities of a Case Study Research Design

Case studies have been criticized for lacking scientific rigour and reliability and for not being able to address the issues of generalizability (Noor, 2008:1603). This research also argues that there are some strengths of case study; it enables the researcher to gain a holistic view of certain phenomenon or series of events since many sources of evidence were used. Case studies also allow generalizations because findings from multiple cases can lead to some form of replication. Some scholars (such as, Butterworth et al., 1986:129; Cohen and Lindblom, 1979:84; Lindblom and Splinter, 1990) have summed up the argument by noting that the development of social research is inhibited by the fact that researchers tend to work with problems in which the answer to the question: 'if you are wrong about this, who will notice?' is all too often: 'Nobody'. Bailey (1992:50) calls the outcome of such research 'so what result'. Case study researchers, according to

Flyvberg (2004:294), seek to transcend this problem of relevance by anchoring their research in the context studied. This is by way of remaining close to the community, organization, phenomenon, or group that they studied during data collection, and remain close during the phases of data analysis, feedback, and publication of results. One advantage of this is that the researcher becomes part of the phenomenon studied, without necessarily 'going native'.

Given the limited amount of information available on the topic of mixed-income housing, it was clear from the onset that the research method and approach to be used would lend itself towards an exploratory study, case study approach as well as the accumulation of experts' opinion through the use of Delphi technique.

9.7 The Application of Case Study Research Approach

The case study was chosen for investigating mixed-income housing development model for South Africa in part because it is a contemporary issue that has been around and has unfolded without me having any control of the outcome. In addition, the case study approach enabled the researcher to draw on the multiple data sources to which he had access. Specifically, the investigation was an explanatory case study of mixed-income housing development model in South Africa. According to Fisher and Zivani (2004), explanatory case study methodology has been used to research complex systems in the fields of business, public policy and urban planning. The case study fits the description of a single case, as the researcher studied mixed-income housing development in Johannesburg, with unique geopolitical configuration. This forms the 'unit' of analysis. This one case study was chosen as it was sufficiently diverse in terms of planning and development of mixed-income housing development and strategies. The essence of a case study, the central tendency among all types of case studies as used here, is that it tries to illuminate a decision or set of decisions: why they were taken, how they were implemented, and with what result (Schramm, 1971 cited in Yin, 2014). For an explanatory case study research, three conditions must be met to be deemed suitable. The research project must seek to explain 'how'/'why' a phenomenon occurs and examine a contemporary phenomenon (Yin, 2014). The researcher must have no control over the phenomenon. For explanatory case study research, the data collection and sources include documents (e.g. newspapers, articles, books), archival records (e.g. government reports), interviews (open-ended conversation with key informants, questionnaire), direct observation (e.g. site visit and surveillance), focus group discussions and interview with key stakeholders. The case study research method is stronger, and the validity increases when there are multiple sources of data as it enables triangulation of evidence (Sophie, 2015). The inclusion of multiple data sources, including the Delphi as already shown, allowed for triangulation, and this is meant to ensure construct validity.

9.8 The Case Study of Cosmo City, Location and History

Cosmo City is now a fully fledged approved township well planned and designed under Region C out of the seven regions of the City of Johannesburg Metropolitan Municipality. This region according to the Regional Spatial Development Framework (RSDF) 2010/2012 of the City of Johannesburg Metropolitan Municipality comprises of Rooderpoort, Randburg, Johannesburg North, Olivedale, Northriding, Jukskei Park, Zandspuit, Kloofendale, Contantia Kloof, Bromhof and Bush Hill together with Kloofendale Nature Reserve. It is a green field development that is strategically located and served by three main roads that comprise of Malibongwe (Hans Strijdom), DF Malan and Nothumberland. It covers an area extent of 1,200 hectares. It is one of the flagships mixed-income housing development that came into existence since 2005. The dream, vision and discussions about Cosmo City started as far back as year 2000, when the Department of Housing of the Provincial Government of Gauteng after a very long procurement process shortlisted only five companies among the lists of bidders that submitted development proposal for the development of the housing project. Out of these lists the company Basil Read and Kopano ke Matla were selected and both reached a mutual agreement/accord in view of the scale of this project to form a consortium called Codevco. Another company called Urban Dynamics Pty Ltd was entrusted and assigned to manage the entire land development and Township Establishment processes together with the supervision of other professional consultants. According to Ogra and Onatu (2013) Cosmo City is located north of Johannesburg K553 that goes all the way to Lanseria Airport and Mogale City Municipality. This area is now earmarked and designated for the Smart City development with comprehensive and detailed master plan that is already finalized. This settlement, Cosmo is confirmed to have emerged out of an urgent need and desperation to provide living accommodation and housing opportunities for the informal settlers of Zevenfontein and Riverbend who had been illegally occupying privately owned land 25 km to the North West of the Johannesburg Central Business District CBD (Onatu, 2010). The private owner won the case and the City Council together with all involved had no choice but to get another site for these settlements. These informal settlements were characterized by substandard living conditions, low level of income, high unemployment, low level of education and limited access to basic services including electricity, water and sewer.

9.8.1 The Planning of the Settlements

According to Rifkin and Pridmore (2001) in their book Titled Partners in Planning: Information, Participation and Empowerment, Planning is an instrument that helps us to define our goals, aims and objectives and make detailed action plans. Planning for a settlement requires that we think about three things: 1. Political, 2. Administrative, 3. Personal Issues. The planning for the Cosmo City embodies all these and the settlements started as far back as 2005 as noted above. According to Onatu (2010) the development comprises of the following:

(1) 5,000 low-income houses (income group R0 to R3 500) with 1 504 completed; each unit is 36 m^2 of floor space and consists of two separate bedrooms, bathroom space with a flush toilet and a living area; this is known as RDP houses.
(2) 3,000 financed credit-linked houses (income group R3 501 to R9 670) subsidies are provided for people earning up to R7 000. First National Bank (FNB) is a partner to this section of the project providing 'step up' loans and the DoH will provide the subsidy.
(3) 1,000 social housing rental units (income group R1 500 to R9 670).
(4) 3,300 bonded houses (open market).
(5) 12 schools.
(6) 40 sites for churches, clinics and crèches.
(7) 43 parks and recreational sites.
(8) 30 commercial and retail centres.
(9) 40 ha of industrial park.
(10) 300 ha environmental area.

The estimated value of the RDP houses is between R180 000 to R280 000 based on 2020 market value and the bonded houses from R380 000 up to R800 000. Nine high residential density sites have been provided in order to supply ±1,000 rental housing units. Seventeen school sites have also been provided, as well as other land uses such place of public worship, recreational areas, clinic, satellite policy station and mini taxi rank.

9.9 The Design Principles Guiding the Development

The roads and street pattern design at Cosmo City are very narrow of 6-metre width and with no provision for pedestrian walk areas. It is such that two big trucks or heavy-duty buses can hardly pass each other freely without touching the kerb. The land use zoning scheme that defines Cosmo City's internal composition follows the previous City of Johannesburg Town Planning Scheme of 1979 but now outdated and replaced with the City of Johannesburg Land Use Scheme of 2018. The land uses are classified into Residential, Industrial, Commercial, Public Open Space, Wetlands and Business sites as well as Roads. The settlements were divided into Extension 3, Extension 8, Extension 10, Extension 6 and Extension 2. It is surrounded by Malibongwe Ridge to the North West extreme, Kya Sand to the East, Mostyn Park to the North East and Zandspuit Extension 19 to the South. Fast food and retail facilities as well as the official taxi rank are all located in Cosmo City's northwestern corner and across is the Cosmo Mall. Each settlement is separated from one another by either a buffer or some natural phenomenon. One important aspect of the design/layout of the settlements is that the area is zoned into different extensions, and with street names that cut across countries: America, Africa and South East Asia, the logic behind this could not be discerned from the field work. There has been some agitation from some countries on why they are not included or listed in the street names. But the rationale of this decision by the Corporate Geographical Information of the City of Johannesburg could not be established. The sections for the bonded houses and Finance Linked Individual Subsidies (FLIPS) are named after the states in America, whereas the RDP houses took after the countries in African continent and the reason behind this as it relates to integration and mixed-income development strategies could not be properly established in this book, most especially the logic behind the centralization of the RDP houses to be surrounded by other housing typologies, this has raised a lot of questions in housing debate.

9.10 Public–Private Partnership

According to Patel (2014), one of the outstanding and remarkable features of Cosmo City is the leverage between the public and private sector in the development of the housing project. This comprises the Gauteng Provincial Government, who are responsible for the administration and management of the subsidies as well as the waiting lists, the City of Johannesburg Metropolitan Municipality with responsibility to provide the land, bulk infrastructure and approval of the land use application for the Township Establishment and the Codevco who are the private sector for the project management and construction works. Also of importance is Absa who provided the initial seed capital for the development of the bond houses and social housing that is now being managed by Johannesburg Social Housing Company (JOSHCO). This cooperation was hampered initially by protracted court cases that last for 7–8 years filed by the surrounding townships who were against the government approach of establishing a low-cost housing in this area. The project only commenced when the case was worn in 2005 and also coincided with the Breaking New Ground strategies of the National Department of Human Settlements. They were of the view that these houses (RDP, especially) will result to the devaluation of their property and spark increase in crime (Field survey information 2017). This is referred to in housing studies and research as NIMBY factor.

9.11 Social Amenities and Infrastructure

Mixed-income housing units or developments are unique as they are served by the availability of easily accessible social amenities. The settlement is served by a Taxi Rank which is being managed by the Provincial Department of Transport and Infrastructure. Currently there are only pre-school, primary and secondary schools. Some of the schools in existence now are Meridian Cosmo City Independent School, Zandspruit Primary School, Cosmo City 2 Secondary, Far North Secondary School, Cosmo City Junior Primary School, Cosmo City West Primary School, and Jump N Play Private Preschool are some of the educational facilities which offer students of Cosmo City a safe haven for learning. There is also Cosmo City Medical Centre that serves the community in all areas of medical check-ups and consultations. The Provincial Government on occasional bases provides mobile clinics on regular basis in view of the population. There is also

Cosmo Business Park, Churches, Cosmo Community Hall of 22,000 m^2 that provides very exciting shopping opportunities to the residents and form an important arena for social integration and networking. The bridge across Malibongwe provides safe and easy access to the mall for the children, adults and all the shoppers. This is also an important land mark when one is travelling along Malibongwe Road to Cosmo City. There are also notable restaurants such as: Marco Polo Restaurant, KFC, Nandos, Sports Bar, Chicken Licken and Pizza Shops as well as Africa Cousines of Shisa Nyama and Liquor Stores.

9.12 Major Challenges and Achievements

Cosmo City is one of the outstanding mixed-income housing projects that saw the full implementation of the National Government human settlements programme of Breaking New Ground (BNG). The aim of which to create a human settlements space that can cater for all categories of people and a living space for all social clusters irrespective of race, gender and ethnic orientation. The history of South Africa is marred by Apartheid spatial planning that ended up separating and segregating people based on race and colour. The mixed-income housing approach as implemented here is to create a living environment that can change this story and bring people of different race closer to each other. The level of integration of all these people is another area that calls for additional research. For the first time, most of the residents, especially those from the informal settlements that are now beneficiaries of the RDP houses who were relocated here were afforded an opportunity of good shopping experience and decent housing with street address, names, access road and accessible social amenities and play area for their children. This is one of the beginning conversations of the 'Citizenship Rights' (Huchzermeyer, 2009) as alluded by the Right to the City advocates. This settlement has won a number of awards and is one of the successful stories of PPP for the National, Provincial and Local Government of note as it relates to human settlements development and planning. The industrial park is gradually being developed to provide needed job opportunities to the youths and construction workers. The bond houses are reported being sold fast through the cross subsidization based on FLIPS and the social housing components are providing safe environment for families. Housing is an asset and thus the beneficiaries of the RDP houses are seen as contributing to the reduction of the waiting list backlog and to have gained an aspect of social capital. Best Developer of the Year and Best Public–Private Partnership of the Year.

Notable challenges are the mushrooming of backyard shacks and informal trading along all the major roads with no regulation. The need for a free-market area is one aspect that the design of this settlement overlooked. There is also increasing level of noise pollution emanating from cars, Taxis with horns at highest level and loud music from Taverns, Restaurants and hawkers. The incident of crime and breakings into peoples' houses is a regular occurrence and the Satellite Police Station is under pressure from reported cases. This development is also short of enough play areas for children as some of them are seen playing along the street with balls and bicycles. The safety of children is a major concern from motorists. The RDP houses and other housing types do not have enough space for urban agriculture and gardening.

9.13 Conclusions

In this chapter, we looked at what constitutes a case study research design. The various definitions as were expounded by several scholars were also looked into. It was understood that case study apart from investigating contemporary phenomenon but also looks at a problem using triangulation approach that ensures that all aspect of data collection and analysis are employed. The method of conducting case study research was also looked into as well as how it is applied. The chapter also looked at the strengths and weaknesses of case study research. Cosmo City was also discussed as an example of case study. It was shown that it is one of the major flagships of mixed-income housing development in South Africa. The composition, design and level of public–private partnership that constitute the project were also highlighted. The chapter ends by looking at the challenges and opportunities that exist at Cosmo City and the coping mechanism of the residents.

Chapter 10

Mixed-Income Housing Development Framework for South Africa and Global South

10.1 Introduction

The body of literatures and scholarly works that interrogate the mixed-income housing as discussed in the other chapters of this book in a cohesive, impactful and comprehensive way has not been as exhaustive and far reaching as presented here. By compiling and collating these literatures together and positioning all in this discourse to argue in favour or raise additional issues in respect of mixed-income housing development, this book intends to validate the claims made by the proponents and opponents. In doing this, this research will create an avenue to make its own contributions and additional input to the existing body of knowledge out there. In order for the outcome of the findings as elicited from the review of literature to be relevant and meaningful in achieving these tasks, the research has developed a conceptual framework. This chapter therefore presents the findings from the Delphi study. This will form the basis and components of the Mixed-Income Housing Development Project Framework for South Africa. This chapter will answer research question two (*RQ2*) on 'What other housing development framework could be adopted or promoted in South Africa?' It will also describe the framework and the various variables that compose the framework. Though the concept of sustainability has been around for several years, its application to housing, especially mixed-income housing development, has been slow in the light of contestations between several role players. South African government has remained upbeat that it will meet its housing delivery commitments in urban areas, despite a soaring demand for houses. Hence, there is a need for a mixed-income housing development framework that can assist in contributing to the solution on housing challenges both now and in future.

Mixed-Income Housing Development Planning Strategies and Frameworks in the Global South, 141–164
Copyright © 2024 George Okechukwu Onatu, Wellington Didibhuku Thwala and Clinton Ohis Aigbavboa
Published under exclusive licence by Emerald Publishing Limited
doi:10.1108/978-1-83753-814-020231010

10.2 Composition and Breakdown of the Variables

The conceptual framework, as noted by scholars in various studies, are classified as composition of systems from various concepts, with various assumptions as well as theories which go a long way to guide and to focus ones research paradigm (Miles and Huberman, 1994; Robinson, 2011). Its main aim is to showcase in a visual manner a sort of product that is written, one that can be able to provide explanations, in either a graph or in story pattern, the objective and main focus of a study – the principal factors, conceptualizations or attributes and the expected relations among each of them. Conceptual framework is noted to play an important role in helping in justifying or proving an empirical research and it is constructed and not found. Prior experience, existing theories, literatures reviewed and pilot case studies all form the major important sources of the designing of the conceptual framework for this book. In order to integrate different approaches, line of investigations, results and theories as highlighted in the literature review chapters, this research will examine the various conceptual model that inform mixed-income housing development. An example of this is the work of de Souza Briggs and Keys (2009), in which the author reviews the 'causes and effects of mixed-income housing'. Briggs notes some influencing factors for mixed-income housing, which includes characteristics of the metropolitan area, availability of jobs and transport, social integration of housing programme, etc. Botha and Steyn (2008) identifies the key variables that influence the development of mixed-income housing as the existing institutions, mode of transport or mobility services, the built environment, economic systems and housing structures as well as socializations together with norms. Tunstall and Lupton (2010), in supporting the debate, argue for the need for the diversification of housing type and tenure further. The conclusion from their research highlighted the need to take note of important features, such as appropriate tenure security systems, changes in the composition of the population in residential areas, socialization and integrations, etc. This study supports the work of these two scholars and the features so identified. This will assist in informing the development of the mixed-income housing development project framework for the present study. Coming from a detailed review of relevant literature on variables that affect mixed-income housing development project, this study recognizes the impact of nearness to social services with 14 variables; community involvement and participation with 11 variables; town planning approval and policy with 10 variables; occupants' social interaction with 11 variables; access to affordable housing with 9 variables; and intergovernmental support and collaborations (IGSC) with 14 variables. However, this book identifies access to affordable housing and town planning approval and policy as gaps that have not been well explored, especially in developing nations.

10.3 Nearness to Social Services (NSS)

The location of mixed-income housing is argued to depend on the nearness to social amenities. Social amenities and services, as used in this context, is comprised of schools, transport systems, playground/open spaces, police station, municipal complaint centres, health facilities, electricity, water supply, fire station, community hall, shopping mall and facilities for physically challenged . This point also relate very well with recent report by The Department of Human Settlements of Western Cape in 2010 recognized this point when it reported in an annual review that strategically located land are very difficult to come by for any human settlements development in the country. The only readily available and cheap land are found and located within the urban edge or peri-urban areas where development is rare and social facilities very scanty, with poor linkages to major towns and cities. These poor integrations give rise to a whole range of social issues including urban sprawl, gentrifications as well as fragmented apartheid spatial planning. This problem and relevance of nearness of human settlement development to social services is further illustrated in the matter between the Governments of the Republic of South Africa v. Grootboom the Constitutional Court case of 2000. The court interpreted the right to have access to adequate housing as follows:

> Housing goes beyond the mere bricks and mortar. It entails and involves the availability of service land, appropriate good social services such as the provision of water and the removal of sewage and the financing of all these, including the building of the house itself. For a person to have access to adequate housing all of these conditions need to be met: there must be land, there must be services, and there must be a dwelling. The right of access to adequate housing also suggests that it is not only the State that is responsible for the provision of houses, but that other agents within society, including individuals themselves, must be enabled by legislative and other measures to provide housing.

Further illustration of this is found in the articles of the United Nations Department of Economic, Social and Cultural Rights, which stipulated the fact that legal security of tenure, affordability, availability of services, materials, facilities and infrastructure, habitability, accessibility, location and cultural adequacy are necessary for a meaningful enjoyment of the right to housing. In a similar vein, Lukhele (2014), in comparing mixed income in South African cities, pointed out that evidenced from Cornubia settlement shows that good location and proximity to viable economic nodes are prerequisite to a sustainable integrated human settlements development in South Africa. Hence, proximity to essential services play an important role in reducing travelling time and to bringing people close to both work and recreational amenities. Fig. 10.1 shows one of the social amenities that is Cosmo City Junior Primary School that is serving the communities and adjoining settlements.

Table 10.1 shows the various items and descriptors that characterize nearness to social services as it relates to mixed-income housing development.

Fig. 10.1. Picture of Cosmo City Primary School. *Source:* Authors Photograph (2016).

Table 10.1. Items for the Nearness to Social Services Construct.

Code	Item Description
NSS1	Availability of schools for the children
NSS2	Integrated public transport system
NSS3	Playground and open spaces
NSS4	Police station
NSS5	Housing customer complain centre
NSS6	Provision of health facilities and clinics
NSS7	Provision of electricity supply
NSS8	Provision of water supply and sanitation
NSS9	Provision of fire station/emergency
NSS10	Availability of community hall or social hall
NSS11	Proximity of houses to hospital/clinic
NSS12	Housing stock take disabled need into consideration
NSS13	Proximity of houses to shopping area
NSS14	Proximity of houses to playground/recreational facilities

Source: Author Primary Data Reporting (2016).

10.4 Community Involvement and Participation (CIP)

Community involvement and participation is found to play a vital role and part in mixed-income housing development. An instance is the concept of the 'Right to the City', as explained in earlier chapters. It is noted by Lefebvre (1967 cited by Boer and Vries, 2009:1321) that this can form an important link to bring together actors and stakeholders with different socio-economic, ideological or ethnic background to cooperation. As Balibar (1968 cited in Goonewardena et al., 2008: 261) remarks, the notion and manner this concept is carried forward requires a radical and automatic changes in the structures that result to an urban space. According to Beider (2007 cited in Thwala, 2007:6), in a public policy debate in the United Kingdom, the term community is used in three general senses. These include Descriptive: a group or network of people who share something in common or interact with each other; Normative: community as a place where solidarity, participation and coherence are found; and Instrumental: community as an agent acting to maintain or change its circumstances, the location orientation of services and policy interventions.

A lot of emphasis and attention is now focusing on community participation within low-cost residential development in South Africa. This is because more recognition is now given and accorded to the issue of participatory urban planning and consultation of the communities and resident associations processes in modern day development. The United Nations is also noted to be encouraging nations, including South Africa together with other countries as well as participating organizations to drive more attention towards public participation process in any human settlement strategy at all levels (Lategan, 2012). According to the UN Habitat Agenda (1996) which states: 'There is increase expectations from all role players, stakeholders and actors in the public, private and community representatives to play active roles at all levels of government structures in the drive for sustainable human settlements and shelter for all initiatives' (UN, 1996:16).

Citizenry involvement both directly/indirectly and all social partners involved as well as interested and affected parties in the affairs of state, governance, administration, planning and the overall welfare development programmes at local or grassroots level is what is called and referred to as community participation (Mafukidze and Hoosen, 2009:12). Planning in a participatory manner is now been recognized and promoted strongly in South African planning approaches and is now a resurfacing issue that come up regularly at every engagement that touches on development planning in the built environment as well as in several legislations and policy documents (Lategan, 2012). De Villiers (2001:7) noted that the South African Constitution do provide an enabling framework for a representative, democratic and participatory system of governance. This is reflected in the Department of Human Settlements document (RSA, 2009:12) which argues that the South African government pursues and drives an enablement strategy and conducive environment in which the human settlement is focusing on people. There is now increase in partnership and cooperation at all fronts. This is promoted further by human settlement strategies that is people-centred and focused which encourages improve housing access and opportunities to all irrespective of social bearings as well as the realization of a sustainable housing vision.

Since the 1994 election, input from the communities affected by planning and housing provision is of immense value (Lategan, 2012). The Reconstruction and

Development Programme (RDP) emphasizes the important and cardinal role of community participation and engagement in ensuring the realization of the objectives of the democratic processes that reaches to the grassroots level (CSIR, 2002). Where stakeholders are involved in decision-making at all stages of a project cycle, development problems and needs will be better understood.

The significant and important role that communities, non-profit organizations (NPOs) and community-based organizations play in ensuring a constructive engagement and interface with government and housing programmes cannot be overemphasized. South Africa Human Settlement White Paper of 1994 illustrates the importance of gender balance and proper representations in all human settlements' efforts and programmes. Community participation and representation entail as highlighted in Table 10.2 as it touches on good outcome as it relates to decision-making, safety and security of our neighbourhoods through vigilantism and patrol groups, information sharing, social support to one another at good time and at bad times, mutual reciprocities as well as in project design and implementations.

Table 10.2 shows the various items and descriptions that characterize community involvement and participation as it relates to mixed-income housing development.

10.5 Town Planning Approval and Policy (TPAP)

The implication for planning as a means to realize social integration and cohesion in a given mixed-income housing development has been extensively discussed by various scholars. Galster (2007) cautioned that planners should assess the social

Table 10.2. Items for the Community Involvement and Participation Construct.

Code	Item Description
CIP1	Decision-making and implementation
CIP2	Involved in the design of the houses and location
CIP3	Effective administration and management
CIP4	Participate in quality management
CIP5	Enforcing municipal by-laws and compliance
CIP6	Information sharing and dissemination
CIP7	Security and safety of residents
CIP8	Welfare and protection of interest of residents
CIP9	Maintaining safe and healthy place to live
CIP10	Monitoring and reporting crime
CIP11	Ensuring the availability of social services

Source: Author Primary Data Reporting (2016).

justice, compliance and how effective a given strategy is before considering adopting it as a framework. Design elements that enhance residents' social relations include public open space with enough room for recreation and relaxation by the residents. In one of their articles Brophy and Smith (1997) used the term 'smooth and identical integration' to explain how each unit can be made to look the same and very difficult to differentiate from other housing typology. To them this will make the entire resident irrespective of income and social standing to feel equal among each other. Fig. 10.2 shows a recreational facility that the children are enjoying and using to keep themselves busy which is an essential social motto for their physical development and upbringing.

Listed below are items that are considered in town planning approval and policies, as it relates to mixed-income housing development, as identified from the literature. Mixed-income housing and good design are a winning combination that has demonstrated the capacity to encourage faster project approvals, attract the support of future residents and overcome the fears of neighbours who are uncertain about the prospects of affordable housing next door (AHURI, 2003:12). On housing policies, there tend to be different opinion among housing researchers. One school of thought argues that housing policy is more of 'government reactions and approaches in housing field'. The difference is that some interventions in the housing field may be directed to objectives outside the field (refer to Chapter 4). This definition is

Fig. 10.2. Cornubia With Limited Social Amenities. *Source:* Authors Fieldwork.

supported by Angel (2000:11), who argues that in the absence of a clear and acceptable definition of what can be regarded as a housing policy, and to whom it is targeted at or attended to it, we can only speak of housing environment. Housing Policy environment is defined as: 'the set of government approaches and strategies that have essential and visible outcome effects on the performance of the housing sector'. This definition is considered 'open and inclusive', as housing is not a discrete entity. While housing production is part of the construction sector, housing investments is part of the overall capital formulation. Table 10.3 shows the various items and descriptors that define and characterize town planning approvals and Policy regulations as evidenced from this study.

10.6 Occupant Social Interaction (OSI)

According to Kleinhans et al. (2000), social interaction between different income groups remains poor, because cultural differences are too great. To address this phenomenon, Lukhele (2014) advocates for 'community solidarity' so as to limit the socio-economic disparity in communities. The social obligation and the voluntary help may include sharing of information on available economic opportunities, particularly by the affluent class to the poor group in the suburb. In this context, Chaskin and Joseph (2011) assume that the middle-income people have better access to both economic and political actors, thus they could assist in bringing change in the lives of the poor people in the urban landscape. Subsequently, when neighbours are supportive to each other, a sense of hope and security is created in the urban neighbourhood. Therefore, social solidarity brings

Table 10.3. Items for the Town Planning Approval and Policy Construct.

Code	Item Description
TPAP1	Regulating informal sector and trading
TPAP2	Enforcing municipal by-laws and regulations
TPAP3	Ensuring that housing construction is according to approved building plan
TPAP4	Conducting inspection of the settlement
TPAP5	Issuing notices and fine to offenders and people that contravene the law
TPAP6	Explain the need for residents to comply to municipal by-laws and Government policies
TPAP7	Maintaining the quality level of the neighbourhood
TPAP8	Demolition of illegal houses and issuance of summons
TPAP9	Managing housing allocation and density
TPAP10	Providing oversight of government facilities and policies

Source: Author Primary Data Reporting (2016).

a sense of hope and security to the neighbours (Mugnano and Palvarini, 2013), and ultimately strengthens the social networks and connections in the cities. Hence, it is argued that the importance of the neighbourhood as a framework for social interaction should not be overestimated.

In conclusion, Van Kempen and Şule Özüekren (1998) have pointed out that assessing concentration areas as good or bad without looking at the opinions of the residents themselves is bad scholarship. Table 10.4 shows the various items and descriptors that define and characterize Occupant Social Interactions (OSI) and relations as evidenced from this study.

10.7 Access to Housing and Affordability (AFA)

When it comes to considering the context of access to affordable housing, new urbanists have a unique perspective that goes well beyond the simple provision of low-income housing as a discrete commodity. In the new urbanism, as highlighted in the literature review on philosophical perspectives guiding housing research in Chapter 4, affordable housing is seen within the context of neighbourhood design, pedestrianism, provision of public spaces and walkable access to services (Johnson and Talen, 2008). The incorporation of affordability into mixed-income housing development projects has been hotly debated. This is because it elevates the issue of diversity as an essential quality (Bohl, 2000). Over the years, the government has been gearing all efforts at fulfilling this goal, especially to the

Table 10.4. Items for the Occupation Social Interaction Construct.

Code	Item Description
OSI1	Neighbours are friendly and exchange greetings
OSI2	Occupants cooperate and assist one another to search for jobs
OSI3	Occupants assist one another to look after the house and baby
OSI4	Occupants children play together and exchange toys activities
OSI5	Occupants' children are attending the same school and board same bus
OSI6	Occupants attend community meeting and discuss matters of mutual interest
OSI7	Occupants support one another in times of need and emergency
OSI8	Occupants run to one another during emergency
OSI9	Occupants engage in sports together and other social functions
OSI10	Neighbours invite each other over for coffee, birthday or any celebrations
OSI11	Neighbours report suspicious movement and behaviours to one another

Source: Author Primary Data Reporting (2016).

poorest of the poor. Housing affordability has become an extremely effective political instrument for most of the East and Central European (ECE) countries, including the Netherlands, even though they are often in quite different stages of the housing transition (Liias, 1998). As a consequence of these changes, housing expenditures in most of the ECE countries continue to burden homeowners more and more severely. As these societies have rapidly changed to nations of home-owners, where more than 90% of the housing stock is owner-occupier, they are plagued by several serious housing problems many of which have grown worse in recent years. Housing policy of the welfare states is typically aimed at providing good and affordable housing to all, rather than being responsible only for people with special needs. Housing affordability is quite poorly defined in both the research papers as well as in the different public documents (Liias, 1998). Often it is even used in quite a meaningless context (Joseph Rowntree Foundation, 1990). The term, housing affordability is a political buzzword: everybody is talking about it but nobody is responsible for it. The pure term 'affordability' or 'housing affordability' is entirely meaningless if the subject is not clearly defined. In most of the political discussions, the question, 'affordable to whom?' has not always been clearly answered (Joseph Rowntree Foundation, 1990). The most common answer to this is 'affordable for the households'.

Mixed-income housing can provide both direct and indirect responses to some of these challenges of providing affordable and accessible housing. Mixed-income development can also contribute indirectly to an overall increase in the availability of affordable housing by generating high-quality housing to win neighbourhood approval, overcoming political barriers, and providing incentives for developers to include affordable units, as never experienced in South Africa before. The features of access to housing and affordability (AFA) as used in the present study are highlighted in Table 10.5.

10.8 Intergovernmental Support and Collaboration (IGSC)

Mixed-income housing development is considered an effective instrument to build and strengthen political constituency for affordable housing, as noted before in the literature review. The high quality of mixed-income housing development may help to create more favourable impression of affordable housing (Smith, 2002). This could result in more funding for affordable housing from various government sectors and more willingness among communities to allow affordable housing to be built in their areas. Johnson (2006:22) argue that rather than appearing to be a waste of 'taxpayers' money, good quality mixed-income housing both aids needy households and may be perceived as a community asset. Well-located mixed-income projects can help to raise standard for good design of affordable housing generally (Myerson, 2003). Simply stated taxpayers and politicians or policymakers are more likely to support housing when a significant number of its residents are people who 'work hard and play by the rules' (Wilkins, 2001:3 cited in Johnson, 2006:22). It is also highly debated in the literature that mixed-income housing is an essential tool that can aid in attracting

Table 10.5. Items for the Access to Housing and Affordability Construct.

Code	Item Description
AFA1	The units are affordable and not too expensive
AFA2	People are now able to own their own house with Title Deed
AFA3	It provides opportunity for people without income, low income and medium income to own houses
AFA4	It gives people opportunity to live close to place of work
AFA5	It is an aspect of social transformation and poverty alleviation strategy
AFA6	It enables people of various tribes or nationality group to live together and share
AFA7	It is an aspect of human settlements aimed at neighbourhood revitalization
AFA8	The housing units are of good design and of quality
AFA9	Livelihood strategies of the poor are taken into consideration in the implementation of mixed-income housing

Source: Author Primary Data Reporting (2016).

broad political support for affordable housing. Ensuring a good support base for affordable housing requires expanding the political constituency for housing assistance to include working-class and middle-class households (Ibid:23).

The political economy of mixed-income developments examines both the intuitional features as well as the strategies that play out within those rules that lead to the creation of mixed-income development. Joseph et al. (2007:378) also noted that individual and external leveraging of external resources leads to higher quality local services and infrastructure, thus directly promoting an improved quality of life for residents. Feasible exchange between politicians and special interest groups determines the outcomes observed. The institutional context of rules and enforcements under which the neighbourhood develops influence the types, persistence and durability of residential patterns (Schaeffer, 2007). Once neighbourhood coordination problems are viewed as spontaneous orders, the questions then turn to consideration of the institutional environment within which these complex orders emerge. The rules of the game influence the strategies that individual find in their interest to pursue and determine how agents learn strategies and correct poor ones. Mixed-income development policy is predicate, not only on alleviating the effects of concentrations of poverty, but more importantly on doing so where those concentrations have developed in a context of public ownership. Planning also requires coordination across numerous national and provincial departments and state-owned entities to ensure easy access to amenities such as schools, clinics, libraries and sporting facilities, as well as economic

Table 10.6. Items for the Intergovernmental Support and Collaboration Construct.

Code	Item Description
IGSC1	Provision of recreational centre
IGSC2	Taxi rank and public transport
IGSC3	Information and job centres
IGSC4	Police station
IGSC5	Shopping mall and retail centres
IGSC6	Commercial and industrial areas
IGSC7	Social welfare centres
IGSC8	Customer services centre
IGSC9	Provision of fire station
IGSC10	Municipal offices
IGSC11	Primary and secondary schools
IGSC12	Fire station and EMS centres
IGSC13	Vocational training centres

Source: Author Primary Data Reporting (2016).

opportunities. Table 10.6 shows the various items and descriptors that define and characterize IGSC as evidenced from this study.

10.9 The Development of the Framework

This section presents results of the Mixed-Income Housing Development (MIHD) framework, using the structural equation model (SEM) and Stata statistical programme. SEM is a statistical technique used when a researcher wants to test the plausibility of a theory or model about the predictive relationship among variables (Heppner and Heppner, 2004). The constructs, NSS, CIP, TRAP, occupant social interaction (OSI), AFA and IGSC, were treated as measurement variables based on arithmetic mean statistics computed from items retained during confirmatory factor analysis. The latent variable modelled in terms of how it fitted the data was the mixed-income housing delivery. The squares are measured variables, the large oval is latent constructs, the arrows represent relationships and the small circles are residual variances. The diagram of the Mixed-Income Housing Delivery is shown in Fig. 10.3.

The estimated results of the SEM presented in Fig. 10.3 shows that the Mixed-Income Housing Delivery framework significantly fitted the survey data collected on all the constructs, namely NSS, CIP, TPAP, OSI, AFA and IGSC. Note that five item-bundles (or parcels) were used to develop the framework for each of the measurement variables instead of 14 individual items for NSS, 11 individuals for

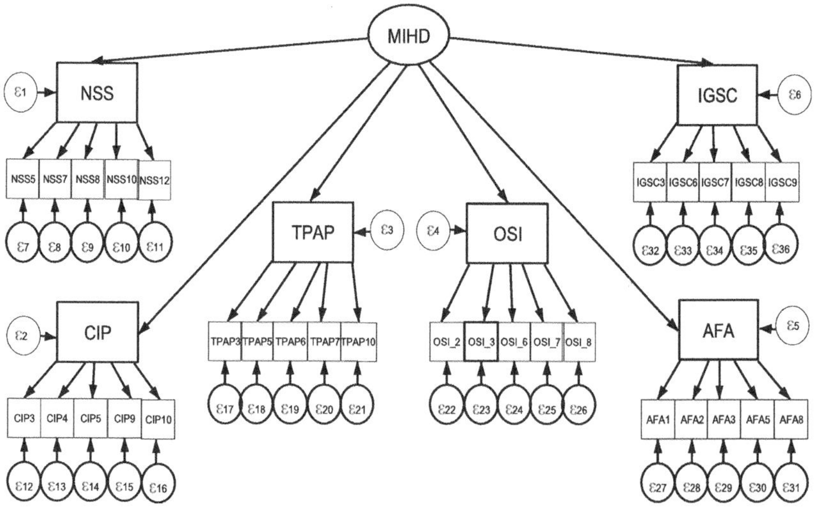

Fig. 10.3. Mixed-Income Housing Delivery Framework.
Source: Author Primary Data Reporting (2016).

CIP, TRAP with 10 individual variables, OSI with 11 individual variables, AFA with 9 and IGSC has 15 individual variables. The use of item-bundles according to Heppner et al. (2002) is significant as it assists researchers to guard against estimating an unnecessary large number of parameters (i.e. factor leadings and errors terms), and more importantly to reduce the possibility of distortions from idiosyncratic characteristics of individual items in fitting the model to the data. Based on computed z-statistics and p-values, the construct, AFA was found to be more significantly associated (z-statistic = 7.38; p = 0.000) with the mixed-income housing development latent variable, followed by OSI (z-statistic = 7.38; p-value = 0.000). Table 10.7 depicts the overall expanded Mixed-Income Housing Development Framework (MIHDF) constructs.

10.10 Interpretation of the Model

Though all the items measuring NSS are significantly associated with the respective construct, results from Table 10.8 shows that nearness to social services was largely associated with NSS 5: housing customer complain centre showing a coefficient of 1.390 (z-statistic = 23.77; p-value = 0.000) and NSS 10: Availability of community hall and social hall showing a coefficient of 1.345 (z-statistic = 21.52; p-value = 0.000).

Community involvement and participation as shown in Table 10.9 was largely significantly associated with CIP3: effective administration and management having a coefficient of 1.125 (z-statistic = 21.95; p-value = 0.01), CIP4: participate in quality

Table 10.7. Overall Expanded MIHD Framework.

	Coef.	OIM Std. Err.	*Z*	*P* > |*z*|	[95% Conf. Interval]	
Structural NSS ← MIHD_cons	1	(constrained)	80.20	0.000	5.701103	5.986754
	5.843929	0.0728713				
CIP ← MIHD_cons	0.6473662	0.1500467	4.31	0.000	0.3532802	0.9414523
	3.318182	0.0799948	41.48	0.000	3.161395	3.474969
TPAP ← MIHD_cons	0.5136655	0.2056827	2.50	0.013	0.1105347	0.9167962
	5.604	0.1131191	49.54	0.000	5.382291	5.825709
OSI ← MIHD_cons	1.203851	0.1630303	7.38	0.000	0.8843171	1.523384
	4.130455	0.0722901	57.14	0.000	3.988769	4.272141
AFA ← MIHD_cons	1.349375	0.1757424	7.68	0.000	1.004927	1.693824
	6.035	0.0779188	77.45	0.000	5.882282	6.187718
IGSC ← MIHD_cons	0.322386	0.1084035	2.97	0.003	0.1099192	0.5348529
	6.268077	0.0600886	104.31	0.000	6.150305	6.385848

Source: Author Primary Data Reporting (2016).

Table 10.8. Nearness to Social Services (NSS).

	Coef.	OIM Std. Err.	*Z*	*P* > |*z*|	[95% Conf. Interval]	
NSS5 ← NSS_cons	1.390895	0.0585025	23.77	0.000	1.276232	1.505558
	−2.908292	0.3471599	−8.38	0.000	−3.588713	−2.227871
NSS7 ← NSS_cons	0.5788161	0.0402307	14.39	0.000	0.4999654	0.6576667
	3.13744	0.2387328	13.14	0.000	2.669533	3.605348
NSS8 ← NSS_cons	0.5854794	0.0409231	14.31	0.000	0.5052717	0.6656872
	3.0935	0.2428416	12.74	0.000	2.617539	3.569461
NSS10 ← NSS_cons	1.345896	0.0625311	21.52	0.000	1.223337	1.468455
	−2.64032	0.3710659	−7.12	0.000	−3.367596	−1.913044
NSS12 ← NSS_cons	1.469855	0.1143049	12.86	0.000	1.245821	1.693889
	−4.104727	0.678297	−6.05	0.000	−5.434165	−2.77529

Source: Author Primary Data Reporting (2016).

Table 10.9. Community Involvement and Participation (CI).

	Coef.	OIM Std. Err.	Z	$P > \|z\|$	[95% Conf. Interval]	
CIP3 ← CIP_cons	1.1255	0.0512826	21.95	0.000	1.024988	1.226012
	−0.8946151	0.179783	−4.98	0.000	−1.246983	−0.542247
CIP4 ← CIP_cons	1.095134	0.0504638	21.70	0.000	0.996227	1.194042
	−0.7688548	0.1769127	−4.35	0.000	−1.115597	−0.4221123
CIP5 ← CIP_cons	1.082171	0.055947	19.34	0.000	0.9725169	1.191825
	−0.6908401	0.1961352	−3.52	0.000	−1.075258	−0.3064222
CIP9 ← CIP_CORS	0.9587531	0.0474513	20.20	0.000	0.8657503	1.051756
	0.403683	0.1663515	2.43	0.000	0.07764	0.729726
CIP10 ← CIP_cons	0.8426159	0.0519232	16.23	0.000	0.7408484	0.9443834
	0.9890472	0.1820287	5.43	0.000	0.6322775	1.345817

Source: Author Primary Data Reporting (2016).

management having a coefficient of 1.095 (z-statistic = 21.70; p-value = 0.000) and CIP9: maintaining safe and healthy place to live (z-statistic = 20.20; p value = 0.015).

Town planning approval and policy as shown in Table 10.10 was largely associated with TPAP7: maintaining the quality level of the neighbourhood showing a coefficient of 1.022 (z-statistic = 45.99; p-value = 0.000), TPAP 10: providing oversight of government facilities and policies showing a coefficient of 1.003 (z-statistic = 44.54; p-value = 0.000), TPAP 6: explain the need for residents to comply with municipal by-laws and government policies maintaining safe and healthy place to live showing a coefficient of (z-statistic = 41.41; p value = 0.000) and TPAP 5: issuing notices and fine to offenders and people that contravene the law showing a coefficient of 1.042 (z-statistic = 40.68; p-value = 0.000).

Occupant social interaction as shown in Table 10.11 was largely significantly associated with OSI 7: occupants support one another in times of need and emergency showing a coefficient of 1.052 (z-statistic = 30.74; p-value = 0.000) and OSI 3: occupants assist one another to look after the house and baby a coefficient of 1.132 (z-statistic = 30.30; p-value = 0.000).

Access to housing and affordability as shown in Table 10.12 was largely significantly associated with AFA 2: occupants support one another in times of need and emergency showing a coefficient of 1.052 (z-statistic = 30.74; p-value = 0.000) and AFA 5: occupants assist one another to look after the house and baby a coefficient of 1.132 (z-statistic = 30.30; p-value = 0.000).

From Table 10.13, the intergovernmental support and collaboration was largely significantly associated with IGSC 9: provision of fire station showing a coefficient of 1.059 (z-statistic = 25.77; p-value = 0.000) and IGSC 7: provision of social welfare centre a coefficient of 1.07925 (z-statistic = 23.04; p-value = 0.000).

The computed R-squared as shown in Table 10.14 is = 0.796 shows that the MIHD framework as developed in this study captured and explained that about 80% of factors that inform policy decisions or factors/parameters considered in developing a mixed-income housing model in South Africa is significantly associated with the construct as developed in this study. According to Heppner and Heppner (2004:293) varieties of goodness-of-fit indexes and their desired levels are important in any research result as it helps in determining the degree to which the hypothesized model fits the actual data. This is an empirical contribution as previous studies as shown in Chapters 2 and 3 all focus only on access to affordable housing, occupants' social interactions and nearness to social services. Very little and limited emphasis is placed on TPAP as well as intergovernmental support and collaborations.

10.11 The Benefit of the Framework

(1) It can be used as a guiding framework in facilitating human settlements development in South Africa and beyond by government sectors, developers, NGOs, consultants and other interested parties and stakeholders, as an

Table 10.10. Town Planning Approval and Policy (TRAP).

	Coef.	**OIM Std. Err.**	***Z***	***P* > |*z*|**	**[95% Conf. Interval]**	
TPAP3 ← TPAP_cons	1.001108	0.0269135	37.20	0.000	0.9483588	1.053858
	0.0097898	0.156848	0.06	0.950	−0.2976265	0.3172062
TPAP5 ← TPAP_cons	1.042653	0.0256309	40.68	0.000	0.992417	1.092888
	−0.3030255	0.1493735	−2.03	0.042	−0.5957922	−0.0102588
TPAP6 ← TPAP_cons	1.031305	0.0249042	41.41	0.000	0.982494	1.080117
	−0.1044349	0.1451383	−0.72	0.472	−0.3889007	0.180031
TPAP7 ← TPAP_cons	1.022232	0.0222266	45.99	0.000	0.9786687	1.065795
	0.0014114	0.1295338	0.01	0.991	−0.2524701	0.2552929
TPAP10 ← TPAP_cons	1.003601	0.0225318	44.54	0.000	0.9594396	1.047763
	0.0258192	0.1313124	0.20	0.844	−0.2315484	0.2831867

Source: Author Primary Data Reporting (2016).

Table 10.11. Occupant Social Interaction (OSI).

	Coef.	OIM Std. Err.	Z	$P > \|z\|$	[95% Conf. Interval]	
OSI_2 ← OSI_cori3	1.063388	0.0447191	23.78	0.000	0.9757398	1.151036
	−0.3822746	0.1902841	−2.01	0.045	−0.7552245	−0.0093247
OSI_3 ← OSI_cons	1.132935	0.0373914	30.30	0.000	1.059649	1.206221
	−0.7145356	0.1591038	−4.49	0.000	−1.026373	−0.4026978
OSI_6 ← OSI cons	1.080214	0.0397826	27.15	0.000	1.002242	1.158186
	−0.3217748	0.1692785	−1.90	0.057	−0.6535546	0.010005
OSI_7 ← OSI_cons	1.05253	0.0342432	30.74	0.000	0.985415	1.119646
	−0.142429	0.1457079	−0.98	0.328	−0.4280113	0.1431532
OSI_8 ← OSI_cons	1.052796	0.0376257	27.98	0.000	0.9790506	1.126541
	−0.1735248	0.160101	−1.08	0.278	−0.487317	0.1402674

Source: Author Primary Data Reporting (2016).

Table 10.12. Access to Housing and Affordability (AFA).

	Coef.	OIM Std. Err.	Z	$P > \|z\|$	[95% Conf. Interval]	
AFA1 ← AFA_cons	1.24238	0.0589264	21.08	0.000	1.126886	1.357874
	−1.647763	0.3615004	−4.56	0.000	−2.356251	−0.5352357
AFA2 ← A FA_cons	1.076702	0.0464603	23.17	0.000	0.5856414	1.167762
	−0.407896	0.2850235	−1.43	0.152	−0.5665318	0.1507358
AFA3 ← AFA_cons	1.137182	0.0539587	21.06	0.000	1.031346	1.243017
	−0.9028523	0.3312703	−2.73	0.006	−1.55217	−0.2536145
AFA5 ← AFA_cons	1.054615	0.0450486	21.50	0.000	0.5584815	1.150745
	−0.3496015	0.3009024	−1.16	0.245	−0.5353553	0.2401564
AFA8 ← AFA_cons	0.95711	0.0797162	12.01	0.000	0.8008651	1.113351
	−0.1561591	0.4890413	−0.32	0.745	−1.114663	0.8023443

Source: Author Primary Data Reporting (2016).

Table 10.13. Intergovernmental Support and Collaboration (IGSC).

	Coef.	OIM Std. Err.	Z	$P > \|z\|$	[95% Conf. Interval]	
IGSC3 ← IGSC_cons	1.120325	0.0527015	21.26	0.000	1.017032	1.223618
	−0.8722853	0.3333591	−2.62	0.009	−1.525657	−0.2189134
IGSC6 ← IGSC_cons	1.086819	0.0474109	22.92	0.000	0.9938949	1.179742
	−0.6322627	0.2998939	−2.11	0.035	−1.220044	−0.0444814
IGSC7 ← IGSC_cons	1.07925	0.04 68333	23.04	0.000	0.9874585	1.171042
	−0.6548232	0.2962405	−2.21	0.027	−1.235444	−0.0742024
IGSC8 ← IGSC_cons	1.042388	0.0480719	21.68	0.000	0.9481689	1.136607
	−0.4937683	0.3040748	−1.62	0.104	−1.089744	0.1022073
IGSC9 ← IGSC_cons	1.059525	0.0411129	25.77	0.000	0.9789451	1.140105
	−0.3761833	0.2600561	−1.45	0.148	−0.8858839	0.1335173

Source: Author Primary Data Reporting (2016).

Table 10.14. Equation Level Goodness of Fit.

.estat eqgof

Equation-Level Goodness of Fit

	Fitted	**Variance Predicted**	**Residual**	***R*-squared**	**mc**	**mc2**
Observed						
NSS	1.062045	0.4149089	0.6471359	0.3906699	0.6250359	0.3906699
CIP	1.279835	0.1738813	1.105953	0.1358623	0.368595	0.1358623
TPAP	2.559184	0.1094746	2.449709	0.0427772	0.2068264	0.0427772
OSI	1.045172	0.6013094	0.4438623	0.5753212	0.7584993	0.5753212
AFA	1.214269	0.755472	0.4587968	0.622162	0.7887725	0.622162
IGSC	0.7221288	0.0431226	0.6790062	0.059716	0.2443685	0.059716
NSS5	2.7816	2.05462	0.7269797	0.7386469	0.8594457	0.7386469
NSS7	0.6996	0.3558148	0.3437852	0.5085974	0.7131602	0.5085974
NSS8	0.719775	0.3640542	0.3557208	0.505789	0.7111884	0.505789
NSS10	2.754375	1.923826	0.8305489	0.6984619	0.8357404	0.6984619
NSS12	5.069774	2.29452	2.775255	0.4525881	0.6727467	0.4525881
CIP3	2.2944	1.621232	0.6731678	0.706604	0.8405974	0.706604
CIP4	2.186775	1.53493	0.6518447	0.7019151	0.8378037	0.7019151
CIP5	2.3	1.498807	0.8011932	0.6516551	0.8072516	0.6516551
CIP9	1.752775	1.176434	0.5763414	0.6711835	0.8192579	0.6711835
CIP10	1.598775	0.9086847	0.6900903	0.5683631	0.7538986	0.5683631
TPAP3	2.9356	2.564859	0.3707409	0.8737087	0.9347238	0.8737087
TPAP5	3.1184	2.782152	0.3362482	0.8921728	0.944549	0.8921728
TPAP6	3.039375	2.721924	0.3174509	0.8955539	0.9463371	0.8955539
TPAP7	2.9271	2.674241	0.2528591	0.9136145	0.9558318	0.9136145
TPAP10	2.8375	2.577649	0.2598508	0.9084226	0.9531121	0.9084226
OSI_2	1.5999	1.181873	0.4180267	0.738717	0.8594864	0.738717
OSI_3	1.633775	1.341521	0.2922541	0.8211173	0.9061552	0.8211173
OSI_6	1.5504	1.219571	0.3308286	0.7866173	0.8869145	0.7866173
OSI_7	1.402975	1.157862	0.2451126	0.8252908	0.9084552	0.8252908
OSI_8	1.454375	1.158446	0.2959289	0.7965251	0.8924825	0.7965251
AFA1	2.7175	1.874234	0.8432662	0.6896904	0.830476	0.6896904
AFA2	1.9319	1.407686	0.524214	0.7286537	0.8536121	0.7286537
AFA3	2.2784	1.570271	0.7081288	0.6891991	0.8301802	0.6891991
AFA5	1.934775	1.350525	0.5842497	0.6980271	0.8354801	0.6980271

Table 10.14. *(Continued)*

.estat eqgof						
Equation-Level Goodness of Fit						
	Fitted	**Variance Predicted**	**Residual**	***R*-squared**	**mc**	**mc2**
AFA8	2.6556	1.112343	1.543257	0.4188668	0.6471992	0.4188668
IGSC3	1.3075	0.9063647	0.4011353	0.6932044	0.832589	0.6932044
IGSC6	1.1776	0.8529603	0.3246397	0.7243209	0.8510705	0.7243209
IGSC7	1.1579	0.8411219	0.3167781	0.7264202	0.8523029	0.7264202
IGSC8	1.1184	0.7846456	0.3337544	0.7015786	0.8376029	0.7015786
IGSC9	1.054775	0.8106567	0.2441183	0.7685589	0.8766749	0.7685589
Overall				0.7962479		

Source: Author Primary Data Reporting (2016).

mc = correlation between depvar and its prediction.

mc2 = mc^2 is the Bentler-Raykov squared multiple correlation coefficient.

important policy tool and guidelines for mixed-income housing development and strategies.

(2) The framework will serve as key criterion that needs to be evaluated and considered in setting up a research agenda for mixed-income housing development. It will go a long way in assisting in the monitoring and evaluation of other service delivery strategies by government because of the increasing spate of service delivery protest and agitation on issues of access to housing.

(3) The framework is user friendly and can be applied to specific situations or case studies because mixed-income housing development project are very complex and complicated, without a proper guiding model or framework can result to project abandonment and an unsustainable development.

10.12 Summary

This chapter presents the result of the research, using SEM. It highlights the various constructs that inform the MIHD framework. These include: NSS with 14 variables, CIP with 11 variables, TPAP with 10 variables, OSI with 11 variables, access to affordable housing with 9 variables and IGSC with 14 variables. The findings show that the computed z-statistics and p-values, that the construct OSI was found to be more significantly associated (z-statistic = 13.73; p = 0.000) with the mixed-income housing development latent variable, followed by AFA (z-statistic = 11.38; p-value = 0.000). In the AFA latent factor the indicator that is significant is that people are now able to own their own houses with title deed. The least significant in the model is the IGSC with z-statistics = 3.40; p = 001. The model will be beneficial to the private sector and public sector as well as other role players in the development and facilitation of mixed-income housing development.

10.13 Conclusion

The findings of this research based on the data analysis and subsequent synthesis of the data collected will provide an important area to guide policy and practice. The first set of data were based on analysis of various document, followed by literature review and the content analysis of policy documents as well as the preliminary Delphi survey of panel of experts in a three-round questionnaire. The second data set were based on the case study visit and interview of the relevant residents of the case study area. The last set of data comprise of the set of questionnaire items to validate the case study and the Delphi survey. The seven research objectives have been achieved and form the basis of the findings. This evidence from this study suggests that mixed-income housing development, as a large-scale urban revitalization project supported by national, provincial and local authorities, has clearly improved the socio-spatial/physical and economic conditions of the low-income earners in South Africa in a broader term. Apartheid geography separated people not only by race, colour and sex but also through segregated and fragmented human settlements and planning. Class-based segregation is a fundamental barrier to urban democracy and social justice.

The high quality and good design of mixed-income housing development may help to create more favourable impression of housing that is affordable. Opportunity to get quality housing that are affordable in cities has been an ongoing challenge for those living in poverty and a big area of debate in public policy issue of most developing countries. Significant contribution is made to existing body of work by noting that mixed-income housing development can lead to more funding for affordable housing from various government sectors and more cooperation from communities to approve and embrace affordable housing to be built in their areas. This will enable good working relationship with government and minimize Not in My Back Yard (NIMBY) factors. Good quality mixed-income housing assists households in dire need of housing support, especially low-income earners and may be perceived as a community asset, thereby discouraging the current trend of selling subsidy houses after it has been allocated to individuals.

The problem of intergovernmental collaborations and support has been noted widely in the literature as lacking in South Africa, especially as it relates to integrated human settlements development. On this issue, this study further contributed through empirical evidence that intergovernmental support and collaboration is necessary for the planning and implementation of mixed-income housing. This is also supported by the evidence from the case study areas as all relevant government departments played very active role in delivering of the mixed-income housing units. Hence, the current finding challenges previous research that concluded that moving people to mixed-income housing project site disadvantages households that are poor who do not have the institutional services and support of their prior neighbourhoods.

Chapter 11

Outcome of the Mixed-Income Housing Development Framework Findings and Results

11.1 Introduction

The essence of this section of the book is to illustrate the key results of the research. The literatures that are reviewed in Chapters 2 and 3 shed lights on the gap that does exist for the mixed-income housing development in South Africa. This summarizes the journey so far as well as the data collection approaches and how it is interpreted in the findings. The discussion is centred on the key objectives that inform this research:

- *OS1*: To find out if the development of mixed-income housing as a large-scale urban revitalization project has clearly improved the socio-spatial/physical and economic conditions of the low-income earners.
- *OS2*: To find out the extent of intergovernmental support and collaboration in the development of mixed-income housing development projects.
- *OS3*: To interrogate the ideals and assumptions behind the mixed-income development policy and explore the ways in which the strategy is playing out on the ground.
- *OS4*: To find out whether any lesson can be learnt from best practices on strategies for mixed-income housing development from international experiences.
- *OS5*: To investigate the community-building strategies implemented to create well-functioning communities within and around the new mixed-income developments.
- *OS6*: To evaluate the linkages between urban land use planning and housing policy on mixed-income housing.

Mixed-Income Housing Development Planning Strategies and Frameworks in the Global South, 165–181
Copyright © 2024 George Okechukwu Onatu, Wellington Didibhuku Thwala and Clinton Ohis Aigbavboa
Published under exclusive licence by Emerald Publishing Limited
doi:10.1108/978-1-83753-814-020231011

- *OS7*: To find out why mixed-income housing development projects are difficult to implement and the factors that are responsible for this.
- *OS8*: To develop a mixed-income housing development framework.

The research is divided into two parts. The first part of the research is comprised of the use of Delphi methods involving three rounds of iterative processes. It involves rounds of questionnaire circulated through a panel that provided opinions regarding an issue. This method is used in this research (Refer to Chapter 9) because, according to Robinson (2011:43), planners and developers together with other experts can use the technique to gather informed opinions around complex questions and subsequently build consensus about key issues such as mixed-income housing development model.

The second phase of the investigation is the survey in which a total of 300 questionnaires were distributed in Cosmo City, one of the case study sites. In this vein, 67%, that is, 200 questionnaires were successfully returned. According to Hogarty et al. (2005), a larger sample size decreases sampling error resulting in more stable solutions. The reason for the choice of this site has already been explained. Random sampling technique was used as each of the research assistant was assigned to cover specific sections of Cosmo City based on zoning. The data collected from this survey were analyzed using SPSS version 24 and Stata version 14. The eight objectives of the study are indicated and, most importantly, to develop a mixed-income housing development framework for South Africa.

The phases of the data collection and the perspectives from multiple respondents increased the opportunity to view the case investigation in a different way. Thus, the development of a model to guide the development of mixed-income housing development project is based on the notion that the pattern from one data source is strengthened by the evidence from another source (Nordin, 2014). The literature review also adds to the robustness of the findings. The discussion will be based on the analysis of the Delphi and the Survey empirical results.

11.2 Analysis of the Delphi Results

The specific question investigated was to establish if mixed-income housing (as a large-scale urban revitalization project) has brought with it (1) local economic development, (2) revitalization of the neighbourhoods or (3) an established environment where other poverty alleviation strategies can be tackled. This is to test the research objective *OS1*. Results derived from the responses of the panel of experts show that majority of the respondents (58%) agree that mixed-income housing development brings along with it local economic development. Forty-two percent of these numbers strongly agree. More so, the majority of the respondents disagree that there is no strong evidence that mixed-housing development revitalizes neighbourhoods. Accordingly, 50% strongly disagree, 25% disagree and 25% agree that mixed-income housing development has no influence in the revitalization of neighbourhood. Concerning poverty alleviation strategies, mixed-income housing was seen as an aspect of poverty alleviation strategies by the government with 58% strongly agreeing and 42% agreeing. This evidence suggests that mixed-income housing development, as a large-scale urban revitalization project, has clearly improved the socio-spatial/physical and economic conditions of the low-income earners. Levy et al. (2010) noted that the primary objective of mixed communities is to address the problems of disadvantaged areas. Mixed communities' policies are seen as solutions for disadvantaged areas, not just as a broad social goal worth pursuing (Tunstall and Lupton, 2010). Mixed-income communities are proposed to restore conditions of integration, cohesion, workability and sustainability, or to create them. According to Schwartz and Tajbakhsh (1997:73) the Hope VI (which was a federal programme for the physical and social revitalization of distressed public housing) was aimed at promoting mixed-income housing.

The study further asked whether it is necessary for strong and good intergovernmental relationship and coordination for the delivery of mixed-income housing development. The result, which addresses the research objective (*OS2*), shows that 17% of the respondent agrees and 83% strongly agree that strong leadership from government is needed for the development and planning of human settlement, including mixed-income housing development. None of the participants disagreed, strongly disagreed or had no opinion at all with respect to this question. This finding is an indication of the need for a strong and effective intergovernmental relationship and coordination at all levels for the implementation and delivery of mixed-income housing development in South Africa. The effective delivery of services and the promotion of development by various government departments, according to the Presidency (2003), are dependent on how collective effort can be harnessed. This requires proper and solid alignment of sectoral plans, joint work collaborations. In promoting government to the national economic space requires thorough co-operative government, the Constitution sets criteria in section 41.1 (c) to stress further this point:

- *Effective government* – co-operative government must entail the effective and efficient use of resources, not wastage and duplication, but the unlocking of synergy of collective effort,
- *Transparent government* – co-operative government should not be an entangled web of committee and consultations, making it difficult to determine who is responsible for what task,
- *Accountable government* – the system and processes of co-operative government should not impede holding executives accountable for their decisions and actions,
- *Coherent government* – government should be rational, informed by best information with due regard to consultation between spheres of government. Contradictory or overlapping policies should not arise by oversight, the absence of consultation or poorly informed decisions.

Intergovernmental support and collaboration have not been an easy thing in South Africa. Tapscott (2000) suggests that given the recency of the transition to democracy and the ongoing process of political transformation, intergovernmental relations in South Africa are in a state of flux and sometimes dysfunction that requires urgent attention.

In interrogating the ideals and assumptions behind the mixed-income housing development policy and exploring the ways in which the strategy is playing out on the ground (*OS3*), respondents were asked whether the return on investment is good for any completed mixed-income housing development. On the issue of the capital return on investment, 67% of the respondents expressed that they agree that it is good and 33% strongly agree with the statement. Market strength is also very crucial in explaining a mixed-income housing development as pointed out by other researchers. According to Brophy et al. (2008), the specific mix of income within any particular development should take into consideration market conditions. Stronger markets can support a wider mix of incomes rather than a weaker market. Smith (2002:15) noted that the market determines to a great extent what mix of incomes is possible. A mixed-income housing development located in a soft market will have a difficult time renting market unit to high-income households. According to Joseph and Feldman (2009) mixed-income can be a way to leverage private sector resources in terms of return on investment when creatively financed through government incentive programme. Developers may find that offering a wider variety of housing products at a range of price points can reduce the overall risk of the project and help increase the absorption rates by widening the scope of the target market. Density bonus as offered to private developers in the United States can enable the provision of affordable units in their project (Ibid, 2009). Several authors (such as Khadduri and Martin, 1997; Schwartz and Tajbakhsh, 1997) have noted that rent collected from market-rate units can provide part of the subsidy needed in the lower income units, thereby reducing the financial input required from the government.

Respondents were asked whether they think mixed-income housing development (through good design and quality products) will change the perception of people towards affordable housing. The aim of the question was to determine whether any lesson can be learnt from the best practices on strategies for mixed-income housing development from international experiences (*see objective OS4*). On the shift to mixed-income housing due to good design and quality of the product, 42% of the respondents agree to this statement and 68% strongly agree. This finding is supported by the literature: in the past when people think of affordable housing, they may imagine the drab, monolithic, concrete high rise that characterize some of the most visible public housing projects of the mid-twentieth century (AHURI, 2003). The reality today is that affordable housing is designed not only to meet the needs of the users; but also, it is responsive to its contents, enhances its neighbourhood, durable and widely accepted by the benefiting communities. For mixed-income housing development, good residential design is often a competitive selling point to attract market-rate residents. Developers are now increasingly aware of the previous stigma attached to low-income housing development. Smith (2002:28) in arguing about this pointed out that 'Painfully aware that the image of troubled public-housing projects is linked to low-income housing, many affordable housing developers and designers have now focused more on building their housing to a very high standard'. Good design and quality housing products are now considered to go a long way to alleviate previous stigmas associated with low-income housing. This is also necessitated by the market pressure to serve higher income population and hence compel developers of mixed-income housing to ensure high standard of the end product. Concerned about the social problems (with the associated poor quality) that accompanies most low-income housing, developers are now forced to design high standard and durable developments without any negative effect to surrounding neighbourhoods. Mixed-income housing and good design are a winning combination that has demonstrated the capacity to encourage faster project approvals, attract the support of future residents and overcome the fears of neighbours who are uncertain about the prospects of affordable housing next door (AHURI, 2003:12).

11.3 Questionnaire Survey Results

As shown in this study, mixed-income housing development is noted to have contributed significantly to an increase in the number and availability of affordable housing provision by ensuring erection of quality housing that can be supported by neighbourhood residents, countering political resistance and providing opportunity for developers to incorporate affordable products. The case studies of Cosmo City depict this argument, and, in so doing, the argument supports the research objectives. The Structural Equation Model (SEM) developed in Chapter 9 indicated that mixed-income housing development project is guided by nearness to social services with 14 variables; Community Involvement and Participation (CIP) with 11 variables; Town Planning Approval and Policy (TPAP) with 10 variables; Occupant Social Interaction (OSI) with 11 variables; Access to Affordable Housing (AFH) with 9 variables and Intergovernmental Support and Collaborations (IGSC) with 14 variables. Hence, as can be illustrated above, the total number of variables or items is 68. To ascertain whether these variables are at all closely related or share certain criteria in common the Cronbach's alpha was used. Cronbach's alpha is a standard used to measure the internal relationship, that is, as a group whether the items are closely related. Cronbach's alpha is used in another word to measure if the scale of measurement is reliable and can be trusted. As mentioned in Section 8.4.1, the value of (α = 0.954) as the Cronbach's alpha coefficient value for the finally selected 68 items was seen to be above the minimum acceptable (α = 0.700) scale reliability score. This result obtained from the data analysis reveals that the listed items indeed carried out measurement of a single unidimensional latent construct. This suggests internal consistency of the items. It is important to note and recommended in most social sciences that results of a reliability coefficient of 0.70 or higher is considered good and 'acceptable'.

To now determine whether the sample as collected is adequate enough we now use the Kaiser-Meyer-Olkin (KMO) criterion. The sampling as collected from the field survey is considered adequate or sufficient if the KMO value is larger than 0.5 (Field, 2000). Since further research has suggested an increased value for KMO, including Pallant (2013) who suggested a KMO of 0.6 and above. The value that is between 0.7 and 0.8 are considered and recommended as very good, value that are between 0.8 and 0.9 are seen as great and values between 0.9 and above are considered superb (Sofronjou and Hutcheson, 1999). On this note since the computed overall KMO value for this research is (= 0.868) for the 68 items in the questionnaire feeding into the Mixed-Income Housing Delivery model in South Africa is a confirmation of the adequacy of the samples of items explored under all the defined constructs. On a similar note, the KMO-MSA value for the following are above the minimum acceptable 0.60 statistical validity score: the disaggregated dimension nearness to social services (NSS), CIP, TPAP, OSI, AFA and IGSC. This indicates the presence of sampling adequacy. Below is a detailed explanation of the items that has the highest score loading among the list of items used in this study.

11.4 Confirmatory Factor Analysis (CFA) as Used in Mixed-Income Housing Development

Here we provide the results of the items retained that have high loadings (factor score ≥0.5) that is statistically considered of significant value in the development and estimation of the Mixed-Income Housing Delivery model for South Africa.

11.4.1 Nearness to Social Services

In the final round iteration evidence shows that there is no need to eliminate any of the items as they did not display complex structure at all, hence they are retained in the datasets. The calculated final results reveal those three items under factor 1 and two items under factor 2 are having the highest in loadings value. Factor loadings that have or that attains highest value of importance are a reflection of the importance the respondents accord to such item in their responses.

For NSS, factor 1 as shown in Table 11.1 reveals that participants highly perceived greatest importance on 'availability of community hall or social hall' (loading = 0.880), 'housing stock take disabled needs into consideration' (loading = 0.826) and 'housing customer complain centre' (loading = 0.820). The items with highest loadings under factor 2 include 'provision of water supply and sanitation' (loading = 0.911) and 'provision of electricity supply' (loading = 0.874). In moderate terms, participants placed value on 'playground and open spaces' (loading = 0.734), 'policy station' (loading = 0.689), 'proximity of houses to hospital/clinic' (loading = 0.683), 'provision of health facilities and clinics' (loading = 0.671) and availability of schools for the children (loading = 0.664). The lowest valued item is the proximity of houses to shopping area. The findings suggest that residents in terms of NSS as it relates to mixed-income housing location attach great importance to the highlighted items except integrated public transport system and proximity to shopping areas. These finding support the work of Kimberlin (2014) that an effective and active mixed-income communities is most likely to be characterized with visible and seamless fitted public open space that is readily reachable by everyone in the community irrespective of social

Table 11.1. Rotated Factor Matrix – Nearness to Social Services.

Rotated Factor Matrix[a]	**Factor**	
	1	**2**
Availability of Schools for the children		0.664
Integrated public transport system		0.618
Playground and open spaces	0.734	
Police station		0.689
Housing customer complain centre	0.820	
Provision of health facilities and clinics	0.671	
Provision of electricity supply		0.874
Provision of water supply and sanitation		0.911
Provision of fire station/emergency	0.637	
Availability of community hall or social hall	0.880	
Proximity of houses to hospital/clinic	0.683	
Housing stock take disabled need into consideration	0.826	
Proximity of houses to shopping area		0.559
Proximity of houses to playground/recreational facilities	0.628	

Source: Author Primary Data Reporting (2016).

[a]Rotation converged in 3 iterations.

Method of Extraction: Varimax with Kaiser Normalization.

orientation and inclination can come and rally round each other in a reciprocity manner. Likely examples that can assist in the social seams include public parks, sports field, community halls, grocery and convenience store, movie theatres, schools and childcare facilities, libraries, cultural and religious institutions. The low-income households and residents who have access to these amenities rub shoulders with the higher income residents and tend to feel elated and motivated. The class of the schools or its quality can be a factor in the retention of higher income families most of whom have high taste. Khadduri and Martin (1997) studies shows that it is a mission and impossible to attract and retain higher income households with children in a given mixed-income housing development. Good school system with amenities can play significant role and help retain families that have housing options. However, during the questionnaire survey, the researcher observed that most of the respondents were excited about the shopping malls as one of the prominent social amenities, but they complained about integrated public transport system as this is still dominated by taxis. The absence of integrated public transport system should be examined in the current drive for integrated human settlements interventions. Table 11.2 shows the rotated matrix analysis of community involvement and participation (CIP).

Table 11.2. Rotated Factor Matrix – Community Involvement and Participation (CIP).

Rotated Factor Matrix[a]

	Factor	
	1	**2**
Involved in the design of the houses and location		0.816
Effective administration and management		0.930
Participate in quality management		0.933
Enforcing municipal by-laws and compliance		0.871
Information sharing and dissemination	0.740	
Security and safety of residents	0.864	
Welfare and protection of interest of residents	0.822	
Maintaining safe and healthy place to live	0.890	
Monitoring and reporting crime	0.897	
Ensuring the availability of social services	0.777	

Source: Author Primary Data Reporting (2016).

[a]3 iterations rotation.
Varimax with Kaiser Normalization.

11.4.2 Community Involvement and Participation (CIP)

Results in Table 11.2 show that none of the questionnaire items displayed any complex behaviour. Accordingly, no bases to get any eliminated from the dataset remaining. Key respondents strongly perceive the importance of community involvement and participation around 'participation in quality management' (loading = 0.933), 'effective administration and management' (loading = 0.930), 'monitoring and reporting crime' (loading = 0.897), 'maintenance of safe and healthy place to live' (loading = 0.890), 'enforcement of municipal by-laws and compliance' (loading = 0.871), 'security and safety of residents' (loading = 0.864), 'welfare and protection of the interests of residents' (loading = 0.822), 'involvement in the design of houses and location' (loading = 0.816) and 'ensuring availability of social services' (loading = 0.777). The high rating as it relates to quality management, monitoring and reporting crime and maintenance of secure and healthy environment to live as well as other factors highlighted is due to the formation of Community or Zone leaders, vigilante groups as well as social groups. These formations meet on regular basis to discuss matters pertaining to residents and this normally takes place in the Community Hall for Cosmo City and at the Primary School for Cornubia or in open areas. There is also *Cosmo Newsletter* to educate residents on what is going on and any other important circular from the developers. These findings are supported by the work of Ibrahim (1987) in Zambia in looking at the upgrade of an Informal Settlements in Lusaka, it is noted that the upgrading process must be seen and recognized as a way in which a local authority supports collective resident's efforts to uplift their living environment. This should serve as a propeller to encourage group savings, skills acquisitions and community initiative. The only two items that has least score is on Information sharing and dissemination with 0.740 and ensuring the availability of social services with 0.777. Other studies differ from this outcome as community involvement and participation has a lot to do with information sharing and dissemination as it relates to job availability. Joseph et al. (2007) in a similar studies identified four ways through which mixed-income environment can contribute in improving the social standings of poor households locked in these neighbourhood by enhanced social network; through job-search, social control improvement; accountability behaviours and attitudes and self-efficacy among low-income residents.

Smith (2002:22) support this findings too by noting that for a typical American low-income earners to overcome the hindrance and setback of a low education, poorly resourced local schools, limited employment opportunities and outright racism attack pose a challenge by any standard. The housing option of mixed-income is also considered a way out and possible solution to reduce these stereotypes and negative behaviours because the higher income households will not allow or condone illegal activities in their housing environment. Argument here is that the authority will listen to the higher income households on matters related to these bad behaviours if they are the ones that reported it as compared to the low-income households. Hence, this section also accomplishes the objectives referring to *OS5*:

11.4.3 Town Planning Approval and Policy (TPAP)

None of the retained items in Table 11.3 demonstrate any complex behaviour. As such, no basis to reject them from the remaining dataset. In terms of TPAP, results show that participants placed considerable importance on all the items/indicators that measured town planning approval and policy. The top five indicators include 'maintaining the quality level of the neighbourhood' (loading = 0.954), 'providing oversight of government facilities and policies' (loading = 0.951), 'explain the need for residents to comply to municipal by-laws and government policies' (loading = 0.942), 'issuing notices and fine to offenders and people that contravene the law' (loading = 0.940) and 'ensuring that housing construction according to approved building plan' (loading = 0.931). Maintaining the quality level of the neighbourhood stood out as the top indicator because this development is a Greenfield development. The township application in terms of the Township Establishment Ordinance of 1986 showing the layout, road network and design of the various housing typologies was approved before the development. It also comprises of all the specialist reports such as the Environmental Impact Assessment (EIA) report, Traffic Impact Assessment (TIA) report, Geo-technical Report, Outline Scheme Report, Electrical capacity requirement report and storm water management report. The development and implementation of the Reconstruction and Development Programme (RDP) components with residents from an informal

Table 11.3. Rotated Factor Matrix – Town Planning Approval and Policy (TPAP).

Factor Matrix[a]

	Factor
	1
Regulating informal sector and trading	0.904
Enforcing municipal by-laws and regulations	0.920
Ensuring housing construction according to approved building plan	0.931
Conducting inspection of the settlement	0.883
Issuing notices and fine to offenders and people that contravene the	0.940
law.	0.942
Explain the need for residents to comply to municipal by-laws and	0.954
Government policies	0.857
Maintaining the quality level of the neighbourhood	0.912
Demolition of illegal houses and issuance of summons	0.951
Managing housing allocation and density	
Providing oversight of government facilities and policies	

Source: Author Primary Data Reporting (2016).
[a]Factor Matrix; Factors extracted.

settlement complied with formal planning or design principles as well as satisfied the local authority planning requirement before it was commissioned. Abbott (2002) in an analysis of the informal settlements upgrade challenge in Cape Town also noted that these settlement houses a significant percentage of the urban population and do contribute a lot, that planning processes for the long-term sustainability of informal settlements should be based on appropriate planning framework. Huchzermeyer and Karam (2006) in comparing this with international best practice refers to this as 'paradigm shift'. It is argued that they were re-enforced by initiatives in response to both United Nations Millennium Declarations and Cities Alliance through the World Bank support to reduce poverty and vulnerability globally as well as increase social inclusion. The current Breaking New Ground of 2004 in South Africa as discussed in Chapter 7 is borne out of this. The new Integrated Urban Development Framework (IUDF) is meant to examine this. As has been noted by CoGTA (2016) that Townships and informal settlements are poorly planned. The importance of planning legislations and framework to guide integrated human settlements development is pushed further by SLUMA (Refer to Chapter 7.) as it highlights in view of the historical context of South Africa on issues of justice in spatial context, sustainability in all sectors, efficiency, resilient and governance of good standings. Hence, another key objective achieved by this study (Refer to OS6) is the evaluation of the linkages between urban land use planning and housing policy on mixed-income housing.

11.4.4 Occupant Social Interaction (OSI)

Table 11.4 demonstrates that all items are loaded under factor 1, indicating that participants perceived that the respective items were positively correlated and were important to housing delivery with regards to occupant social interaction. Based on the values of loading scores, the top five items that were considered to be most important by the participants include 'occupants support one another in times of need and emergency' (loading = 0.97), 'occupants support one another to look after the baby and the house' (loading = 0.904), 'occupants run to one another during emergency' (loading = 0.886), 'occupants attend community meeting together and discuss matters of mutual interests' (loading = 0.876), 'occupants cooperate and assist one another to search for jobs' (loading = 0.849), 'neighbours report suspicious movement and behaviours to one another' (loading = 0.844) and 'occupants engage in sports together and other social functions' (loading = 0.822).

In moderate terms, the occupant social interaction activities which were considered to be important by the participants include 'children play together and exchange toys' (loading = 0.797), 'neighbours invite each other over for

Table 11.4. Rotated Factor Matrix – Occupant Social Interaction (OSI).

Factor Matrix[a]	**Factor**
	1
Neighbours are friendly and exchange greetings	0.699
Occupants cooperate and assist one another to search for jobs	0.849
Occupants assist one another to look after the house and baby	0.904
Occupants' children play together and exchange toys activities	0.797
Occupants' children are attending the same school and board same	0.702
bus	0.876
Occupants attend community meeting together and discuss matters	0.907
of mutual interests.	0.886
Occupants support one another in times of need and emergency.	0.822
Occupants run to one another during emergency	0.789
Occupants engage in sports together and other social functions	0.844
Neighbours invite each other over for coffee, birthday or any celebrations	
Neighbours report suspicious movement and behaviours to one another	

Source: Author Primary Data Reporting (2016).
[a]Factors extracted.

coffee, birthday or any celebrations' (loading = 0.789), 'occupants' children attend the same school and board same bus' (loading = 0.702), and 'neighbours are friendly and exchange greetings' (loading = 0.699). Mixed-income housing development if appropriately planned and designed accordingly do promote and foster social integration and relations among residents of varying income levels/background and give rise to an ample environment that is conducive for informal relations and mutual sharing by all the residents. This relationship is seen mostly in the RDP housing units with regard to occupants supporting one another in times of need and emergency. This is supported by Campbell and Lee (1992) and Fischer (1982) who note that the low-income households maintain and retain social networks more locally as compared to the higher incomes groups. In contrast to the findings of Brophy and Smith (1997), who both noted in their studies in the United States after interviewing property managers and developers that little evidence exists about neighbouring relationship across the various income streams. Though each person lives happily with one another without much quarrel but there is a very limited interaction among them. While reviewing eight scattered sites of public housing around the United States, Hogan (1996) concludes the findings by noting minimal and few identifiable social relations and mixing between those that are in public housing and their new neighbours. Though public housing residents are reported that they feel welcomed and accepted in these new neighbourhoods, report has it of very few instances of socializing or visiting each other.

Rosenbaum et al. (1998) countered this view by pointing out strong evidence of social interaction in mixed-income development at Lake Parc Place in Chicago. Physical interaction was very high at Lake Parc Place as it was noted that households within the same income bands got mixed in every building and on every floor. Similar research studies at Hope VI redevelopment in Seattle, Kliet (2005) found that there are indications of social interaction similar to this. Here, there was 'higher levels of neighbouring' than in other studies. How close these developments are located and shared characteristics (ethnicity, language, education, marital status, owners/renters) were attributed to the social tiers shared. The study also found that children are an important element and serve as bridges that facilitate these interactions among families who also are with children. Where social network and relationship are found existing between residents of varying income levels, questions do arise, whether there exists any positive impact. The answer to this question does not come around easily. Brophy and Smith (1997) further reported no proof of any improvement in the life chance for low-income residents in seven developments they investigated. Hence, documented empirical evidence of linkage that exists between interaction and employment opportunities or job access in a mixed-income housing development is still scanty notwithstanding the positive contribution this can make to South African situation in view of large proportion of the population in search of jobs.

Table 11.5. Rotated Factor Matrix – Access to Housing and Affordability (AFA).

Rotated Factor Matrix[a]

	Factor	
	1	**2**
The units are affordable and not too expensive	0.816	
People are now able to own their own house with Title Deed	0.816	
It provides opportunity for people without income, low income	0.888	
and medium income to own houses	0.621	
It gives people opportunity to live close to place of work	0.790	
It is an aspect of social transformation and poverty alleviation strategy	0.586	
It enables people of various tribes or nationality group to live together and share		
The housing units are of good design and of quality		0.869
Livelihood strategies of the poor are taken into consideration in the implementation of mixed-income housing		0.748

Source: Author Primary Data Reporting (2016).
[a]Factors extracted.

11.4.5 Access to Housing and Affordability (AFA)

Results in Table 11.5 reveal any of the questionnaire listed shows any complex behaviour with regard to the loading pattern in rotated factors. Accordingly, no basis or reasons to set aside any of these items from the remaining dataset. Based on the size of factor loadings, results show that participants strongly hold the perceptions that 'it provides opportunity for people without income, low income and medium income to own houses' (loading = 0.888), 'the housing units are of good design and of quality' (loading = 0.869), 'the units are affordable and not too expensive' (loading = 0.816), 'people are now able to own their own house with Title Deed' (loading = 0.816), 'it is an aspect of social transformation and poverty alleviation strategy' (loading = 0.790), 'livelihood strategies of poor are taken into consideration in mixed-income housing development' (loading = 0.748) and 'it gives people opportunity to live close to place of work' (loading = 0.621). Due to scarce resources and limited finance to tackle the housing needs of low-income families, policy-makers and developers are exploring other avenues to get the needed resources and support to undertake and sort out affordable housing issues. As can be shown from these findings, mixed-income is a means to showcase this. In his study of the promises and reality of mixed-income housing development in the United States, Smith (2002) supports these results and findings. Powered by necessary incentives, the existence of market-rate units in a given site will encourage the developers to construct affordable units with a subsidy below that needed in 100% affordable developments. Smith (2002:14) also added that residential development that is of more than 50 units provide for upto at least 12.5% of the units affordable to moderate income households.

11.4.6 Intergovernmental Support and Collaboration (IGSC)

Table 11.6 shows that no two items had a complex structure in terms of loading into factors. The top five items regarded as most significant are 'provision of fire station' (loading = 0.868), 'police station' (loading = 0.867), 'commercial and industrial areas' (loading = 0.835) 'Social welfare centres' (loading = 0.835) and Taxi rank and public transport (loading = 0.828). The reason why provision of fire station is rated high in this study might be related to the high incidence of fire outbreak in residential areas in winter and the increased lack of or delay in emergency response. Police station is rated highly because of high incidence of crime, especially in low-income residential areas. Similar findings include (Short, 1997; Skogan and Maxfiel, 1981 cited in Smith, 2002:8) also indicate a strong relation between violence and low neighbourhood socio-economic status. Onatu (2010) noted that this problem of crime though rampant can be addressed together with Not in My Back Yard (NIMBY) with multidimensional approach involving cluster security departments working together with the community. Chaskin and Joseph (2010) in a separate investigation on how to build community in mixed-income development pointed out the need for community-level

Table 11.6. Rotated Factor Matrix – Intergovernmental Support and Collaboration (IGSC).

Factor Matrix[a]	**Factor**
	1
Provision of recreational centre	0.742
Taxi rank and public transport	0.828
Information and job centres	0.811
Police station	0.867
Shopping mall and retail centres	0.796
Commercial and industrial areas	0.835
Social welfare centres	0.835
Customer services centre	0.819
Provision of fire station	0.868
Municipal offices	0.779
Primary and secondary schools	0.649
Fire station and EMS centres	0.823
Vocational training centres	0.739

Source: Author Primary Data Reporting (2016).
[a]Factors extracted.

improvement through 'increase in safety'. This is because respondent talked about the kinds of positive neighbourhood change, they expect to see in a mixed-income development, and among these are a 'decrease in crime'. The research also noted the need for interaction among various cluster groups including, planning, governance and decision-making bodies. The result also noted low rating on the availability of Primary and Secondary schools with 0.649 availability, Vocational Training Centres with 0.739 availability and Provision of Recreation Centre with 0.742 availability. This is interpreted as evidence of lack of intergovernmental support and collaboration as the Department of Education and the Department of Labour as well as Social Development are supposed to be on board to ensure cluster collaboration in the provision of this social amenity.

11.5 Recommendations

Recommendation from this research project is as follows:

(1) Neighbourhood Group/Ward Committee: An important association to pay much attention to in any given mixed-income housing development is a well-supported neighbourhood associations which could go a long way to promote greater commitment and solidarity. A resident or ward association that grows out of this kind of initiative could enter into savings scheme arrangement or neighbourhood watch group and in no time contribute to the peoples housing initiatives and safety of the area on their own.

(2) Low-cost Housing Provision: Mixed-income housing as can be seen in this research with an increasing effort of the government driving towards that direction should aim also at the use of housing that is cheap and affordable to help poor as well as marginalized households to become home owners. To provide good living space that can give people dignity and respect in housing is one of the greatest challenges that present South Africa government faces.

(3) Social Services Support Centres: Establishment of childcare and care giver in the form of neighbourhood childcare co-operative in our housing approaches, especially in mixed-income housing areas. This will serve as sustainable poverty reduction strategy. An example is the Action Foundation founded by Maria in Kibera slums in Kenya. This enables disabled children to see good life and become active citizens. Facilities in this area houses special needs and physically challenged children whose families are losing hope on how to cope with them and even lack needed resources, skills and training to take care of them. Here they provide various kinds of health services and therapy. Feed a Child that provides Nutrimeal at R10.00 per meal and other social services should be promoted in a mixed-income housing development project.

(4) Job Placement and vocational areas: Mixed-income housing can serve as a multipurpose area to enable the school leavers and low skill residents to be empowered. Housing provision as it is currently driven cannot do this as there is wide range of challenges that low-income people and the youths

living here are facing, especially in South Africa. There is a need for an inclusive long-term job placement and employment education programme. This can also incorporate vocational training activities and artisan workshop to expose interested youths to technical works such as plumbing, electrical wiring, brick laying and entrepreneur skills. An example is in Chicago, job seekers are not just trained and placed, but are provided with ongoing training and contacts as well as monitoring and evaluation after placement to help them retain their job.

(5) Inter-sectoral collaboration: The entire government departments should see housing provision as a national problem that cut across all spheres of government at all levels. The provision of integrated human settlements can only be a reality if needed social services are readily not available. It is recommended that all government departments should join hand to ensure that mixed-income housing development achieves the set goals and objectives by bringing people of all cadre together to live and work together. The dream of integrated development planning will only remain a wish list if we continue the business as usual.

(6) Innovation and smart cities: The National Building Regulation (NBR) should be reviewed and updated to come to speed with innovation, Fourth Industrial Revolution and new ways of building, designs and construction. The issue of bricks and mortar in the role out of RDP that takes ages to complete with creeping of corruptions can be dispelled with modular housing that can be completed within days. There is a need to revisit smart cities initiatives as it is now the other of the day in China, the United States and the UAE with new satellite towns and residential buildings completed at recorded short time without undue delays. The process of tendering and award of contacts need to be improved so that small, medium and micro enterprise (SMME) do not suffer due to no payment and frequent system failures that bring most project to half completion.

(7) The long-term future of subsidy housing and Breaking New Ground (BNG) need to be decided and the sustainability of this need to be measured and thoroughly interrogated.

(8) Constant policy review and adjustment brought about by change of government and the fiscus is not moving the Department of human settlement forward. Continuity is essential in any human endeavour. The National Development Plan (NDP) should be given more attention and all cluster agencies to support and promote the agenda.

(9) The skill shortages in South Africa's human settlement drive are a reoccurring issue. Limited human settlements graduates and skilled personnel is a very big problem that impacts heavily in all areas. Tertiary institutions should work closely with the human settlements department in area of research to identify areas of need and more efforts to be put into the Professionalization of human settlements to promote ethical behaviours and good practice.

11.6 Conclusions

This chapter seeks to provide answers for objectives 5, 6 and 7. In an attempt to do this, this study investigate the community-building strategies implemented to create well-functioning communities within and around the new mixed-income developments (*OS5*). When asked whether mixed-income housing development can lead to strong community building and correct previous apartheid segregated settlements and planning, only 42% agree to this statement. Forty-two percent also strongly agree that mixed-income housing development can lead to strong community building and correct previous apartheid segregated settlements and planning. Sixteen percent of them indicated that they do not have any opinion. While no one among the respondents strongly disagree or disagree to the statement. The study concludes that 84% of the respondents suggest that mixed-income housing development can lead to strong community building and correct previous apartheid segregated areas and planning. Analysis of the comments from the respondents suggest that while this can be achieved theoretically and rhetorically, the reality is that on its own mixed-income developments cannot achieve this in South Africa given South African history. However, supplemented by other supportive programmes and activities such as adequate communal and sporting facilities, parks, food festivals, campaigns against any form of social and political exclusions and violence, etc. then the goals can be approached. This point is supported by other works as noted by Mafukidze and Hoosen (2009) that community participation may have negative impacts and shortcomings if not undertaken in the correct manner and, when not carried forward, might result in sensitive issues concerning housing to be unresolved. They conclude in their studies that community participation give rise to unintended outcomes like social unrest, unhappiness, conflict and societal fragmentation. Facilitators of a participation process need necessary skills and have to equip themselves with adequate sociocultural and historical knowledge of a community so as to counter any negative outcomes. Aigbavboa and Thwala (2011, 2013) extend the debate further by pointing out that beneficiary participation theory have received considerable academic attention.

Appendices

Appendix 1: Instrument Used for the Research – Delphi Round 1

Delphi Survey – Round 1 (Q1)

This questionnaire is drawn for a *PhD thesis on Mixed-Income Housing Development Model for South Africa*. The questionnaire is intended to solicit the opinion of experts' and their views on this topic in an anonymous manner not known to other contributors that are part of the sample group. All the information provided will be used solely for this purpose. The confidentiality of the participants will be guided and protected in line with ethics of research. We appreciate your acceptance to partake on the Delphi panel for this research. Thank you so much for your understanding, time and expected valued response.

This is the first round of the three series of questionnaire that will inform this research and at this stage it is intended to be completed just in approximately 20–25 minutes. Subsequent surveys will require significantly less time to complete. Please return your response, in Word format, to gonatu@uj.ac.za by 20th of March 2015.

You will be given the opportunity to change your response later on after all Delphi participants have completed the first Round survey and results have been analyzed. Results will be in simple statistics, e.g. median response, average, range and percentage.

Instructions

(1) Please indicate your response by placing an 'X' in the appropriate boxes. This survey is self-explanatory and you are requested to rate the prospect of the elements that affects the mixed-income housing development strategies, South Africa human settlement policies, impact factors, implementation and advancement as well as prospects.

(2) Experts are also required to state their levels of agreement using a 5-point Likert Scale with certain statement and to support their choices where necessary with regards to South Africa human settlement policy, programme, issues and the future of mixed-income housing in order to arrive at a consensus.

(3) The influence (probability) scale is presented below and only a number should be used for a probability range. For instance, if you consider the influence (probability) range to be between 61% and 70% of the feature's influence then you should mark 'X' under the box '7'. If the impact is considered to be high, then the 'X' should be marked under the '7' or '8' box depending on whether your opinion is inclined more towards high or very high impact (See below).

Objective of This Delphi Method

- To find out if Mixed-Income housing development units are assets to the community it is located in.
- To identify the major factors or attributes that attract higher income population group to Mixed-Income Housing Development.
- To predict or forecast when the government intend to switch over to Mixed-Income Housing Development.
- To find out if Mixed-Income Housing Development can provide solutions to the increasing problems of concentrated poverty in Informal Settlements.
- The opinion of experts with respect to access to Land for Mixed-Income Housing Development.
- To ascertain the challenges that developers encounter in accessing land for Mixed-Income Housing Development.
- To find out the opinion of experts on the impact of Mixed-Income on the property value of surrounding neighbours.

Sample Questions

1: The neighbourhood that an individual lives affects them (either positively or negatively) and also makes the returns he or she receives from the residential choices contingent on the behaviour of others around him.

True	False
	X

1.2: If you strongly disagree to the previous statement (False), what do you think?

What other factors that affects them.	

List of Questions for the Research

1: Kindly use your experience, expertise and judgement to rate what you consider to be the impact of the mixed-income housing development on community building strategies of the municipalities in South Africa.

No impact		Low impact		Medium impact		High impact		Very high impact	
1	2	3	4	5	6	7	8	9	10

2: How do you judge the effects/impact of Mixed-Income Housing development strategies in an attempt to correct the previous consequences of Apartheid segregated planning/concentrated poverty as witnessed in South African urban environment?

0-10%	11- 20%	21- 30%	31- 40%	41- 50%	51- 60%	61-70%	71-80%	81-90%	91-100%
1	2	3	4	5	6	7	8	9	10

Please state some of your
reasons. . . . .

Q3: Residents of mixed-income housing developments are satisfied with the quality, maintenance and the management of the units?

Agreement:

☐ Strongly disagree
☐ Disagree
☐ No opinion
☐ Agree
☐ Strongly Agree

Q4: The social amenities and opportunities to promote interaction among residents of various background and income group living in mixed-income housing development are not enough?

Agreement:

☐ Strongly disagree
☐ Disagree
☐ No opinion
☐ Agree
☐ Strongly Agree

Q5: Economic Features: This refers to the economic opportunities and value capture of the housing product or unit and the neighbourhood.

Mixed-Income residential attributes	What is the **Impact** of each of the listed economic features on the Overall residential satisfaction of mixed-income housing development? (1=no impact, 10=very high impact)										
	No impact		**Low impact**		**Medium impact**		**High impact**		**Very High impact**		
	1	2	3	4	5	6	7	8	9	10	
Property value											
Neighbourhood socio-economic status											
Access to Shops											
Living Cost											
Location											
Retail Areas											
Out Door Life											

Q6: Social/Community Services Provided by the Government: This refers to the services provided by the government to each housing development projects and the institutional arrangement that operates in a mixed-income housing development projects.

Services Attributes	What is the **Impact** of each of the listed services provided by the government on the **Overall residential satisfaction** of South Africa low-income housing beneficiaries' if the listed features are lacking? (1=no impact, 10=very high impact)										
	No impact		**Low impact**		**Medium impact**		**High impact**		**Very High impact**		
	1	2	3	4	5	6	7	8	9	10	
Health Care Centre											
Garbage and waste collection system											
Tenure Status and Occupancy rate											
Visible Policing or Police Posts											
Emergency protection and response											
Maintenance and repair services											
Convenience of bus and public transportation											
Electricity supply											
Water supply											
Repair of Roads and Signage											
Telephone services											
Community Information centres											
Management responds to necessary repairs											
Property Management and Control											
Open Spaces and Environmental Management											
Enforcement of rules by the Department of housing											
Participation by the community											
Skills Development Centre											
Community Hall											
Education and Care centres											
Sports and Recreation Areas											

Q7: Intergovernmental Relationship: This refers to the relationship between the spheres of government involved in the development of mixed-income housing. Do you think that it is necessary for good intergovernmental relationship and cooperation?

Agreement:

☐ Strongly disagree
☐ Disagree
☐ No opinion
☐ Agree
☐ Strongly Agree

Q8: Housing Project Development: This refers to the factors that need to be considered in a human settlement project development and roll out.

Attributes	What is the **Impact** of each of the listed factors on the **mixed-**income housing residential development'? (1=no impact, 10=very high negative impact)										
	No impact		**Low impact**		**Medium impact**		**High impact**		**Very High impact**		
	1	2	3	4	5	6	7	8	9	10	
Local Housing Market											
Access to Finance											
Planning Regulation											
Strong Leadership from Government											
Good cooperation											
Legislative and Policy framework											
Goal of the developer											

Q9: Developer and Government Relations: This refers to the interpersonal relationship and coexistence between the project developer and sphere of government.

Public – Private relationship attributes	What is the **Impact** of each of the listed attributes on the development of mix-income housing development'? (1=no impact, 10=very high negative impact)										
	No impact		**Low impact**		**Medium impact**		**High impact**		**Very High impact**		
	1	2	3	4	5	6	7	8	9	10	
Mistrust											
Negative emotions											
Respect of the role and responsibility of one another											
Pessimism											
Good cooperation and support											

Q10: Planning and Design Forms: This refers to the Town Planning and design layout such as the appearance, height, etc.

Mixed-income residential development attributes	What is the **Impact** of each of the listed planning and urban design principles on the **mix**-income housing development strategies'? (1=no impact, 10=very high negative impact)										
	No impact		**Low impact**		**Medium impact**		**High impact**		**Very High impact**		**Rank**
	1	2	3	4	5	6	7	8	9	10	
Size of the development (Hectares)											
Percentage of low-cost housing (RDP)											
Percentage of social housing units											
Percentage of market rate bond units											
Land use schemes and town planning											
None inclusion of social amenities											
Mode of transport network											
Design of streets and orientation of buildings											
Height, density, coverage and Floor Area											

Q11: Location: This refers to the area where the project is situated.

Mixed-income development	What is the **Impact** of the following locational attributes on the **South** Africa mix-income- housing '? (1=no impact, 10=very high impact)									
	No impact		**Low impact**		**Medium impact**		**High impact**		**Very High impact**	
	1	2	3	4	5	6	7	8	9	10
Plot and unit size										
Ease of access by public transport										
Geotechnical Conditions										
Nearness to social amenities										
Nearness to slums										
Nearness to economic opportunities										
Nearness to upmarket housing units										

Q12: Are there attributes that in your opinion affect satisfaction that has not been addressed? If any, please state the attributes below

Attributes not listed	

Q13: Implementation of Mixed-income Housing: To find out the level of demand for mixed-income housing products.

Attributes	Why are there few demand for mixed-income housing development products in South Africa? (1=no impact, 10=very high impact)										
	No impact		**Low impact**		**Medium impact**		**High impact**		**Very High impact**		
	1	2	3	4	5	6	7	8	9	10	
High cost of construction											
Affordability of the housing products											
Complex Housing Environment											
Occupancy Rate and return on investment											
Lack of skills to handle the project											
Lack of Finance and support											
High Cost of Land											
Lack of Good management											
Poor inter-sectoral collaboration											
Lack of Capacity											
Poor Economic Environment											
Political involvement											
High Objection rate and Public Participations											
Policy Inconsistencies											
Bureaucratic capacity											
Town Planning requirements and approval of plans											

Q14: Are there factors that in your opinion **IMPACT** on the implementation of mixed-income housing development in South Africa that has not been addressed? If any, please state the factor and rank the **IMPACT**.

Attributes not listed:	

Q15: Housing Policy Instruments: To identify the combination of Housing Policy instrument that will better serve the South Africa low-income group.

Housing Policy instruments	What is the **influence** of the following housing policy instruments on **mixed-income housing** in South Africa? (1=low influence, 10=high influence)										
	1	2	3	4	5	6	7	8	9	10	
Public housing (subsidy schemes)											
Social (Medium-density) Housing Instrument											
Integrated Human Settlement											
National Homebuilders Regulations and standards											
Social Housing Regulatory Authorities											
Informal Settlement Upgrade Support											
Financial Charter and Housing credit											
Community Residential Units/ FLIPS											
Incremental housing											

Q16: Are there any housing policy instruments that in your opinion **IMPACT** public housing delivery in South Africa that has not been addressed? If any, please state the factor and rate the **IMPACT**

Housing Policy Instruments not listed:	

Q17: Do you think that South Africa Housing Policy through the mixed-income housing development approach will be able to address the issue of segregation, gated communities and racial separation of the built environment?

Agreement:

☐ Strongly disagree
☐ Disagree
☐ No opinion
☐ Agree
☐ Strongly Agree

Q18: Mixed-income housing can provide both direct and indirect positive response to the challenge of providing affordable housing to the 'poorest of the poor'.

Agreement:

☐ Strongly disagree
☐ Disagree
☐ No opinion
☐ Agree
☐ Strongly Agree

Q19: Do you think that mixed-income housing development is an essential tool that can aid in attracting broad political support and change in policy debate for affordable housing?

Agreement:

☐ Strongly disagree
☐ Disagree
☐ No opinion
☐ Agree
☐ Strongly Agree

Q20: Do you think that mixed-income housing development through good design and quality delivery will at any stage in the future change the perception of people towards affordable housing?

Agreement:

☐ Strongly disagree
☐ Disagree
☐ No opinion
☐ Agree
☐ Strongly Agree

Q21: Can mixed-income housing development at any point in time from your opinion ever going to be considered as an asset to the community?

Agreement:

☐ Strongly disagree
☐ Disagree
☐ No opinion
☐ Agree
☐ Strongly Agree

Q22: Please identify any critical issues affecting the provision of housing for the low-income group in South Africa through mixed-income housing strategies that is currently implemented in different municipalities.

Critical issues:	

Q23: The greater the supply of affordable, moderate and middle-income housing, the greater the range of housing options available to these households and more difficult it is for mixed-income housing to attract them?

Agreement:

☐ Strongly disagree
☐ Disagree
☐ No opinion
☐ Agree
☐ Strongly Agree

Q24: Which of the following conditions do you consider to be of extreme importance in attracting higher income households in mixed-income housing development to reduce vacancy rate?

Determinants of Mixed-Income		**Rank**
Location of the development	1	
Cost of the units	2	
Design and aesthetics	3	
Size of the house	4	
Social Amenities	5	
Condition of the Neighbourhood	6	

Comment:	

Q25: Which of the following housing delivery models will best respond to the needs of the low-income, middle-income and high-income group in South Africa?

Housing delivery models		**Rank**
Public housing (through the provision of free subsidy)	1	
Self-help housing	2	
Enabling the market to work	3	
Mixed-income housing	4	
Provision of social housing (rental option)	5	
Hostel Upgrade / CRU	6	
National Upgrade Support Programme	7	

Q26: Do you consider the viability of mixed-income housing to depend to a great extent on the state of region's housing market and physical attributes of the development?

Agreement:

☐ Strongly disagree
☐ Disagree
☐ No opinion
☐ Agree
☐ Strongly Agree

Q27: To attract market-rate tenants and minimize vacancy losses developers of mixed-income housing may need to invest more resources in quality schools and social amenities?

Agreement:

☐ Strongly disagree
☐ Disagree
☐ No opinion
☐ Agree
☐ Strongly Agree

Q28: When do you predict government will end the current model of housing delivery to the poor and switch to mixed-income housing development strategy in South Africa?

Agreement:

- ☐ 6 months' time
- ☐ 1 – 2 years' time
- ☐ 3 – 5 years' time
- ☐ 6 – 8 years' time
- ☐ 9 – 10 years and above
- ☐ 10 years and above

Q29: Why is the demand for market-rate units in mixed-income housing lower than affordable units?

Comments:	

Q30: What do you envisage will be the turnaround strategies of the South Africa Housing policy in the next 10–15 years?

Pivotal context:	

Q31: Please list and rank accordingly the prospects or what to be expected from the development of mixed-income housing development at the National, Provincial, and the local government housing agencies in South Africa (1 being most important, 5 being least important).

Rank

____ A.) ____________________

____ B.) ____________________

____ C.) ____________________

____ D.) ____________________

____ E.) ____________________

Q32: Please list and rank accordingly the challenges and obstacles that affects prospects of the development of mixed-income housing development at the National, Provincial and the local government housing agencies in South Africa (1 being most important, 5 being least important).

Rank

____ A.)

____ B.)

____ C.)

____ D.)

____ E.)

Q33: Please list and rank the housing development strategies and management issues that will affect mixed-income housing development at the National, Provincial and the local government agencies in the next 10 years or in the future in South Africa plan (1 being most important, 5 being least important).

Rank

____ A.)

____ B.) ____

____ C.) ____

____ D.)

____ E.) ____

Q34: The problem of unemployment and side effects of concentrated poverty in urban areas can be addressed with proper planned mixed-income housing development?

Agreement:

☐ Strongly disagree
☐ Disagree
☐ No opinion
☐ Agree
☐ Strongly Agree

Q35: If you strongly disagree to the previous statement, what do you think?

To address issue of urban poverty :	

Q36: Mixed-income housing development impact negatively to the surrounding neighbourhood in terms of decrease in property value?

Agreement:

☐ Strongly disagree
☐ Disagree
☐ No opinion
☐ Agree
☐ Strongly Agree

Q37: If you disagreed to the previous statement, what do you think?

The impact of mixed-income:	

Q38: Which of the following characteristics in the South African mixed-income housing projects do you consider that might impede social interaction'?

Attributes		**Rank**
Race	1	
Ethnicity and Language	2	
Socio-economic status	3	
Gender	4	
Housing Typology	5	

Q39: Access to housing and a place to live is on top of the priorities of the poor and low-income group in South Africa?

Agreement:

☐ Strongly disagree
☐ Disagree
☐ No opinion
☐ Agree
☐ Strongly Agree

Q40: If you disagreed to the previous statement, what do you think should be the paramount needs of the poor and low-income group in South Africa that the government should give priority?

Principal needs:	

Q41: Public participation and the need to get everyone on board is a big challenge to the developer and affordable housing development, including mixed-income housing?

Agreement:

☐ Strongly disagree
☐ Disagree
☐ No opinion
☐ Agree
☐ Strongly Agree

Q42: Statutory Town Planning regulations and municipal compliance tend to delay the development of mixed-income housing development and impact on the project cost?

Agreement:

☐ Strongly disagree
☐ Disagree
☐ No opinion
☐ Agree
☐ Strongly Agree

Q43: Access to strategic prime land for human settlement development is a very big obstacle to the successful roll out and provision of affordable housing, especially mixed-income housing?

Agreement:

☐ Strongly disagree
☐ Disagree
☐ No opinion
☐ Agree
☐ Strongly Agree

Q44: Access to reliable finance is a very big obstacle to the developers for rapid roll out of mixed-income housing units?

Agreement:

☐ Strongly disagree
☐ Disagree
☐ No opinion
☐ Agree
☐ Strongly Agree

Q45: If you disagreed to the previous statement, what other factors hinder the development?

Comments:	

Personal Information of Expert Panel Member

Title (Mr., Mrs., Ms., Dr., Prof.)	
Highest qualification	
Field of specialisation	
Professional registration (SACPLAN, RTPI, SCPQSP, FCIOB, SACPCMP, ECSA etc.)	
Years of experience (housing studies, development studies, project management, construction, developer, planner policy analyst etc.)	
Province, State, Country and Metropolitan Municipality currently residing	
Country	
Continent	
Have you lived in other Metropolitan Municipality(s) before	
If yes, kindly state	

Thank you for taking your time to fill out this first round survey. The second round of the Delphi process will begin on 25 February 2015.

Please do not hesitate to contact me or my promoter **Professor Wellington Didibhuku Thwala** if you have any questions about this survey or about the research project in general. Kindly see contact details below.

Contact details:
George Onatu
PhD Candidate
Department of Town and Regional Planning, University of Johannesburg
Doornfontein Campus 2028;
Johannesburg, South Africa.
Tel.: +27115596428;
Mobile: +27733630388
Email: gonatu@uj.ac.za

Promoter

Professor Wellington Didibhuku Thwala PhD (Eng.) Pr CPM, FCIOB, Pr. Pln, MSAPI
Professor of Construction Project Management
Masters Programme Co-ordinator
Tel: +27 (0)11 559 6048
Fax: +27 (0) 11 559 6630
Mobile: +27 83 383 5537
Email: didibhukut@uj.ac.za
Website: http://www.uj.ac.za/EN/Faculties/engineering/departments/cmqs/about/Staff/Pages/DidibhukuThwala.aspx
Department of Construction Management and Quantity Surveying
Faculty of Engineering and the Built Environment
University of Johannesburg
South Africa

Appendix 2: Instrument Used for the Research – Delphi Round 2

Delphi Survey – Round 2 (Q2)

This questionnaire is drawn for a PhD thesis on Mixed-Income Housing Development Model for South Africa. The questionnaire is intended to solicit the opinion of experts and their views on this topic in an anonymous manner not known to other contributors that are part of the sample group. All the information provided will be used solely for this purpose. The confidentiality of the participants will be guided and protected in line with ethics of research. We appreciate your acceptance to partake on the Delphi panel for this research. Thank you so much for your understanding, time and expected valued response to the first round of questionnaire.

This is the second round of the three series of questionnaire that will inform this research and at this stage it is intended to be completed just in approximately 20–25 minutes. The last round after this will even require significantly less time to complete. Please return your response, in Word format, to gonatu@uj.ac.za by 20th of June, 2015.

Instructions

4. Please indicate your response by placing an 'X' in the appropriate boxes.
5. Experts are also required to state their levels of agreement using a 5-point Likert Scale with certain statement and to support their choices where necessary with regards to South Africa human settlement policy, programme, issues and the future of mixed-income housing in order to arrive at a consensus.

List of Questions for This Research

Q1: Mixed-income housing development in South Africa is designed to enhance and promote integrated human settlements to accommodate households with disparate incomes band.

☐ Strongly disagree
☐ Disagree
☐ No opinion
☐ Agree
☐ Strongly Agree

Q2: Mixed-income housing development can lead to strong community building and correct previous Apartheid segregated settlement and planning.

Agreement:

☐ Strongly disagree
☐ Disagree
☐ No opinion
☐ Agree
☐ Strongly Agree

Q3: It is necessary for there to be strong and good intergovernmental relationship and coordination for the delivery of mixed-income housing development.

Agreement:

☐ Strongly disagree
☐ Disagree
☐ No opinion
☐ Agree
☐ Strongly Agree

Q4: An important issue that is lacking in the development of mixed-income housing development is the level of cooperation between the public sector and private sector.

Agreement:

☐ Strongly disagree
☐ Disagree
☐ No opinion
☐ Agree
☐ Strongly Agree

Q5: If you strongly disagree to the previous statement, what do you think?

Your comment	

Q6: Strong Leadership from Government is of high importance in any human settlement project development and planning including mixed-income housing.

Agreement:

☐ Strongly disagree
☐ Disagree
☐ No opinion
☐ Agree
☐ Strongly Agree

Q7: Access to finance is not a major obstacle or impediment for the developer in the implementation of mixed-income housing development.

Agreement:

☐ Strongly disagree
☐ Disagree
☐ No opinion
☐ Agree
☐ Strongly Agree

Q8: If you strongly disagree to the previous statement, what do you think?

Your comment	

Q9: Access to integrated Public Transport system and provision of social amenities are important elements to be considered in a mixed-income housing development project.

Agreement:

☐ Strongly disagree
☐ Disagree
☐ No opinion
☐ Agree
☐ Strongly Agree

Q10: Of current concern is the percentage of Low-cost units (RDP) that is permissible in a given mixed-income housing development project and its impact on the viability of the project.

Agreement:

☐ Strongly disagree
☐ Disagree
☐ No opinion
☐ Agree
☐ Strongly Agree

Q11: Of current concern is the increase in cost that the delay and long process in getting Town Planning approvals and adhering to the Land use regulations is having on mixed-income housing development projects.

Agreement:

☐ Strongly disagree
☐ Disagree
☐ No opinion
☐ Agree
☐ Strongly Agree

Q12: Of great concern to the roll out of more mixed-income housing development is the high cost of prime land for development.

Agreement:

☐ Strongly disagree
☐ Disagree
☐ No opinion
☐ Agree
☐ Strongly Agree

Q13: Nearness to upmarket housing units can slow the approval and implementation of mixed-income housing development due to objections and resistance from neighbours.

Agreement:

☐ Strongly disagree
☐ Disagree
☐ No opinion
☐ Agree
☐ Strongly Agree

Q14: The occupancy rate in any completed mixed-income housing development is very slow and unsustainable.

Agreement:

☐ Strongly disagree
☐ Disagree
☐ No opinion
☐ Agree
☐ Strongly Agree

Q15: If you strongly disagree to the previous statement, what do you think?

Your comment	

Q16: Backyard shacks are not major issues for consideration in the implementation of mixed-income housing development.

Agreement:

☐ Strongly disagree
☐ Disagree
☐ No opinion
☐ Agree
☐ Strongly Agree

Any other comments	

Q17: Mixed-income housing development is believed to enhance and broaden affordability of housing in South Africa.

Agreement:

☐ Strongly disagree
☐ Disagree
☐ No opinion
☐ Agree
☐ Strongly Agree

Q18: The return on investment is good for any completed mixed-income housing development.

Agreement:

☐ Strongly disagree
☐ Disagree
☐ No opinion
☐ Agree
☐ Strongly Agree

Any other comments:		

Q19: Compliance to the National Homebuilders Registration Council and other statutory regulations is a major obstacle to the increase in roll out of mixed-income housing development.

Agreement:

☐ Strongly disagree
☐ Disagree
☐ No opinion
☐ Agree
☐ Strongly Agree

Q20: Government support for integrated human settlement is currently shifting towards mixed-income housing development.

Agreement:

☐ Strongly disagree
☐ Disagree
☐ No opinion
☐ Agree
☐ Strongly Agree

Q21: Mixed-income is considered to bring along with it local economic development to the surrounding areas.

Agreement:

☐ Strongly disagree
☐ Disagree
☐ No opinion
☐ Agree
☐ Strongly Agree

Q22: The aesthetic beauty of the housing units and the layout design will attract high income earners.

Agreement:

☐ Strongly disagree
☐ Disagree
☐ No opinion
☐ Agree
☐ Strongly Agree

Q23: The location of the development is of concern on whether it will attract higher income earners or not?

Agreement:

☐ Strongly disagree
☐ Disagree
☐ No opinion
☐ Agree
☐ Strongly Agree

Q24: Do you think that mixed-income housing development through good design and quality product will at any stage in the future change the perception of people towards affordable housing?

Agreement:

☐ Strongly disagree
☐ Disagree
☐ No opinion
☐ Agree
☐ Strongly Agree

Q25: Availability of good quality school and other social amenities will increase the occupancy rate of mixed-income by high income earners?

Agreement:

☐ Strongly disagree
☐ Disagree
☐ No opinion
☐ Agree
☐ Strongly Agree

Q26: The social acceptance of mixed-income housing development is very low in South Africa.

Agreement:

☐ Strongly disagree
☐ Disagree
☐ No opinion
☐ Agree
☐ Strongly Agree

Q27: In 9–10 years from now Government will shift totally to mixed-income housing development.

Agreement:

☐ Strongly disagree
☐ Disagree
☐ No opinion
☐ Agree
☐ Strongly Agree

Q28: If you strongly disagree to the previous statement, what do you think?

Your comment	

Q29: Factors at the National, Provincial and Local levels all impact on mixed-income housing development as the projects typically involves complicated multilevel coordination

Agreement:

☐ Strongly disagree
☐ Disagree
☐ No opinion
☐ Agree
☐ Strongly Agree

Comment:	

Q30: The problem associated with informal settlements and social ills of concentrated poverty can be addressed with mixed-income housing development.

Agreement:

☐ Strongly disagree
☐ Disagree
☐ No opinion
☐ Agree
☐ Strongly Agree

Q31: Mixed-income housing development initiatives if well implemented can play an active role in creating foundational environment in which other poverty alleviation strategies can be tackled.

Agreement:

☐ Strongly disagree
☐ Disagree
☐ No opinion
☐ Agree
☐ Strongly Agree

Q32: There is no strong evidence about the revitalization of neighbourhood by mixed-income housing development.

Agreement:

☐ Strongly disagree
☐ Disagree
☐ No opinion
☐ Agree
☐ Strongly Agree

Q33: Of great concern is the lack of Public participation and community involvement in the decision-making for mixed-income housing development.

Agreement:

☐ Strongly disagree
☐ Disagree
☐ No opinion
☐ Agree
☐ Strongly Agree

Q34: Of concern is that inner-city mixed-income housing initiatives are not interventions to serve low-income households, but methods to grow city economies by substantial increase in land values.

Agreement:

☐ Strongly disagree
☐ Disagree
☐ No opinion
☐ Agree
☐ Strongly Agree

Q35: Good management of the differing needs of income diverse residents as well as ability to manage the challenges associated with effective coordination between public and private sectors is seen as essential to mixed-income success.

Agreement:

☐ Strongly disagree
☐ Disagree
☐ No opinion
☐ Agree
☐ Strongly Agree

Q36: Do you think that the drive towards mixed-income housing development will eradicate informal settlements in the near future?

Agreement:

☐ Strongly disagree
☐ Disagree
☐ No opinion
☐ Agree
☐ Strongly Agree

Q37: Mixed-income housing development is a good initiative in that it creates healthy and safe place to live, work and play.

Agreement:

☐ Strongly disagree
☐ Disagree
☐ No opinion
☐ Agree
☐ Strongly Agree

Q38: The lack of bulk infrastructure is seen as one of the impediments and obstacle to the development of mixed-income housing development.

Agreement:

☐ Strongly disagree
☐ Disagree
☐ No opinion
☐ Agree
☐ Strongly Agree

Q39: There is lack of capacity within Government and other municipal structures to drive mixed-income housing development.

Agreement:

☐ Strongly disagree
☐ Disagree
☐ No opinion
☐ Agree
☐ Strongly Agree

Q40: If you strongly disagree to the previous statement, what do you think?

Your comment	

Q41: Proper branding and setting up mixed-income housing development steering committee or mechanism is seen as an important approach to the sustainability of projects.

<u>Agreement:</u>

☐ Strongly disagree
☐ Disagree
☐ No opinion
☐ Agree
☐ Strongly Agree

Q42: If you disagreed to the previous statement, what do you think?

Any other comments:	

Q43: The turnaround in Human Settlements policy in South Africa in the near future is a shift from subsidy housing towards self-help/assisted housing programme.

<u>Agreement:</u>

☐ Strongly disagree
☐ Disagree
☐ No opinion
☐ Agree
☐ Strongly Agree

Q44: If you disagreed to the previous statement, what do you think?

Any other comments:	

Q45: Gender is considered an issue with respect to social interaction within the mixed-income housing development.

<u>Agreement:</u>

☐ Strongly disagree
☐ Disagree
☐ No opinion
☐ Agree
☐ Strongly Agree

Q46: If you disagreed to the previous statement, what do you think?

Any other comments:	

Q47: The state of the economy has a negative impact on the development of the mixed-income housing development.

Agreement:

☐ Strongly disagree
☐ Disagree
☐ No opinion
☐ Agree
☐ Strongly Agree

Q48: If you disagreed to the previous statement, what do you think?

Any other comments:	

Personal Information of Expert Panel Member

Title (Mr., Mrs., Ms., Dr., Prof.)	
Highest qualification	
Field of specialisation	
Professional registration (SACPLAN, RTPI, SCPQSP, FCIOB, SACPCMP, ECSA etc.)	
Years of experience (housing studies, development studies, project management, construction, developer, planner policy analyst etc.)	
Province, State, Country and Metropolitan Municipality currently residing	
Country	
Continent	
Have you lived in other Metropolitan Municipality(s) before	
If yes, kindly state	

Thank you for taking your time to fill out this second round survey. The third round of the Delphi process will begin on 25 June, 2015.

Please do not hesitate to contact me or my promoter **Professor Wellington Didibhuku Thwala** if you have any questions about this survey or about the research project in general. Kindly see contact details below.

Contact details:

George Onatu
PhD Candidate
Department of Town and Regional Planning, University of Johannesburg
Doornfontein Campus 2028;
Johannesburg, South Africa.
Tel.: +27115596428;
Mobile: +27733630388
Email: gonatu@uj.ac.za

Promoter

Professor Wellington Didibhuku Thwala PhD (Eng.) Pr CPM, FCIOB, Pr. Pln, MSAPI
Professor of Construction Project Management
Masters Programme Co-ordinator
Tel: +27 (0)11 559 6048
Fax: +27 (0) 11 559 6630
Mobile: +27 83 383 5537
Email: didibhukut@uj.ac.za
Website: http://www.uj.ac.za/EN/Faculties/engineering/departments/cmqs/about/Staff/Pages/DidibhukuThwala.aspx
Department of Construction Management and Quantity Surveying
Faculty of Engineering and the Built Environment
University of Johannesburg
South Africa

Appendix 3: Instrument Used for the Research – Delphi Round 3

Delphi Survey – Round 3 (Q3)

This questionnaire is drawn for a PhD thesis on Mixed-Income Housing Development Model for South Africa. The questionnaire is intended to solicit the opinion of experts' and their views on this topic in an anonymous manner not known to other contributors that are part of the sample group. All the information provided will be used solely for this purpose. The confidentiality of the participants will be guided and protected in line with ethics of research. We appreciate your acceptance to partake on the Delphi panel for this research. Thank you so much for your understanding, time and expected valued response to the first and second round of questionnaire.

This is the third and final round of the three series of questionnaire that will inform this research and will take approximately 20–25 minutes to complete. In this round, you will find statement from the second round where consensus was not reached. Results of feedback and answers from all the experts that has been participating in this research survey are listed below each statement. You have the opportunity at this stage to change any of your answers you gave in the second round if you wish or choose not to. Also, if you find that your answer to any item is an outlier from those of other experts and do not wish to change your response, or if you feel that you want to contribute more additional information on any of the statements, you have the option to do so in the comments section below. Please return your response, in Word format, to gonatu@uj.ac.za by 15th of October, 2015. Since this is the final round, your answers will be analyzed with those of other participants and at the end of the study we shall send to you the compiled data and outcome for your personal use.

Once again, thank you so much for your kindness on this journey so far.

Instructions

(6) Please indicate your response by placing an 'X' in the appropriate boxes.
(7) Experts are also required to state their levels of agreement using this 5-point Likert Scale.

List of Questions for This Research

Q1: Mixed-income housing development in South Africa is designed to enhance and promote integrated human settlements to accommodate households with disparate incomes band.

☐ Strongly disagree
X ☐ Disagree
☐ No opinion
☐ Agree **5**
☐ Strongly Agree **7**

Comment … **The challenge in SA is the base spatial structure created by apartheid. Initiatives are being done as stand-alone projects and do not have influence on the macro & meso-spatial structure rather impact the micro and precinct level. This is good but not adequate in addressing the fundamentals associated with mixed housing development**……………………………

Q2: Mixed-income housing development can lead to strong community building and correct previous Apartheid segregated settlement and planning.

Agreement:

☐ Strongly disagree
☐ X Disagree
☐ No opinion **2**
☐ Agree **5**
☐ Strongly Agree **5**

Comment While theoretically and rhetoric supports this, the reality is that on its own mixed income developments cannot achieve this in SA given the SA history. However supplemented by other supporting programmes and activities such as adequate communal and sporting facilities; fan parks; food festivals; campaigns against any form of social and political exclusions and violence etc. then the goals can be approached……………………………

Q3: It is necessary for there to be strong and good intergovernmental relationship and coordination for the delivery of Mixed-income housing development.

Agreement:

☐ Strongly disagree
☐ Disagree
☐ No opinion
☐ Agree
☐ X Strongly Agree **12**

Comment.............. **This is necessary to address the big framework housing agenda issues such as inclusion, integration, and construction friendly technology transfer platforms etc. as well as good governance. These act as preconditions for sustainable mixed housing development and replication** ....

Q4: An important issue that is lacking in the development of mixed-income housing development is the level of cooperation between the public sector and private sector.

Agreement:

☐ Strongly disagree
☐ Disagree
☐ No opinion
☐ X Agree **10**
☐ Strongly Agree **2**

Comment...

Q5: Strong Leadership from Government is of high importance in any human settlement project development and planning including mixed-income housing.

Agreement:

☐ Strongly disagree
☐ Disagree
☐ No opinion
☐ Agree **2**
☐ X Strongly Agree **10**

Comment...

Q6: Access to finance is not a major obstacle or impediment for the developer in the implementation of mixed-income housing development.

Agreement:

☐ X Strongly disagree **8**
☐ Disagree **2**
☐ No opinion **2**
☐ Agree
☐ Strongly Agree

Comment...

Q7: Access to integrated Public Transport system and provision of social amenities are important elements to be considered in a mixed-income housing development project.

Agreement:

☐ Strongly disagree **2**
☐ Disagree
☐ No opinion
☐ Agree **5**
☐ X Strongly Agree **5**

Comment...

Q8: Of current concern is the percentage of Low-cost units (RDP) that is permissible in a given mixed-income housing development project and its impact on the viability of the project.

Agreement:

☐ Strongly disagree
☐ X Disagree **5**
☐ No opinion **5**
☐ Agree
☐ Strongly Agree **2**

Comment...

Q9: Of current concern is the increase in cost that the delay and long process in getting Town Planning approvals and adhering to the Land use regulations is having on mixed-income housing development projects.

Agreement:

☐ X Strongly disagree
☐ Disagree
☐ No opinion
☐ Agree **3**
☐ Strongly Agree **9**

Comment...**with SPLUMA roll out the landscape should slowly shift in this regard**...

Q10: Of great concern to the roll out of more mixed-income housing development is the high cost of prime land for development.

Agreement:

☐ Strongly disagree
☐ Disagree
☐ No opinion
☐ Agree **3**
☐ X Strongly Agree **9**

Comment. . . . .

Q11: Nearness to upmarket housing units can slow the approval and implementation of mixed-income housing development due to objections and resistance from neighbours.

Agreement:

☐ Strongly disagree
☐ Disagree **2**
☐ No opinion **2**
☐ Agree **6**
☐ X Strongly Agree **2**

Comment. . . . .

Q12: The occupancy rate in any completed mixed-income housing development is very slow and unsustainable.

Agreement:

☐ Strongly disagree **5**
☐ Disagree **5**
☐ No opinion
☐ X Agree **2**
☐ Strongly Agree

Comment. . . . .

Q13: Backyard shacks are not major issues for consideration in the implementation of mixed-income housing development.

Agreement:

☐ X Strongly disagree **5**
☐ Disagree
☐ No opinion
☐ Agree **2**
☐ Strongly Agree **5**

Comment. . . . .

Q14: Mixed-income housing development is believed to enhance and broaden affordability of housing in South Africa.

<u>Agreement:</u>

☐ Strongly disagree
☐ X Disagree **3**
☐ No opinion
☐ Agree **8**
☐ Strongly Agree **1**

Comment. . . . .

Q15: The return on investment is good for any completed mixed-income housing development.

<u>Agreement:</u>

☐ Strongly disagree
☐ Disagree
☐ X No opinion
☐ Agree **8**
☐ Strongly Agree **4**

Comment. . . . .

Q16: Compliance to the National Homebuilders Registration Council and other statutory regulations is a major obstacle to the increase in roll out of mixed-income housing development.

<u>Agreement:</u>

☐ X Strongly disagree **2**
☐ Disagree **6**
☐ No opinion
☐ Agree **2**
☐ Strongly Agree **2**

Comment. . . . .

Q17: Government support for integrated human settlement is currently shifting towards mixed-income housing development.

<u>Agreement:</u>

☐ Strongly disagree
☐ Disagree
☐ No opinion **4**
☐ X Agree **4**
☐ Strongly Agree **6**

Comment. . . . .

Q18: Mixed-income is considered to bring along with it local economic development to the surrounding areas.

Agreement:

☐ Strongly disagree
☐ Disagree
☐ No opinion
☐ X Agree **7**
☐ Strongly Agree **5**

Comment. . . . .

Q22: The aesthetic beauty of the housing units and the layout design will attract high-income earners.

Agreement:

☐ Strongly disagree
☐ Disagree
☐ No opinion
☐ Agree **8**
☐ X Strongly Agree **4**

Comment. . . . .

Q23: The location of the development is of concern on whether it will attract higher income earners or not?

Agreement:

☐ Strongly disagree
☐ Disagree
☐ No opinion
☐ Agree **8**
☐ X Strongly Agree **4**

Comment. . . . .

Q24: Do you think that mixed-income housing development through good design and quality product will at any stage in the future change the perception of people towards affordable housing?

Agreement:

☐ Strongly disagree
☐ Disagree
☐ No opinion
☐ X Agree **5**
☐ Strongly Agree **7**

Comment. . . . .

Q25: Availability of good quality school and other social amenities will increase the occupancy rate of mixed-income by high-income earners?

Agreement:

☐ Strongly disagree
☐ Disagree **2**
☐ No opinion
☐ X Agree **5**
☐ Strongly Agree **5**

Comment. . . . .

Q26: The social acceptance of mixed-income housing development is very low in South Africa.

Agreement:

☐ Strongly disagree
☐ X Disagree **8**
☐ No opinion **2**
☐ Agree **2**
☐ Strongly Agree

Comment. . . . .

Q27: In 9–10 years from now Government will shift totally to mixed-income housing development.

Agreement:

☐ Strongly disagree
☐ Disagree
☐ No opinion **2**
☐ X Agree **5**
☐ Strongly Agree **5**

Comment. . . . .

Q28: Factors at the National, Provincial and Local levels all impact on mixed-income housing development as the projects typically involves complicated multilevel coordination

Agreement:

☐ Strongly disagree
☐ Disagree
☐ No opinion **12**
☐ Agree
☐ X Strongly Agree

Comment. . . . .

Q30: The problem associated with informal settlements and social ills of concentrated poverty can be addressed with mixed-income housing development.

<u>Agreement:</u>

☐ Strongly disagree
☐ X Disagree
☐ No opinion
☐ Agree **4**
☐ Strongly Agree **8**

Comment. . . . .

Q31: Mixed-income housing development initiatives if well implemented can play an active role in creating foundational environment in which other poverty alleviation strategies can be tackled.

<u>Agreement:</u>

☐ Strongly disagree
☐ Disagree
☐ No opinion
☐ Agree **5**
☐ X Strongly Agree **7**

Comment. . . . .

Q31: There is no strong evidence about the revitalization of neighbourhood by mixed-income housing development.

<u>Agreement:</u>

☐ Strongly disagree **6**
☐ X Disagree **3**
☐ No opinion
☐ Agree **3**
☐ Strongly Agree

Comment. . . . . **Grey evidence exists, the problem is it is scant and far and in between**. . . . .

Q33: Of great concern is the lack of Public participation and community involvement in the decision-making for mixed-income housing development.

<u>Agreement:</u>

☐ Strongly disagree **2**
☐ Disagree **5**
☐ No opinion
☐ Agree
☐ X Strongly Agree **2**

Comment. . . . .

Q34: Of concern is that inner-city mixed-income housing initiatives are not interventions to serve low-income households, but methods to grow city economies by substantial increase in land values.

Agreement:

☐ Strongly disagree
☐ Disagree
☐ No opinion **5**
☐ X Agree **5**
☐ Strongly Agree **2**

Comment. . . . .

Q35: Good management of the differing needs of income diverse residents as well as ability to manage the challenges associated with effective coordination between public and private sectors is seen as essential to mixed-income success.

Agreement:

☐ Strongly disagree
☐ Disagree
☐ No opinion
☐ X Agree **4**
☐ Strongly Agree **8**

Comment. . . . .

Q36: Do you think that the drive towards mixed-income housing development will eradicate informal settlements in the near future?

Agreement:

☐ Strongly disagree **2**
☐ X Disagree **8**
☐ No opinion
☐ Agree
☐ Strongly Agree **2**

Comment. . . . .

Q37: Mixed-income housing development is a good initiative in that it creates healthy and safe place to live, work and play.

Agreement:

☐ Strongly disagree
☐ X Disagree
☐ No opinion
☐ Agree **4**
☐ Strongly Agree **8**

Comment . . . **The outcome is not linear and is dependent on other factors. Mixing income groups sometimes accentuates the differences and increases the likelihood of the less privileged targeting the privileged through covert and disguised crime syndicates, etc**. . . . .

Q38: The lack of bulk infrastructure is seen as one of the impediments and obstacle to the development of mixed-income housing development.

Agreement:

☐ Strongly disagree
☐ Disagree
☐ No opinion
☐ X Agree **5**
☐ Strongly Agree **7**

Comment. . . . .

Q39: There is lack of capacity within Government and other municipal structures to drive mixed-income housing development.

Agreement:

☐ Strongly disagree
☐ Disagree
☐ No opinion
☐ Agree **5**
☐ X Strongly Agree **7**

Comment. . . . .

Q40: Proper branding and setting up mixed-income housing development steering committee or mechanism is seen as an important approach to the sustainability of projects.

Agreement:

☐ Strongly disagree
☐ Disagree
☐ No opinion **2**
☐ Agree **5**
☐ X Strongly Agree **5**

Comment. . . . .

Q41: The turnaround in Human Settlements policy in South Africa in the near future is a shift from subsidy housing towards self-help/assisted housing programme.

Agreement:

☐ Strongly disagree
☐ Disagree **2**
☐ No opinion
☐ Agree **2**
☐ X Strongly Agree **8**

Comment. . . . . **State funding is increasingly dwindling and can never be expected to be enough to address all the housing issues in any country, South Africa included**. . . . .

Q42: If you disagreed to the previous statement, what do you think?

Any other comments:	

Q43: Gender is considered an issue with respect to social interaction within the mixed-income housing development.

<u>Agreement:</u>

☐ X Strongly disagree **3**
☐ Disagree **3**
☐ No opinion **3**
☐ Agree **3**
☐ Strongly Agree

Comment ... **SA societies are increasingly becoming multiracial and are indeed cosmopolitan hence the new and emerging challenges of managing and incorporating international migrants (i.e. in terms of Xenophobia and its housing dimensions especially in the context of this study)**
....

Q44: The state of the economy has a negative impact on the development of the mixed-income housing development.

<u>Agreement:</u>

☐ Strongly disagree **2**
☐ Disagree
☐ No opinion **4**
☐ X Agree **6**
☐ Strongly Agree

Comment ... **Housing and construction development by its nature requires a lot of investment. Consequent a slow economy has limited options for experimenting and developers will go for tried and tested standard housing solutions that may exclude mixed income housing**..

Personal Information of Expert Panel Member

Title (Mr., Mrs., Ms., Dr., Prof.)	
Highest qualification	
Field of specialisation	
Professional registration (SACPLAN, RTPI, SCPQSP, FCIOB, SACPCMP, ECSA etc.)	
Years of experience (housing studies, development studies, project management, construction, developer, planner policy analyst etc.)	
Province, State, Country and Metropolitan Municipality currently residing	
Country	
Continent	
Have you lived in other Metropolitan Municipality(s) before	
If yes, kindly state	

Thank you for taking your time to fill out this third round survey and we shall make available to you the outcome of this important research work.

Please do not hesitate to contact me or my promoter **Professor Wellington Didibhuku Thwala** if you have any questions about this survey or about the research project in general. Kindly see contact details below.

Contact details:

George Onatu
PhD Candidate
Department of Town and Regional Planning, University of Johannesburg
Doornfontein Campus 2028;
Johannesburg, South Africa.
Tel.: +27115596428;
Mobile: +27733630388
Email: gonatu@uj.ac.za

Promoter

Professor Wellington Didibhuku Thwala PhD (Eng.) Pr CPM, FCIOB, Pr. Pln, MSAPI
Professor of Construction Project Management
Masters Programme Co-ordinator
Tel: +27 (0)11 559 6048
Fax: +27 (0) 11 559 6630
Mobile: +27 83 383 5537
Email: didibhukut@uj.ac.za

Website: http://www.uj.ac.za/EN/Faculties/engineering/departments/cmqs/about/Staff/Pages/DidibhukuThwala.aspx
Department of Construction Management and Quantity Surveying
Faculty of Engineering and the Built Environment
University of Johannesburg
South Africa

References

Abbott, J. (2002). An analysis of informal settlement upgrading and critique of existing methodological approaches. *Habitat International*, vol. 26, pp. 303–315.

Abdulai, R.T. (2006). Is land title registration the answer to insecure and uncertain property rights in sub-Sahara Africa? *RICS Research Paper Series*, vol. 6, no. 4, pp. 1–28.

Abercrombie, N., Hill, S. & Turner, S.T. (1984). *Dictionary of sociology*. Harmondsworth: Penguin.

Adams, M., Kalabamu, F. & White, R. (2003). Land tenure policy and practice in Botswana-Governance lessons for southern Africa. *Journal fur Entwicklungspolitik*, vol. 19, no. 1, pp. 55–74.

Adarkwa, K. (2012). The changing face of Ghanaian towns. *African Review of Economics and Finance*.

Adarkwa, K.K. (ed.) (2014). *Human settlements and service delivery in Ghana*. Kumasi: Kwame Nkrumah University of Science and Technology.

Addo, I.A. (2014). Urban low income housing development in Ghana: Politics, policy and challenges. In *Urban planning: Practices, challenges and benefits*, pp. 89–118.

Adler, M. & Ziglio, E. (1996). *Gazing into the oracle: The Delphi methods and its application to social policy and public health*. London: Jessica Kingsley Publishers.

Agbola, T. (1998). The housing of Nigeria. 'A review of policy development and implementation'. Research Report 14, Development Policy Centre, Ibadan, Nigeria.

AHURI. (2003). *What bearing do different form of housing have on social re-integration*. Australian Housing and Urban Research Institute (AHURI).

Aigbavboa, C.O. & Thwala, W.D. (2011). Quality of low income houses in Kliptown Johannesburg. In *Procs NMMU Construction Management 40 Conference (CM 40)*, Port Elizabeth, South Africa.

Aigbavboa, C.O. & Thwala, D. (2013). An integrated beneficial centred satisfaction model for publicly funded housing schemes in South Africa. PhD. (Engineering Management). [Unpublished]. University of Johannesburg. Cited from https://ujdigispace.uj.ac.za. Accessed on 10th of August, 2017.

Akiyode, O. (2011). Urbanisation trend and water insecurity in developing economy mega-city: A case study of Lagos, Nigeria. *Journal of Sustainable Development in Africa*, vol. 13, no. 3, pp. 194–212.

Albers, M., Agarwal, R. & Tanniru, M. (1994). The practice of business process reengineering: Radical planning and incremental implementation in an IS organization. In *SIGCPR'84. Proceedings of the 1994 computer personnel research conference on reinventing IS: Managing information technology in changing organizations*. Arlington, VA: ACM Press, pp. 87–96.

Ali, A.K. (2005). Using the Delphi technique to search for empirical measures of local planning agency power. *Qualitative Report*, vol. 10, no. 4, pp. 718–744.

Allison, G.T. (1971). *Essence of decision-making: Explaining the Cuban Missile Crisis*. Boston, MA: Little Brown.

Anderson, J. (1993). Is a communicative approach practical for teaching English in China? Pros and cons. *System*, vol. 21, no. 4, pp. 471–480.

Anderson, S. & Panell, R. (2006). Adverse credit mortgages. *Housing Finance*, Vol. 10. London: CML/Paragon.

Anderson, S.T. & West, S.E. (2006). Open space, residential property values, and spatial context. *Regional Science and Urban Economics*, vol. 36, no. 6, pp. 773–789.

Angel, S. (2000). *Housing policy matters: A global analysis*. Oxford: Oxford University Press.

Arku, G. (2006). Housing and development strategies in Ghana, 1945–2000. *Journal of International Development Planning Review*, vol. 28, no. 3, pp. 333–358.

Armstrong, M.A. (1989). *The Delphi technique*. Princeton Economic Institute. Cited from http://www.pei-intl.com/Research

Arthurson, K. (2004). Social mix and disadvantaged communities. *Urban Policy and Research*, vol. 22, no. 1, pp. 101–106.

Arthurson, K. (2010). Operationalising social mix: Spatial scale, lifestyle and stigma as mediating points in residents interaction. *Urban Policy and Research*, vol. 28, no. 1, pp. 49–63.

Arthurson, K. (2012). Social mix and the city. Challenging the mixed communities' consensus in housing and urban planning policies. Melbourne: CSIRO.

Atkinson, R. (2008). Commentary: Gentrification, segregation and the vocabulary of affluent residential choice. *Urban Studies*, vol. 45, no. 12, pp. 2626–2636.

Atkinson, R. & Jacobs, K. (2008). Public housing in Australia: Stigma, home and opportunities. Housing and community research unit, Hobart, Discussion Paper No. 1, pp. 1–23.

Atkinson, R. & Kintrea, K. (2000). Owner occupation, social mix and neighbourhood impacts. *Policy and Politics*, vol. 28, pp. 93–108.

August, M. (2008). Social mix and Canadian public housing redevelopment: Experiences in Toronto. *Canadian Journal of Urban Research*, vol. 17, no. 1, pp. 35–73.

Ball, M. (1998, September). Institutions in British property research: A review. *Urban Studies*, vol. 35, no. 9, pp. 1501–1517.

Barton, S.E. (1977). The urban housing problems, Marxist theory and community organising. *Review of Radical Political Economics*, vol. 9, no. 4.

Banks, E.J. (2011). *Elementary and middle school bullying: A Delphi analysis of successful prevention programming*. Capella University.

Barube, A. (2005). *Mixed communities in England: A US perspectives on evidence and policy prospectus*. Joseph Rowntree Foundation.

Bassett, K. & Short, J.R. (1980). *Housing and residential structure: Alternative approaches*. London: Routledge.

Bayor, R.H. (2003). The second ghetto: Then and now. *Journal of Urban History*, vol. 29, pp. 238–242.

Beckhoven, E. & Kempen, R.V. (2003). Social effects of urban restructuring: A case study in Amsterdam and Utrecht, The Netherlands. *Housing Studies*, vol. 18, no. 6, pp. 853–875.

Beech, B. (1999). Go the extra mile: Use the Delphi technique. *Journal of Nursing Management*, vol. 7, no. 5, pp. 281–288.

Benbasat, I. (1984). An analysis of research methodologies. In F.W. McFarlan (ed.). *The information systems research challenge*. Boston: Harvard Business School Press, pp. 47–85.

Bengtsson, B., Annaniassen, E., Jensen, L., Ruonavaara, H. & Sveinsson, J.R. (2006). *Why so divergent? Nordic housing policy in a comparative historic light*. Malmo: Egalite.

Berkman, L.F. & Kawachi, I. (2000). *Social epidemology*. Oxford: Oxford University Press.

Bertaud, A. (2004). The spatial organization of cities: Deliberate outcome or unforeseen consequences? Institute of Urban and Regional Development, IURD Working Paper Series 2004-01, pp. 1–32.

Bhattacherjee, A. (2012). *Social science research: Principles, methods, and practices*. Textbooks collection. 3. Cited from http://scholarcommons.usf.edu/oa_textbooks/3. Accessed on 24th of June, 2016.

Boer, R.W. & de Vries, J. (2009). The right to the city as a tool for urban social movements: The case of Barcelona. In *The 4th international conference of the international forum on urbanism (IFoU)*, Delft/Amsterdam. Cited from http://ifou.org. Accessed on 5th of January, 2016.

Bohl, C.C. (2000). New Urbanism and the city. Potential applications and implications for distressed inner-city neighborhoods. *Housing Policy Debate*, vol. 11, no. 4, pp. 761–801.

Bolt, G. (2004). Over spreidingsbeleid en drijfzand [On dispersal policy and quicksand]. *Migrantenstudies*, vol. 20, no. 2, pp. 60–73.

Bolt, G., Burgers, J. & Kemper, R. (1998). On the social significance of spatial location, spatial segregation and social inclusions. *Netherlands Journal of Housing and Built Environment*, vol. 13, no. 1, pp. 83–95.

Bolt, G., van Kempen, R. & van Ham, M. (2008). Minority ethnic groups in the Dutch housing market: Spatial segregation, relocation dynamics and housing policy. *Urban Studies*, vol. 45, no. 7, pp. 1359–1384.

Bond, L., Sautkina, E. & Keans, A. (2011). Mixed messages about mixed tenure: Do reviews tell the real story? *Housing Studies*, vol. 26, no. 1, pp. 69–94.

Bonoma, T.V. (1985). Case research in marketing: Opportunities, problems, and a process. *Journal of Marketing Research*, vol. 22, no. 2, pp. 199–208.

Boston, T.D. (2005). *Environment matters: The effect of mixed-income revitalization on the socioeconomic status of public housing residents: A case study of Atlanta*. Atlanta: Georgia Institute of Technology. Working Paper no. 1.

Botha, R.P. & Steyn, H. (2008). Decision-making and management of pre-investment in a programme of projects. *South African Journal of Industrial Engineering*, vol. 19, no. 2, pp. 135–148.

"Botswana". (2014, March 30). Central Intelligence Agency. Cited from https://www.cia.gov/library/publications/the-world. Accessed on the 26th of March, 2019.

Bourdieu, P. (1986). The forms of capital. In J.G. Richardson (ed.), *Handbook of theory and research for the sociology of education*. New York, NY: Greenwood Press, pp. 241–258.

Bradbury, M., Peterson, M.N. & Liu, J. (2014). Long-term dynamics of household size and their environmental implications. *Population and Environment*, vol. 36, pp. 73–84.

Breheny, M. (1992). The compact city and transport energy consumption. *Transaction of the Institute of British Geographers, New Series*, vol. 20, no. 1, pp. 81–101.

Breheny, M. (1995). *The compact city and transport energy consumption*. Transactions of the institute of British Geographers, pp. 81–101.

Briggs, X. (1997). Moving up versus moving out: Neighbourhood effects in housing mobility programms. *Housing Policy Debate*, vol. 8, no. 1, pp. 195–234.

Briggs, X.S. (1998). Brown kids in white suburbs: Housing mobility and the many faces of social capital. *Housing Policy Debate*, vol. 9, no. 1, pp. 177–221.

Briggs, X.S., Duncan, G., Edin, K., Joseph, M., Mare, R.D., Mollenkopf, J., Pattillo, M., Quillian, L., Sampson, R., Solari, L., Tach, L. & Venkatesh, S. (2009). *Research designs for the study of mixed-income housing*. California Center for Population Research, On-Line Working Paper Series, May, CCPR-2009-011. University of California, Los Angeles.

Brophy, P.C., Garcia, M. & Karen, P. (2008). Mixed-income housing: A promising approach to improved housing and neighborhoods. Unpublished manuscript.

Brophy, P.C. & Smith, R.N. (1997). Mixed-income housing: Factors for success. *Cityscape*, vol. 3, no. 2, pp. 3–31.

Brown, A.D. & Jones, M. (1998). Doomed to failure: Narrative of inevitability and conspiracy in a failed IS project. *Organizational Studies*, vol. 19, no. 1, pp. 73–88.

Brown, A. & Lloyd-Jones, T. (2002). Spatial planning, access and infrastructure. In C. Rakodi & T. Lloyd-Jones (eds.), *Urban livelihoods: A people-centred approach to reducing poverty*. London: Earthscan, pp. 188–204.

Bunyi, J. (2010). Concentric model. Cited from https://pt.slidesshare.net/morgannnx38. Accessed on 4th of January, 2016.

Burchell, R.W., Listokin, D. & Galley, C.G. (2000). Smart growth: More than a ghost of urban policy past, less than a bold new horizon. *Housing Policy Debate*, vol. 11, no. 4, pp. 821–878.

Burgess, E. (1925). The growth of the city: An introduction to a research project. In R. E. Park, E.W. Burgers & R.D. McKenzie (eds.). *The city*. Chicago: University of Chicago Press.

Burgess, R. (1977). Self-help housing: A new imperialist strategy? A critique of the turner school. *A Radical Journal of Geography*, vol. 9, no. 2, pp. 50–59.

Burgess, R. (1978). Petty commodity housing or dwellers control? A critique of John Turners views on housing policy. *World Development*. vol. 6, pp. 1105–1133.

Burgess, R. (1982). Self-help housing advocacy: A curious form of radicalism. A critique of the work of John F. C. Turner. In P.M. Ward (ed.), *Self-help housing. A critique*. London: Mansell, pp. 55–97.

Burgess, R. (1985). The limits of state self-help housing programmes. *Development and Change*, vol. 16, pp. 271–312.

Burton, E. (2000). Housing for an urban renaissance: Implications for social equity. *Journal of Housing Studies*, vol. 18, no. 4, pp. 537–562.

Burton, E. (2003). Housing for an urban renaissance: Implications for social equity. *Housing Studies*, vol. 18, no. 4, pp. 537–562.

Butterworth, B., Campbell, R. & Howard, D. (1986). The uses of short-term memory: A case study. *The Quarterly Journal of Experimental Psychology*, vol. 38, no. 4, pp. 705–737.

California Centre for Population Research CCPR. (2009). *Research design for the study of mixed-income housing*. Online Working Paper Series. Los Angeles: California University Press.

Campbell, K.E. & Lee, B.A. (1992). Sources of personal neighbor networks: Social integration, need, or time? *Social Forces*, vol. 70, no. 4, pp. 1077–1100.

Chapham, D.F., Clark, W.A. & Gibb, K. (2012). *The SAGE handbook of housing*. London: SAGE Publication Ltd.

Chaskin, R., Khare, A. & Joseph, M. (2009). Building community in mixed-income development. In *Mixed-income development study*, The University of Chicago and Case Western Reserve University, Research Brief.

Chaskin, R.J. & Joseph, M.L. (2010). Building community‘ in mixed-income developments: Assumptions, approaches, and early experiences. *Urban Affairs Review*, vol. 45, no. 3, pp. 299–335.

Chaskin, R.J. & Joseph, M.L. (2011). Social interaction in mixed-income developments: Relational expectations and emerging reality. *Journal of Urban Affairs*, vol. 33, no. 2, pp. 209–237.

Chaskin, R.J. & Joseph, M.L. (2013). Positive gentrification, social control and the ‘right to the city’ in mixed-income communities. *International Journal of Urban and Regional Research*, vol. 37, no. 2, pp. 480–502.

Chen, H., Jia, B. & Lau, S. (2008). Sustainable urban form for Chinese compact cities: Challenges of rapidly urbanizing economy. *Habitat International*, vol. 32, pp. 28–40.

Chesire, P. (2007). *Segregated neighbourhoods and mixed communities. A critical analysis*. Joseph Rowntree Foundation. London School of Economics.

Christenson, C. (1976). Proposal for a programme of empirical research into the properties of triangles. *Decision Sciences*, vol. 7, no. 3, pp. 631–648.

Christie, C.A. & Barela, E. (2005). The Delphi technique as a method for increasing inclusion in the evaluation process. *Canadian Journal of Program Evaluation*, vol. 20, no. 1, pp. 105–122.

Clampet-Lundquist, S. (2004). Hope VI relocation: Moving to new neighborhoods and building new ties. *Housing Policy Debate*, vol. 15, no. 2, pp. 415–447.

Clapham, D. (2016). *Housing policy. Encyclopedia of urban studies*. New York, NY: SAGE Publications Inc.

Clapham, D.F., Clark, W.A.V. & Gibb, K. (eds.) (2012). *The SAGE handbook of housing studies*. London: SAGE.

Clapman, D. (2001). Bringing actors back in: Towards an institutional perspective. *Housing, Theory and Society*, vol. 17, pp. 15–16.

Clayton, M. (1997). Delphi: A technique to harness expert opinion for critical decision-making tasks in education. *Journal of Educational Psychology*, vol. 17, no 4, pp. 373–386.

Coleman, J.S. (1990). *Foundations of social theory*. Cambridge, MA: Harvard University Press.

Coulton, C.J. & Pandey, S. (1992). Geographic concentration of poverty and risk to children in urban neighborhoods. *American Behavioral Scientist*, vol. 35, no. 3, pp. 238–257.

Council for Scientific and Industrial Research (CSIR). (2002). *National survey*. Pretoria: Mimeo, CSIR.

Cowan, J.S.P. (2009). *Environmental justice after Hurricane Katrina: A Delphi approach to determining the ethics and future of public housing policies in New Orleans*. Oklahoma State University.

Crane, J. (1991). Effects of neighborhood on dropping out of school and teenage childbearing. In C. Jencks & P. Perterson (eds.), *The urban underclass*. Washington, DC: Brookings Institution.

Crane, J. (1991). Effects of neighborhood on dropping out of school and teenage childbearing. In C. Jencks & P. Peterson (eds.), *The urban underclass*. Washington, DC: Brookings Institution.

Creswell, J.W. (2003). *Research design: Qualitative, quantitative and mixed methods approaches*. 2nd edition. London: SAGE Publications.

Curley, A.M. (2005). Theories of urban poverty and implication for public housing policy. *Journal of Sociology & Social Welfare*, vol. 32, no. 2, pp. 97–117.

Cyert, R.M., Simon, H.A. & Trow, D.B. (1956). Observation of a business decision. *The Journal of Business*, vol. 29, no. 4, pp. 237–248.

Dalkey, N. & Helmer, O. (1963). An experimental application of the Delphi method to the use of experts. *Management Science*, vol. 9, no. 3, pp. 458–467.

Darcy. (2009). De-concentration of disadvantaged and mixed income housing: A critical discourse approach.

Darcy, M. (2010). De-concentration of disadvantage and mixed-income housing: A critical discourse approach. *Housing, Theory and Society*, vol. 27, no. 1, pp. 1–22.

de Souza Briggs, X. & Keys, B.J. (2009). Has exposure to poor neighbourhoods changed in America? Race, risk and housing locations in two decades. *Urban Studies*, vol. 46, no. 2, pp. 429–458.

De Villiers, M.R., De Villiers, P.J.T. & Kent, A.P. (2005). The Delphi technique in health sciences education research. *Medical Teacher*, vol. 27, no. 7, pp. 639–643.

DeFelippis, J. & Fraser, J. (2008). Why do we want mixed-income housing and neighborhoods? In J. S Davies & D. L. Imbroscio (eds.), *Critical urban studies: New directions*. New York, NY: Sunny Press.

Deitrick, S. & Ellis, C. (2004). New urbanism in the inner city: A case study of Pittsburgh. *Journal of the American Planning Association*, vol. 70, no. 4, pp. 426–442.

Delbecq, A.L., Van de Ven, A.H. & Gustafson, D.H. (1975). *Group techniques for program planning: A guide to nominal group and Delphi processes*. Glenview, IL: Scott, Foresman.

Delbecq, A.L., Van de Ven, A.H. & Gustafson, D.H. (1986). *Group techniques for programme planning: A guide to national group and Delphi processes*. Middleton, WI: Green Briar Press.

Democratic Alliance. (2013, December). *Building firm foundation: DA policy on integrated human settlements for South Africa.* Cited from http://www.da.org.za/doc/human settlements

Denzin, N.K. & Lincoln, Y.S. (1994). *Handbook of qualitative research*. London: SAGE Publication.

Department of Cooperative Governance and Traditional Affairs (CoGTA). (2016). *Integrated urban development framework*. CoGTA.

Department of the Environment, Transport and the Regions (DERT). (2000). *Quality and choice: A decent home for all*. London: DERT.

Department of Monitoring and Evaluation. (2010). *For outcome 8 delivery agreement: Sustainable human settlements and improved quality of household life*. Cited from http://www.dpme.gov.za/publications/outcomes. Accessed on 6th of June, 2017.

Dikec, M. (2001). Justice and the spatial imagination. *Environment and Planning*, vol. 33, pp. 1785–1805.

Dietz, T. (1987). Methods for analyzing data from Delphi panels: Some evidence from a forecasting study. *Technological Forecasting and Social Change*, vol. 31, no. 1, pp. 79–85.

Dillman, D.A. (2000). *Mail and Internet surveys. The tailored design methods*. 2nd edition. New York, NY: Wiley.

Dorling, D. & Rees, P. (2003). A nation still dividing: The British census and social polarization. *Environmental and Planning*, vol. 35, pp. 1287–1313.

Elkin, T., McLean, D. & Hillman, M. (1991). *Reviving the inner city. Towards sustainable urban development*. London: Friends of the Earth.

Ellickson, R. (2010). The false promise of the mixed-income housing project. *UCLA Law Review*, vol. 57, pp. 983–1021.

Elliot, J.R., Gotham, K.F. & Milligan, M.J. (2004). Framing the urban: Struggles over HOPE VI and new urbanism in a historical city. *City and Community*, vol. 3, no. 4, pp. 373–394.

Enzer, S., Boucher, W.I. & Lazer, F.D. (1971). *Futures research as an aid to government planning in Canada: Four workshops demonstrations*. Middleton, CT: Institute for the Future.

Epp, G. (1996). Emerging strategies for revitilising public housing communities. *Housing Policy Debate*, vol. 7, no. 3, pp. 563–588.

Eysenck, H.J. (1976). *Case studies in behavioural therapy*. London: Routledge and Kegan Paul.

Faggio, G. & Nickell, S. (2003). The rise in inactivity among adult men. In R. Dickens, P. Gregg & J. Waldsworth (eds.), *The labour market under new labour: The state of working Britain II*. London: LSE Centre for Economic Performance.

Fainstein, S. (2005). Directions in planning theory. *Urban Affairs Review*, vol. 35, no. 4, pp. 461–475.

Farvacque-Vitkovic, C., Raghunath, M., Eghoff, C. & Boakye, C. (2008). *Development of the cities of Ghana: Challenges, priorities and tools*. African regional working papers series. Washington, DC: The World Bank.

Fein, J.A., Lavelle, J.M., Ginsburgt, K.R. & Giardino, A.P. (1997). A methodology to maximize resident input in improving a pediatric rotation. *The Archives of Pediatrics & Adolescent Medicine*, vol. 151, pp. 840–844.

Fellowes, M. (2005). *The price is wrong: Getting the market right for working families in Philadelphia*. Washington, DC: Brookings Institution.

Field, A. (2000). *Discovering statistics using SPSS for Windows*. London: Sage.

Fischer, C.S. (1982). *To dwell among friends*. Chicago: University of Chicago Press.

Fisher, I. & Zivani, J. (2004). Explanatory case studies: Implications and applications for clinical research. *Australian Occupational Therapy Journal*, vol. 51, no. 4, pp. 185–191.

FinMark Trust. (2007). Cosmo city and re-development. Workshop Organised by FinMark Trust.

Flyvbjerg, B. (2004). Five misunderstandings about case study research. In C. Seal, D. Silverman, J. Gubrium & G. Gobo (eds.), *Qualitative research practice*. London: SAGE.

Franz, C.R. & Robey, D. (1984). An investigation of user-led system design: Rational and political perspectives. *Communication of the ACM*, vol. 27, no. 12, pp. 1202–1217.

Fraser, J. & Kick, E. (2007). The role of public, private, non-profit and community sectors in shaping mixed-income housing outcomes. *Urban Studies*, vol. 44, no. 12, pp. 2357–2377.

Furtado, L. & Frietas, C. (2015). *The use of Building Information Modeling to set parameters for inclusionary zoning in Brazil*. Capes Research Publications.

Galster, G. (2007, March). Neighbourhood social mix as a goal of housing policy: A theoretical analysis. *European Journal of Housing Policy*, vol. 7, no. 1, pp. 19–43.

Galster, G.C., Booza, J.C. & Cutsinger, J.M. (2008). Income diversity within neighborhoods and very low-income families. *Cityscape: A Journal of Policy Development and Research*, vol. 10, no. 2, pp. 257–300.

Gans, H.J. (1961). The balanced community: Homogeneity or heterogeneity in residential areas? *Journal of the American Planning Association*, vol. 27, no. 3, pp. 176–184.

Ghana Statistical Service. (2012). *Population and housing census. Summary report final results*. Accra: Ghana Statistical Services.

Giannatou, L. & Zervas, E. (2014). Using Delphi techniques to build consensus in practice. *International Journal of Business Science and Applied Management*, vol. 9. ISSN: 1753-0296.

Gibbons, S. (2002). *Geography, resources and primary school performance*. London: LSE Centre for the Economic of Education.

Gibson, K. (2007) The relocation of the Columbia villa community: View from residents. *Journal of Planning Education and Research*, vol. 27, pp. 5–19.

Giddens, A. (2006). *Sociology*. 5th edition. Cambridge: Polity Press.

Given, L.M. (ed.) (2008). *The SAGE encyclopaedia of quantitative research methods*. Vol. 1 &2. London: SAGE Publications Inc.

Goetz, E. (2003). Housing dispersal programs. *Journal of Planning Literature*, vol. 18, no. 1, pp. 3–16.

Goetz, E. (2005). Comment: Public housing demolition and the benefits to low-income families. *Journal of the American Planning Association*, vol. 7, no. 14, pp. 407–410.

Goodchild, B. & Cole, I. (2001). Social balance and mixed neighborhood in Britain since 1979. *Environmental and Planning: Society and Spaces*, vol. 19, pp. 103–121.

Goonewardena, K., Kipler, S., Milgrom, R. & Schmid, C. (2008). *Space, difference, everyday life: Reading Henri Lefebvre*. New York, NY: Routledge.

Gordon, P. & Richardson, H. (1997). Are compact cities a desirable planning goal? *Journal of the American Planning Association*, vol. 63, no. 1, pp. 95–109.

Gough, K.V. & Yankson, P.W. (2000). Land markets in African cities: The case of peri-urban Accra, Ghana. *Urban Studies*, vol. 37, no. 13, pp. 2485–2500.

Government of the Republic of South Africa and Others v Grootboom and Others. (2000). (11) BCLR 1169, para 41.

Greenstein, R., Sabatini, F. & Smolka, M. (2000, November). Urban spatial segregation: Forces, consequences and policy responses. *Land Line*, vol. 12, no. 6.

Guenther, K.S. (2015). Competing voices: Negotiating power and places in mixed-income housing development. Unpublished PhD thesis, Loyola University Chicago, Chicago.

Gumbo, T. & Onatu, G. (2015). Interrogating South Africa's people's housing process: Towards comprehensive collaborative and empowering aided self-help housing approaches. *Journal of the Korean Housing Association*, vol. 26, no. 6, pp. 27–34. (IBSS).

Gupta, U.G. & Clarke, R.E. (1996, October). Theory and applications of the Delphi technique: A bibliography (1975–1994). *Technological Forecasting and Social Change*, vol. 53, no. 2, pp. 185–211.

Guy, R.F., Edgley, C.E., Arafat, I. & Allen, D.E. (1987). *Social research methods: Puzzles and solutions*. Boston, MA: Allyn & Bacon.

Guy, S. & Henneberry, J. (2000). Understanding urban development processes: Integrating the economic and the social in property research. *Urban Studies*, vol. 37, no. 13, pp. 2399–2416.

Hackett, S., Masson, H. & Phillips, S. (2006). Exploring consensus in practice with youth who are sexually abusive: Findings from a Delphi study of practitioner views in the United Kingdom and the Republic of Ireland. *Child Maltreatment*, vol. 11, no. 2, pp. 146–156.

Halasz, E. (2008). *As murder migrates, neighbors point to high-rise demolition*. Chicago: Medill Reports. Cited from http://news.medill.northwestern.edu/chicago/news.aspx?id=89113

Hanafin. (2004). *Review of literature on the Delphi technique*. Readkong. Cited from https://www.readkong.com/page/review-of-literature-on-8619502. Accessed on the 12th of January, 2020.

Handy, S. (2005). Smart growth and the transportation land use connection: What does the research tell us? *International Regional Sciences Review*, vol. 28, no. 2, pp. 146–167.

Hardoy, J.E. & Satterthwaite, D. (1997). Building the future city. In J. Gugler (ed.), *Cities in the developing world. Issues, theory, and policy*. New York, NY: Oxford University Press, pp. 265–279. *Habitat International*, vol. 22, no. 2, pp. 165–189.

Harms, H. (1992). *Self-help housing in developed and Third World countries*. in: K.

Harris, R. (1998). The silence of the experts: "Aided self-help housing", 1939–1954. *Habitat International*, vol. 22, no. 2, pp. 165–189.

Harris, R. (1999a). Slipping through the cracks: The origins of aided self-help housing, 1918-53. *Housing Studies*, vol. 14, no. 3, pp. 281–309.

Harris, R. (1999b). *Aided self-help housing, a case of amnesia: Editor's introduction*, pp. 277–280.

Harris, R. (2003). A double irony: The originality and influence of John F. C. Turner. In *Habitat international*. Vol. 27, no. 2. Elsevier, pp. 245–269.

Harvey, D. (1997, 1 November). The New Urbanism and the communitarian trap. *Harvard Design Magazine*. Cited from http://mitpress.mit.edu. Accessed on 4th of May, 2016.

Harvey, D. (2003). The right to the city. *International Journal of Urban and Regional Research*, vol. 27, no. 4, pp. 939–941.

Harvey, D. (2008, September–October). The right to the city. *New Left Review*, vol. 53. Cited from http://newleftreview.org/./53/david-harvey-the right to the city. Accessed on 7th of November, 2017.

Hasic, P. (2000). Sustainable urban matrix. In K. Williams, E. Burton & M. Jenks (eds.), *Achieving sustainable urban form.* Spon Press.

Hasson, F., Keeny, S. & McKenna, H. (2006). Research guidelines for the Delphi survey technique. *Journal of Advance Nursing Research*, vol. 32, no. 4, pp. 1008–1015.

Heather, B. (2005). Urban land and housing challenges in Brazil. Land Lines. Lincoln Institute of Land Policy. October edition, vol. 17, no. 4.

Hemel, J., Dufour, S. & Fortin, D. (1993). *Case study methods.* Newbury Park, CA: SAGE Publications.

Heppner, P.P. & Heppner, M.J. (2004). *Writing and publishing your thesis, dissertation, and research: A guide for students in the helping professions.* Thomson/Brooks/Cole.

Heppner, P.P., Pretorius, T.B., Wei, M., Lee, D.G. & Wang, Y.W. (2002). Examining the generalizability of problem-solving appraisal in Black South Africans. *Journal of Counseling Psychology*, vol. 49, no. 4, p. 484.

Hill, K.Q. & Fowles, J. (1975). The methodological worth of the Delphi forecasting technique. *Technological Forecasting and Social Change*, vol. 7, pp. 179–192.

Hogan, J.B. (1996). *Scattered-site housing: Characteristics and consequences (Report No. HUD-7470).* Washington, DC: U.S. Department of Housing and Urban Development, Office of Policy Development and Research.

Hogarty, K.Y., Hines, C.V., Kromrey, J.D., Ferron, J.M. & Mumford, K.R. (2005). The quality of factor solutions in exploratory factor analysis: The influence of sample size, communality, and overdetermination. *Educational and Psychological Measurement*, vol. 65, no. 2, pp. 202–226.

Housing Authority of New Orleans (HANO). (1996). New St. Thomas/Lower Garden District HOPE VI application. New Orleans.

Housing Authority of New Orleans (HANO). (1999). St. Thomas Revitalization Plan.

Huchzermeyer, M. (2001). Housing for the poor? Negotiated housing policy in South Africa. *Habitat International*, vol. 25, pp. 303–331.

Huchzermeyer, M. (2004). *Unlawful occupation: Informal settlements and urban policy in South Africa and Brazil.* African World Press, pp. 317–324.

Huchzermeyer, M. (2009). The struggle for in situ upgrading of informal settlements: A reflection on cases in Gauteng. *Development Southern Africa*, vol. 26, no. 1, pp. 59–73.

Huchzermeyer, M. & Karam, A. (2006). *Informal settlement: A perpetual challenge.* Juta Publication (Pty) Ltd.

Hudak, R.P., Brooke, P.P., Finstuen, K. & Riley, P. (1993). Health care administration in the year 2000: Practitioners' views of future issues and job requirements. *Hospital and Health Services Administration*, vol. 38, no. 2, pp. 181–195.

Hughes, M.A. (1987). Moving up and moving out: Confusing ends and means about ghetto dispersal. *Urban Studies*, vol. 24, no. 6, pp. 503–517.

Hughes, M.A. (1989). Misspeaking truth to power: A geographical perspective on the "underclass" fallacy. *Economic Geography*, vol. 65, no. 3, pp. 187–207.

Hulse, K. & Saugeres, L. (2007). Beyond positivism: Giving a voice to low-income renters in research about housing assistance and paid work. In *Paper presented at 2nd AHRC conference.*

Hulse, K. & Saugeres, L. (2008). *Housing insecurity and precarious living: An Australian study*. Australian Housing and Urban Research Institute, Final Report no. 124.

Hussler, C., Muller, P. & Rondé, P. (2011). Is diversity in Delphi panelist groups useful? Evidence from a French forecasting exercise on the future of nuclear energy. *Technological Forecasting and Social Change*, vol. 78, no. 9, pp. 1642–1653.

Ibrahim, R.A. (1987). Structural dynamics with parameter uncertainties. *Applied Mechanics Review*, vol. 40, no. 3. Online Publication. 1st of March.

Imbroscio, D. (2008). "Unintended and actuated by some common impulse of passion": Challenging the dispersal consensus in American housing policy research. *Journal of Urban Affairs*, vol. 30, no. 2, pp. 111–113.

Jacobs, K., Arthurson, K., Cica, N., Greenwood, A. & Hastings, A. (2011). *The stigmatisation of social housing: Findings from a panel investigation*. Australian Housing & Urban Research Institute, Final Report no. 166.

Jacobs, K. & Manzi, T. (2000). Evaluating the social constructionist paradigm in housing research. *Housing, Theory and Society*, vol. 17, no. 1, pp. 35–42.

Janis, I.L. (1972). *Victims of group thinking: A psychological study of foreign policy decisions and fiascos*. Boston, MA: Houghton Mifflin.

Jargowsky, P. & Bane, M. (1991). 'Ghetto poverty in the United States', 1970–1980. In Christopher & P. Peterson (eds.), *The urban underclass*. Washington, DC: Brookings Institution.

Jeffery, D., Ley, A., Bennun, I. & McLaren, S. (2000). Delphy survey of opinion on interventions, services principles and services organisation for severe mental illness and substance misuse problems. *Journal of Mental Health*, vol. 9, no. 4, pp. 371–384.

Jenks, C. & Peterson, P. (1991). *The urban underclass*. Washington, DC: Brooklings Institution.

Jillson, I.A. (1975). III. B. 3. The national drug-abuse policy delphi: Progress report and findings to date. In *The Delphi method: Techniques and applications*, p. 124.

Johnson, E.S.J. (2006). Mixed income housing: A conceptual model and critical discource analysis. An Unpublished PhD Dissertation submitted to the University of Colorado at Denver in partial fulfilment of the Doctor of Philosophy in Design and Planning. Cited from https://www.yumpu.com/en/document/view/11521053/mixed-income-housing-a-conceptual-model. Accessed on 2nd of February, 2014.

Johnson, J.S. & Talen, E. (2008). Affordable housing in new urbanist communities: A survey of developers. *Housing Policy Debate*, vol. 19, no. 4, pp. 583–613.

Jones, R.K. & Luo, Y. (1999, 1 September). The culture of poverty and African American culture: An empirical assessment. *Sociological Perspectives*. SAGE Publications. Cited from https://doi.org/10.2307%2F1389697

Joseph, M., Chaskin, R.J. & Webber, H.S. (2007). The theoretical basis for addressing poverty through mixed-income development. *Urban Affairs Review*, vol. 42, no. 3, pp. 369–409.

Joseph, M. & Feldman, J. (2009). Creating and sustaining successful mixed-income communities: Conceptualizing the role of schools. *Education and Urban Society*, vol. 41, no. 6. Sage Publications.

Joseph, M.L. (2006). Is mixed-income development the antidote to urban poverty? *Housing Policy Debate*, vol. 17, no. 2, pp. 209–234.

Joseph Rowntree Foundation. (1990). Affordable housing in Britain and America, Housing Finance Series.

Joshi, H., et al. (2000). Putting health inequalities on the map: Does where you live matter, and why? In E. Graham (ed.). *Understanding health inequalities.* Milton Keynes: Open University Press.

Kabir, B. & Bustani, S.A. (2009). A review of housing delivery efforts in Nigeria. In *Paper presented at the ISA International Housing Conference*, University of Glasgow, Scotland, September 1st–4th. Cited from http://www.gla.ac.uk/media/media_129767_en.pdf

Kahneman, D. & Tversky, A. (1979). Prospect theory: An analysis of decision under risk. *Econometrica*, vol. 47, pp. 263–291.

Karley, N.K. (2008). Ghana residential property delivery constraints and affordability analysis. *Housing Finance International*, vol. 22, no. 4, p. 22.

Katz, B. (1999). *Beyond city limits: The emergence of a new metropolitan agenda.* Washington: Brookings Institution. Unpublished manuscript.

Katz, L., Kling, J. & Liebman, J. (1999). Moving to opportunity in Boston. Early impact of a housing mobility programme. In *Paper presented at the conference: Neighbourhood effects on low income families: Joint centre for poverty research*, North Western University/University of Chicago, Chicago, IL.

Keil, M., Tiwana, A. & Bush, A. (2002). Reconciling user and project manager perceptions of IT project risk: A Delphi study 1. *Information Systems Journal*, vol. 12, no. 2, pp. 103–119.

Kemeny, J. (1988). Defining housing realities: Ideologies hegemony and power in housing research. *Housing Studies*, vol. 3, no. 4, pp. 2015–2018.

Kemeny, J. (1992). *Housing and social theory*. London: Routledge.

Keiting, L. (2000). Redeveloping public housing: Relearning urban renewals immutable lessons. *Journal of the American Planning Association*, vol. 66, pp. 384–397.

Khadduri, J. (2001). Deconcentration: What do we mean? What do we want? *Cityscape: A Journal of Policy Development and Research*, vol. 5, no. 2, pp. 69–84.

Khadduri, J. & Martin, M. (1997). Mixed-income housing in the HUD multifamily stock. *Cityscape*, vol. 3, no. 2, pp. 33–69.

Kimberlin, S. (2014). *Building and sustaining thriving mixed income communities.* Cited from https://www.community-wealth.org. Accessed on the 6th of April, 2019.

King, P. (2009). Using theory or making theory: Can there be theories of housing? *Housing, Theory and Society*, vol. 26, no. 1, pp. 41–52.

Kittell-Limerick, P. (2005). *Perceived barriers to completion of the academic doctorate: A Delphi study.* Texas: Texas A&M University-Commerce.

Kleinhans, R.J., Veldboer, L. & Duyvendak, J.W. (2000). *Integratie door differentiatie? Een onderzoek naar de sociale effecten van gemengd bouwen (Integration through Redifferentiation? A Study of Social Effects of Diversified Construction)*. The Hague: Ministry of Housing, Planning and Environment.

Kleit, R.G. & Carnegie, N.B. (2011). Integrated or isolated? The impact of public housing redevelopment on social network homophily. *Social Networks*, vol. 33, no. 2, pp. 152–165.

Kliet, R. (2005). HOPE VI new communities: Neighborhood relationships in mixed-income housing. *Environment and Planning A*, vol. 37, pp. 1413–1441.

Klienhans, R. (2004). Social implication of housing diversification in urban renewal: A review of recent literature. *Journal of Housing and the Built Environment*, vol. 19, pp. 367–370.

Kunstler, S. (1996). *Italy and the South German Baroque*. Australia: Monash University.

Kuusi, O. (1999). Expertise in the future use of generic technologies. In *Epistemic and methodological considerations concerning Delphi studies*. Helsinki: HeSe Prints.

Kwame-Bediako, N. (2014). How can Ghana increase its use of domestically sourced construction inputs? Nana Kwame Bediako CEO, Kwarleyz Group: Interview. Cited from https://oxfordbusinessgroup.com/articles-interviews/increasing-affordability

Laakso, K. (2012, April). On improving emergency preparedness and management with Delphi. In *Proceedings of the 9th international ISCRAM conference*, Vancouver, Canada.

Landman, K. & Napier, M. (2010). Waiting for a house or building your own? Reconsidering state provision aided and unaided self-help in South Africa. *Habitat International*, vol. 34, no. 3, pp. 299–305.

Lategan, L.G. (2012). A study of the current South African housing environment with specific reference to alternative approaches to improve living conditions. Unpublished Master's thesis, North West University, South Africa.

Lategan, L.G. (2017). Informality and sustainability: Reflecting on South Africa's informal backyard rental sector from a planning perspective. Unpublished PhD Theis submitted to the North-West University Potchefstroom.

Lawrence, P.L. & Lorsch, J.W. (1986). *Organisation and environment*. Boston, MA: Harvard Business School Press.

Leavitt, J. & Loukaitou-Sideris, A. (1995). A decent home and a suitable environment: Dilemmas of public housing residents in Los Angeles. *Journal of Architectural and Planning Research*, vol. 12, no. 3, pp. 221–239.

Lee, A.S. (1989). Case studies as natural experiments. *Human Relations*, vol. 42, no. 2, pp. 117–137.

Lees, L., Slater, T. & Wylyl, E. (2008). *Gentrification*. New York, NY: Routledge.

Lennon, S.J. & Burns, L.D. (2000). Diversity of research in textiles, clothing, and human behavior: The relationship between what we know and how we know. *Clothing and Textiles Research Journal*, vol. 18, no. 4, pp. 213–226.

Lerise, F.S. (2009). Case method and narratology in practice: Studying and reporting on politics of resources management in rural Tanzania. Unpublished PhD thesis, Ardhi University, Dar es Salaam.

Levi, M. (1997). A model, a method, and a map: Rational choice in comparative and historical analysis. *Comparative Politics: Rationality, Culture, and Structure*, vol. 28.

Levy, J.M. (2009). *Contemporary urban planning*. 8th edition. Pearson Prentice Hall.

Levy, D.K., Abravanel, M., Been, V., Dumlao, K., Fisher, L., Franks, K., Knapp, G., Pindus, N., Rosenthal, L. & Sartori, J. (2010). *Benefits and costs of inclusionary zoning programs in the United States: A literature review to inform assessment of inclusionary zoning programs*. Project 33 deliverable submitted to the U.S. Department of Housing and Urban Development, Office of Policy Design and Research. Unpublished report.

Levy, D.K., Belder, H. & Price, D. (2010). *Case studies of housing and community redevelopment in the United States and the United Kingdom*. Report to the John D and Catherine T. MacArthur Foundation and the Birmingham City.

Levy, D.K., McDade, Z. & Dumlao, K. (2010). Effects from living in mixed-income communities for low-income families: A review of the literature. Washington, DC: Urban Institute. Support from Annie.E.Casey Foundation.

Lewis, O. (1965). The culture of poverty. *American*, vol. 215, no. 4. Cited from http://lchc.ucsd.Edu. Accessed on 02nd February, 2016.

Liias, R. (1998). Housing in Estonia. Creating market through conflicts. *The Finnish Journal of Urban Studies*, vol. 36, pp. 22–23.

Lindblom, L. & Splinter, R.J. (1990, January 1). The accuracy of the relativistic Cowling approximation. *The Astrophysical Journal, Part 1*, vol. 348, pp. 198–202. ISSN 0004-637X.

Lindert, P.V. (1991). Social mobility as a vehicle for housing advancement? Some evidence from La Paz, Bolivia. In K. Mathéy (ed.), *Beyond self-help housing*. London: Mansell, pp. 157–179.

Linstone, H.A. & Turoff, M. (1975). *The Delphi methods: Techniques and applications*. London: Addison-Wesley.

Loo, R. (2002). The Delphi method: A powerful tool for strategic management. *Policing*, vol. 25, no. 4, pp. 762–769.

Loury, G.C. (1992). The economics of discrimination: Getting to the core of the problem. *Harvard Journal of African American Public Policy*, vol. 1, pp. 91–100.

Lukhele, T.M. (2014). Mixed-income housing, urban transformation and social cohesion in post-apartheid South Africa. *Mediterranean Journal of Social Sciences*, vol. 5, no. 25, p. 36.

Lunsford, D.A. & Fussell, B.C. (1993). Marketing business services in central Europe. *Journal of Services Marketing*, vol. 7, no. 1, pp. 13–21.

Lupton, R. & Tunstall, R. (2003, June). *Is targeting deprived areas an effective means to reach poor people? An assessment of one rationale for area-based funding programmes*. CASE Paper 70. London: Centre for the Analysis of Social Exclusion.

MacIntyre, A. (1984). *After virtue: A study in moral theory*. 2nd edition. Notre Dame, IN: University of Notre Dame Press.

Madsen, J. (2012). A behavioral model of house prices. *Journal of Economic Behavior & Organization*, vol. 82, no. 1, pp. 21–38.

Mafukidze, J.K. & Hoosen, F. (2009, November). Housing shortages in South Africa: A discussion of the after-effects of community participation in housing provision in Diepkloof. *Urban forum*, vol. 20, pp. 379–396. Springer Netherlands.

Mahoney, M. (1990). Law and racial geography: Public housing and the economy in New Stanford, Orleans. *Stanford Law Review*, vol. 42, no. 5, pp. 1251–1290.

Mahoney, J. (2000). Path dependence in historical sociology. *Theory and Society*, vol. 29, no. 4, pp. 507–548.

Malnar, J.M. & Vodvarka, F. (1992). *The interior dimension: A theoretical approach to enclosed space*. New York: John Wiley.

Malpass, P. (2011). Path dependence and the measurement of change in housing policy. *Housing Theory and Society*, vol. 28, no. 4, pp. 305–319.

Malta, F. (2006, April). Low-income housing in Brazil: The case of Sao Sebastiao. *Focus*, vol. 3. Cited from http://digitalcommons.calpoly.edu/focus/vole/iss1/8. Accessed on 5th of January, 2015.

Mangin, W. (1967). Squatter settlements. *Scientific America*, vol. 217, no. 4, pp. 21–29.

Marais, L., Ntema, J. & Venter, A. (2008). *State control in self-help housing: Evidence from South Africa*. Centre for Development Support University of the Free State.

Marais, L. & Venter, A. (2006). Hating the compound, but . . . mineworker housing needs in post-apartheid South Africa. *African Insight*, vol. 36, no. 1.

Maricato, E. (2005). *Housing and cities in Brazil and Latin America: Globalisation, poverty and some reasons for hope*. Cited from http://courses.arch.ntua.gr/fsr/135683/brazil. Accessed on 10th of June, 2017.

Marsh, A. & Gibb, K. (2011). Uncertainty, expectations and behavioural aspects of housing market choices. *Housing, Theory and Society*, vol. 28, no. 3, pp. 215–235.

Massey, D. & Denton, N. (1993). *American apartheid*. Cambridge, MA: Harvard University Press.

Massey, D.S. & Kanaiaupuni, S. M. (1993). Public housing and the concentration of poverty. *Social Science Quarterly*, vol. 74, pp. 109–122.

Massey, D.S., Shawn, M. & Kanaiaupuni, S.M. (1993). Public housing and the concentration of poverty. *Social Science Quarterly*, vol. 74, pp. 109–123.

Matjiya, A.T. (2009). *Assessing the housing policy framework in promoting inclusionary housing developments*, University of the Witwatersrand, Johannesburg.

McKenna, H. (1989). The selection by ward managers of an appropriate nursing models. *Journal of Advanced Nursing*, vol. 14, pp. 762–775.

McNamara, J.F. (1994). *Surveys and experiments in education research*. Technomic Publications. University of Michigan.

Melis, G., Mara, G. & Gelormino, E. (2013). Housing and social mix. Work package 6: Literature review. *Equity Action*.

Melis, G.G. & Galormino, E. (2013). Housing and social mix. Work package 6- literature review. *Equity Action*. Cited from http://health-inequalities.eu/wp-content/uploads/2016/05/Literature-Review-housing_social-mix-final-1.pdf. Accessed on 18th of September, 2017.

Miles, M.B. & Huberman, A.M. (1994). *Qualitative data analysis: An expanded sourcebook*. Sage.

Miller, J.B. (1976). *Towards a new psychology of women*. Boston, MA: Beacon Press.

Miller, A.B. (2014). *Public housing works: Lessons from Vienna and Singapore*. Cited from http://www.shareable.net. Accessed on 12th of January, 2016.

Mindali, O., Raveh, A. & Salomon, I. (2004). Urban density and energy consumptions: A new look at old statistics. *Transportation Research Part A: Policy and Practice*, vol. 38, no. 2, pp. 143–162.

Ministry of Local Government Lands and Housing. (1997). *Review of the National Policy on Housing*. Prepared by Saad Yahya & Associates and FMA Architects (Pty) Ltd.

Ministry of Water Resources, Works and Housing (MWRWH). (2009). *Draft National Shelter Policy*.

Mitchell, M. & Jolley, J. (1992). *Research design explained* (2nd edition). Forth Worth, TX: Harcourt Brace Jovanovich College Publishers.

Moreira, T. (2009). The national housing project and the new national housing policies in Brazil: Proposal and advances for the right of housing. *International Journal for Housing Science*, vol. 33, no. 2, pp. 89–98.

Moser, G., Rorgers, S., Van Til, R., Robin, K. & Lukonga, I. (1997). *Experience with structural adjustment*. International Monetary Fund.

Mosha, A.C. (2010). Making land and housing accessible to the urban low income Botswana. Paper presented at *the regional symposium organized by Ardi University and Royal Institute of Chartered Surveyors (RICS) UK on land reforms and the right of the urban poor to housing (Ownership/Renting)* on 15th–16th, February.

Mugnano, S. & Palvarini, P. (2013). "Sharing space without hanging together": A case study of social mix policy in Milan. *Cities*, vol. 35, pp. 417–422.

Murie, A., Niner, P. & Watson, C. (1976). Housing policy and the housing system. *Urban and Regional Studies*, no. 7. London: Allen & Unwin.

Murray, C. (1996). Underclass: The developing debate. *The IEA Health and Welfare Unit ChoiceWelfare*, no. 33. Cited from http://www.civitas.org.uk. Accessed on 3rd of July, 2016.

Murray, J.W. & Hammons, J.O. (1995). Delphi: A versatile methodology for conducting qualitative research. *The Review of Higher Education*, vol. 18, p. 423. Cited from https://doi.org/10.1353/rhe.1995.0008

Musterd, S. (2008). Residents' views on social mix: Social mix, social networks and stigmatisation in post-war housing estates in Europe. *Urban Studies*, vol. 45, no. 4, pp. 897–915.

Musterd, S. & de Winter, M. (1998). Conditions for spatial segregation: Some European perspectives. *International Journal of Urban and Regional Research*, vol. 22, no. 4, pp. 665–673.

Myerson, D.L. (2003). *Mixed-income housing: Myth and fact*. ULI-the Urban Land Institute.

Nehamas, A. (1985). *Nietzsche: Life as literature*. Cambridge, MA: Harvard University Press.

Neiderman, F., Brancheau, J.C. & Wetherbe, J.C. (1991). Information systems management issues for the 1990s. *MIS Quarterly*, vol. 15, no. 4, pp. 474–500.

Newman, K. & Ashton, P. (2004). Neoliberal urban policy and new paths of neighborhood change in the American inner city. *Environment and Planning A*, vol. 36, no. 7, pp. 1151–1172.

Newman, P. & Kenworthy, J. (2000). Sustainable urban form: The big picture. In K. Williams, E. Burton & M. Jenks (eds.), *Achieving sustainable urban form*. London: Spon Press, pp. 109–120.

Nientied, P. & Van Der Linden, J. (1988). Approaches to low-income housing in the Third World: Some comments. In Gugler 3 (ed.), *The urbanism of the Third World*. New York, NY: Oxford University Press.

Noor, K.B.M. (2008). Case study: A strategic research methodology. *American Journal of Applied Sciences*, vol. 5, no. 11, pp. 1602–1604.

Nordin, R.B. (2014). A framework of fighting corruption through transparency initiatives for public construction projects. Unpublished PhD thesis, Universiti Teknologi Mara.

North, D. C. (1998). Economic performance through time. In M. Brinton & V. Lee (eds.). *The new institutionalism in sociology* (pp. 247–249). Sage Publication.

Nueman, W. (2006). *Social research methods: Qualitative and quantitative approaches*. 6th edition. Boston: Pearson Education Inc.

Nworie, J. (2011). Using the Delphi technique in education technology research. *Tech Trends*, vol. 55, no. 5, pp. 24–30.

Obeng-Odoom, F. (2009a). Transforming third world cities through good urban governance: Fresh evidence. *Theoretical and Empirical Researchers in Urban Management*, vol. 1, no. 10.

Obeng-Odoom, F. (2009b). The future of our cities. *Cities: The International Journal of Urban Policy and Planning*, vol. 26, no. 1, pp. 49–53.

Obeng-Odoom, F. & Amedzro, L. (2011). Inadequate housing in Ghana. *Urban Challenge (Urban izziv)*, vol. 22, no. 1, pp. 127–137.

OECD. (2011). Society at a Glance 2011. *Social Indicators*. Cited from www.oecd.org/social/societyat a glance 2011.htm. Accessed on 20th of May, 2017.

Office of the Deputy Prime Minister: Housing, Planning, Local Government and the Regions Committee (ODPM). (2005). *Affordability and the supply of housing*. Vol. 1. London: House of Commons.

Ogra, A. & Onatu, G. (2013). *Metropolitan housing development in urban fringe areas – A case study of three metropolitan cities of South Africa*. Johannesburg: Ekurhuleni and Tshwane.

Olayiwola, L.M., Adeleye, O. & Ogunshakin. (2005). Public housing in Nigeria. Problems and Challenges. Repository. Up.ac.za.

Olshfski, D. & Joseph, A. (1991). Assessing training needs of executives using the Delphi technique. *Public Productivity and Management Review*, vol. 14, no. 3, pp. 297–301.

Onatu, G. (2010). Mixed-income housing development strategy: Perspective on Cosmo City, Johannesburg, South Africa. *International Journal of Housing Markets and Analysis*, vol. 3, no. 3, pp. 203–215.

Onatu, G. & Thwala, D. (2014). Mixed-income housing development and neighbourhood revitalisation: A case of Cosmo City. In *Peer Review paper delivered at conference on infrastructure investments in Africa organised by CARINBE in Livingstone*, Zambia 25–26 September.

Onsrud, H.J., Pinto, J.K. & Azad, B. (1992). Case study research methods for geographic information systems. *URISA Journal*, vol. 4, no. 1, pp. 32–44.

Onibokun, A. (1985). *Housing in Nigeria: (A book of readings)*. Ibadan: Nigerian Institute for Social and Economic Research (NISER).

Palmer, I., Moodley, N. & Parnel, S. (2017). *Building a capable state: Service delivery in Post Apartheid South Africa*. Bloomsbury Publishers.

Pallant, J. (2013). *SPSS survival manual: A step by step guide to data analysis using IBM 395 SPSS*. 5th edition. Crows Nest: Allen & Unwin.

Parnell, S. & Hart, D. (1999). Self-help housing as a flexible instrument of state control in 20th-century South Africa. *Housing Studies*, vol. 14, no. 3.

Patel, Y. (2014). *Public private collaboration: Case study – Cosmo City*. Seminar Presentation on Urban Regeneration, 5th November, at Maboneng, Johannesburg.

Patillo, M. (2007). *Black on the block: The politics of race and class in the city*. Chicago: University of Chicago Press.

Patricios, N. (2002). Urban design principles of the original neighborhood concepts. *Urban Morphology*, vol. 6, no. 1, pp. 21–32.

Patulny, R.V. & Morris, A. (2012). Questioning the need for social mix: The implications of friendship diversity amongst Australian social housing tenants. *Urban Studies*, vol. 49, no. 15, pp. 3365–3384.

Payne, G. (1997, August). *Urban land tenure and property rights in developing countries: A review*. London: IT Publications/ODA, p. 73.

Pierson, P. (2000). Increasing returns, path dependence and the study of politics. *American Political Science Review*, vol. 94, no. 2, pp. 251–267.

Platt, J. (1992). "Case study" in American methodological thoughts. *Current Sociology*, vol. 40, no. 1, pp. 17–48.

Polikoff, A. (1994). Comments on Alex M. Johnson, Jr.'s destabilizing race. *University of Pennsylvania Law Review*, vol. 143, p. 1685.

Popkin, S.J., Gwiasda, V.E., Olson, L.M., Rosenbaum, D.P. & Buron, L. (eds.). (2000). *The hidden war: Crime and the tragedy of public housing in Chicago*. New Brunswick: Rutgers University Press.

Popkin, S.J., Katz, B., Cunningham, M., Brown, K.D., Gustafson, J. & Turner, M. (2004). *A decade of Hope VI: Research findings and policy challenges*. Washington: Urban Institute and Brookings Institution.

Pugh, C. (1997). The changing role of self-help in housing and urban policies: 1950–1996; experience in developing countries. *Third World Planning Review*, vol. 19, no. 1.

Pugh, C. (2001). The theory and practice of housing sector development for developing countries, 1950–1999. *Housing Studies*, vol. 16, no. 4, pp. 399–423.

Punch, M. (1998). Politics and ethics in qualitative research. In N. Denzin & Y. Lincoln (eds.), *The landscape of qualitative research*. London: SAGE, pp. 83–99.

Purcell, M. (2002). Excavating Lefebvre: The right to the city and its urban politics of the inhabitant. *Geojournal*, vol. 58, no. 3, pp. 99–108.

Purcell, M. (2008). *Recapturing democracy: Neoliberalization and the struggle for alternative urban futures*. London: Routledge.

Putnam, R.D. (1993). The prosperous community: Social capital and public life. *American Propects*, vol. 13, pp. 35–42.

Quercia, R. & Galster, G. (1997). Threshold effects and the expected benefits of attracting middle income households to the central city. *Housing Policy Debate*, vol. 8, no. 2, pp. 409–435.

Quigley, J.M. (2000). A decent home: Housing policy in perspective. *Brookings–Wharton Papers on Urban Affairs*, vol. 1, no. 1, pp. 53–100.

Quigley, J. & Raphael, S. (2004). Is housing unaffordable? Why isn't it more affordable? *The Journal of Economic Perspectives*, vol. 18, no. 1, pp. 191–214.

Radhakrishna, R.B. (2007). Tips for developing and testing questionnaire/instruments. *Journal of Extension*, vol. 45, no. 1.

Randolph, B. & Wood, M. (2004). *The benefits of tenure diversification, Final report*. Melbourne: Australian Housing and Urban Research Institute.

Raskin, M.S. (1994). The Delphi study in field instruction revisited: Expert consensus on issues and research priorities. *Journal of Social Work Education*, vol. 30, no. 1, pp. 75–89.

Rayens, M.K. & Hahn, E.J. (2000). Building consensus using the policy Delphi method. *Policy, Politics, & Nursing Practice*, vol. 1, no. 4, pp. 308–315.

Reichel, A.J. (1999). Learning from St. Thomas: Community, capital, and the redevelopment of public housing in New Orleans. *Journal of Urban Affairs*, vol. 21, no. 2, pp. 169–187.

Republic of South Africa. (2008). *Social Housing Act. No. 16. Government Publications*. Pretoria: RSA, Department of Housing.

Republic of South Africa. Department of Housing (DOH). (1994). *White Paper on Housing: A new housing policy and strategy for South Africa, Government Gazette No. 16178*. Pretoria: RSA Department of Housing.

Republic of South Africa. Department of Housing (DOH). (2000). *National Housing Code*. Pretoria: RSA Department of Housing.

Republic of South Africa. Department of Housing (DOH). (2004). Breaking New Ground: A comprehensive plan for the development of sustainable human settlements. *South African Cabinet approved document*. Pretoria: RSA Department of Housing.

Rérat, P., Söderström, O. & Piguet, E. (2010). New forms of gentrification: Issues and debates. *Wiley Online*, vol. 16, no. 5.

Richetts, E. & Sawhill, I. (1988). Defining and measuring the underclass. *Journal of Policy Analysis and Management*, vol. 7, pp. 316–325.

Rifkin, S.B. & Pridmore, P. (2001). *Partners in planning: Information, participation and empowerment*. (No Title).

Robinson, D. (2005). The search for community cohesion: Key themes and dominant concepts of the public policy agenda. *Urban Studies*, vol. 42, pp. 1411–1427.

Robinson, O.C. (2011). Relational analysis: An add-on technique for aiding data integration in qualitative research. *Qualitative Research in Psychology*, vol. 8, no. 2, pp. 197–209.

Rockart, J.F. & Flannery, L.S. (1983). The management of end-user computing. *Communications of the ACM*, vol. 26, no. 10, pp. 776–784.

Rodrigue, J.P. (1998). *The geography of transport systems*. Cited from https://people.hofstra.edu. Accessed on 4th of January 2016.

Roethlisberger, F.J. (1977). *The elusive phenomena*. Boston: Harvard Business School, Division of Research.

Rosenbaum, J., Stroh, L. & Flynn, C. (1996). *Lake parc place: A study of the first four years of a mixed-income housing program*. Working Paper WP–96–7. Evanston: Center for Urban Affairs and Policy Research, Northwestern University.

Rosenbaum, J.E., Stroh, L.K. & Flynn, C.A. (1998). Lake Parc Place: A study of mixed-income housing. *Housing Policy Debate*, vol. 9, no. 4, pp. 703–740.

Rowley, J. (2002). Using case studies in research. *Management Research News*, vol. 25, no. 1, pp. 16–27.

RSA. (2009). *National housing code*, vol. 1. Pretoria: Department of Human Settlements.

Ruonavaara. (2012). Tenure as an institution. In S. J. Smith (ed.), *International encyclopedia of housing and home*. Amsterdam: Elsevier.

Ruming, K. (2011). Understanding of social mix and community opposition to social housing constructed under the Nation Building Economic Stimulus Plan. Cited from http://soac.fbe.unsw.edu.au. Accessed on 7th of January, 2015.

Ruming, K.J., Mee, K. & McGuirk, P. (2004). Questioning the rhetoric of social exclusion: Courteous community of hidden hostility? *Australian Geographical Studies*, vol. 42, pp. 234–248.

Sackman, H. (1974). *Delphi assessment: Experts opinion, forecasting, and group process*. A report prepared for the United States Air Force Project Rand. R-1283-pr. Santa Monica, CA: Rand Corporation.

Saint-Germain, M.A., Ostrowski, J.W. & Dede, M.J. (2000). Oracle in ether: Using an e-mail Delphi to revise an MPA curriculum. *Journal of Public Affairs Education*, vol. 6, no. 3, pp. 161–172.

Saito, M. & Sinha, K. (1991). Delphi study on bridge conditions ratings and effects of improvements. *Journal of Transportation Engineering*, vol. 117, pp. 320–334.

Sandercock. (1977). *Cities for sale property, politics and urban planning in Australia.* Melbourne University Press.

Sarkissian, W. (1976). The idea of social mix in town planning: An historical review. *Urban Studies*, vol. 13, pp. 231–246.

Sarkissian, W., Foryth, A. & Heine, W. (1990). Residential 'social mix': The debate continues. *Australian Planner*, vol. 28, no. 1.

Schaeffer, E.C. (2007). *Mixed-income development housing: What's left in neighborhood economic planning?* Unpublished PhD Dissertation, George Mason University.

Schmidt, R. (1997). Managing Delphi surveys using nonparametric statistical techniques. *Decision Sciences*, vol. 28, no. 3, pp. 763–774.

Schramm, W. (1971). *Notes on case studies of instructional media projects.*

Schubert, M.F. & Thresher, A. (1996). Lessons from the field: Three case studies of mixed-income housing development. In *A Great Cities Institute Working Paper prepared for the John D. and Catherine T.* MacArthur Foundation, no. GCP-96-4.

Schwartz, A. & Tajbakhsh, K. (1997). Mixed-income housing: Unanswered questions. *Cityscape: A Journal of Policy Development and Research*, vol. 3, no. 2, pp. 71–92.

Selvanayagam, R. (2012). *Why Brazils affordable housing strategy is weak.* Habitation for the Planet: In association with Fez Ta Pronto.

Simmonds, D. & Coombe, D. (2000). The transport implication of alternative urban form. In K. Williams, E. Burton & M. Jenks (eds.), *Achieving sustainable urban form.* London: E&FN Spon, pp. 121–130.

Skulmoski, G.J., Hartman, F.T. & Krahn, J. (2007). The Delphi method for graduate research. *Journal of Information Technology Education: Research*, vol. 6, no. 1, pp. 1–21.

Smith, H. (1999). *Networks and spaces of negotiation in low-income housing: The case of Costa Rica.* Unpublished PhD. Thesis. Edinburgh: School of Planning and Housing, Hariot-Watt University.

Smith, J. (2000). The space of local control in the devolution of US public housing policy. *Geografiska Annaler*, vol. 82, pp. 221–233.

Smith, A. (2002). *Mixed-income housing developments: Promise and reality.* Joint Centre for Housing Studies of Harvard University Neighborhood Reinvestment Corporation.

Smith, J.S. (2011). Home price dynamics: A behavioural economy. *Journal of Housing, Theory and Society*, vol. 28, no. 11, pp. 236–261.

Smith, D. M. & Shawky, H. A. (eds.). (2011). *Institutional money management: An inside look at strategies, players, and practices.* Vol. 16. John Wiley & Sons.

Social Exclusion Unit. (2004). *Jobs and enterprise in disadvantaged areas.* London: ODPM.

Sofroniou, N. & Hutcheson, G.D. (1999). The multivariate social scientist: Introductory statistics using generalized linear models. *The Multivariate Social Scientist.*

Soliman, A.M. (2004). *A possible way out: Formalising housing informality in Egyptian cities.* New York, NY: University Press of America, Inc.

Sophie newsletter: Explanatory case study research method. (2015, June). Cited from http://www.slidesshare.net/sophieprojects/. Accessed on 10th of June, 2016.

South African Human Rights Commission. (2002). *3rd economic and social rights report.* Johannesburg: South African Human Rights Commission. Cited from https://www.sahrc.org.za/home/21/files/Economic/. Accessed on 3rd of June, 2018.

South Africa National Development Plan. (2012). *National Development Plan 2030.* National Planning Commission.

Spencer, L. (1993). Rethinking the social role of public housing. *Housing Policy Debates*, vol. 4, no. 3, pp. 355–368.

Spinelli, T. (1983). The Delphi decision-making process. *The Journal of Psychology*, vol. 113, pp. 73–80.

Steffel Johnson, J. E. (2006). *Mixed-income housing: A conceptual model and critical discourse analysis.* Cited from http://search.proquest.com.ezproxy.cul.columbia.edu/docview/304947802. Accessed on 18th of April, 2017.

Steggell, C.D., Binder, S.K., Davidson, L.A., Vega, P.R., Hutton, E.D. & Rodecap, A.R. (2001). The role of theory in the study of housing. *Housing and Society*, vol. 28, no. 1–2, pp. 87–100.

Steggell, C.D., Yamamoto, T., Bryant, K. & Fidzani, L. (2006). The use of theory in housing research. *Housing and Society*, vol. 33, no. 1, pp. 5–20.

Stein, C.S. (1939). *Towards new towns for America.* Cambridge, MA: MIT Press.

Stitt-Gohdes, W.L. & Crews, T.B. (2004). The Delphi technique: A research strategy for career and technical education. *Journal of Career and Technical Education*, vol. 20, no. 2, pp. 55–67. ERIC.

Strauss, H.J. & Zeigler, L.H. (1975). The Delphi technique and its uses in social sciences research. *Journal of Creative Behaviour*, vol. 9, pp. 253–259.

Streeck, W. & Thelen, K. (ed.) (2005). *Beyond continuity: Institutional change in advanced political economies.* Oxford: Oxford University Press.

Tach, L.M. (2009). More than Bricks and Mortar: Neighborhood frames, social processes, and the mixed-income redevelopment of a public housing project. *City and Community*, vol. 8, no. 3, pp. 273–303.

Talen, E. (2002). The social goals of new urbanism. *Housing Policy Debate*, vol. 13, no. 1, pp. 165–188.

Taniguchi, M. & Ikeda, T. (2005). The compact city as a means of reducing reliance on the car: A model-based analysis for a sustainable urban layout. In K. Williams (ed.), *Spatial planning, urban form, and sustainable transport.* London: Ashgate.

Tapscott, C. (2000). Intergovernmental relations in South Africa: The challenges of co-operative government. *Public Administration and Development*, vol. 20, no. 2, pp. 119–127.

Tech-Hong, T. (2011). Sustainability and housing provision in Malaysia. *Journal of Strategic Innovation and Sustainability*, vol. 7, no. 1, pp. 62–71.

Tellis, W. (1997). Introduction to case study. *The Qualitative Report*, vol. 3, no. 2, pp. 1–14.

The City of Winnipeg. (2013, September). *Housing policy.* Cited from http://winnipeg.ca

Thompson, T.C. (1995). A comparison of Delphi studies to determine the principal character traits descriptive of a positive American work ethic. Unpublished PhD Thesis. Oklahoma State University, USA.

Thwala, W.D. (2007). Employment creation through public works programme: New agenda: Third quarter. *South African Journal of Social and Economic Policy*, p. 27.

Tienda, M. & Haya, S. (1991). Joblessness and shiftlessness: Labor force activity in Chicago's Inner City. In C. Jencks & P. Peterson (eds.), *The urban underclass*. Washington, DC: Brookings Institution.

Tienda, M. & Stier, H. (1991). Joblessness and shiftlessness: Labor force activity in Chicago's inner city. In C. Jencks and P. Peterson (eds.). *The urban underclass*. Washington: Brookings Institution.

Tipple, A.G. & Korboe, D. (1998). Housing policy in Ghana: Towards a supply-oriented future. *Habitat International*, vol. 22, no. 3, pp. 245–257.

Tissington, K. (2011). *A resource guide to housing in South Africa, 1994–2010: Legislation, policy, programme and practice*. Social Economic Right Institute of South Africa. Cited from https://housingfinanceafrica.org/app/uploads/SERI_A-Resource-Guide-to-Housing-in-South-Africa_Feb11.pdf. Accessed on 2nd of June, 2018.

Topa, G. (2001). Social interaction, local spillover and unemployment. *The Review of Economic Studies*, vol. 68, no. 2, pp. 261–295.

Touliatos, J. & Compton, N. (1988). *Research method in human ecology/home economics*. Ames, IA: Iowa State University Press.

Townsend, P. (1979). *Poverty in the United Kingdom*. London: Allen Lane and Penguin Books.

Tunstall, R. & Lupton, R. (2010). Mixed communities: Communities and local government. *Evidence Review*. Cited from www.communities.gov.uk. Accessed on 5th of January, 2015.

Turbov, M. & Piper, V. (2005). *HOPE VI and mixed-finance redevelopments: A catalyst for neighborhood renewal*. Washington, DC: Brookings Institute.

Turner, J.C. (1966, April). A new view of the housing deficit. San Juan Seminar Paper, Social Sciences Research Centre, University of Puerto Rico. Cited from http://www.communityplanning/TJ

Turner, J.C. (1967). Barriers and channels for housing development in modernizing countries. *Journal of the American Institute of Planners*, vol. 33, no. 3, pp. 167–181.

Turner, J.C. (1968). Housing priorities, settlements patterns and urban development in modernizing countries. *Journal of the American Institute of Planners*, vol. 33, no. 3, pp. 167–181.

Turner, J.F.C. (1976). *Housing by people. Towards autonomy in building environments*. London: Marion Byers.

Turner, J.F.C. & Fichter, R. (1972). *Freedom to build: Dwellers control of the housing process*. New York, NY: Macmillian.

Turoff, M. (1970). The design of a policy Delphi. *Technological Forecasting and Social Change*, vol. 2, no. 2, pp. 149–171.

United Nations Human Settlements Programme. (2003). *The challenge of slums: Global report on human settlements 2003*. London: Earthscan Publications.

UN-Habitat. (1996). *United Nations conference on human settlements: Habitat II*. Nairobi, Kenya: United Nations Human Settlements Publications.

UN-Habitat. (2009). Planning sustainable cities: Global report on human settlements 2009 global report on human settlements. London: Earthscan Publications.

UN-Habitat. (2010). *State of African cities 2010, governance, inequalities and urban land market*. Nairobi: United Nations Human Settlements Publications.

UN-Habitat. (2012). *Sustainable housing for sustainable cities: A policy framework for developing countries*. Nairobi: UN-HABITAT.

UN-Habitat Report. (2013). *Global Activities Report: Our presence and partnerships*. Nairobi: United Nations for Human Settlements Publication.

United Nations Development Programme. (2014). *Human development report summary: Sustaining human progress: Reducing vulnerability and building resilience*. UNDP.

United Nations Educational, Scientific and Cultural Organization. (1997). Decisions adopted by the Executive Board at its 151st session. Cited from http://unesdoc.unesco.org/images/0010/001065/106582e.pdf. Accessed 12th of April, 2020.

United Nations Human Settlements Programme. (2010). *Housing as a strategy for poverty reduction in Ghana*. Nairobi: UN-HABITAT.

United States Department of Housing and Urban Development (HUD). (2003, December 27). Housing choice voucher programme. *Federal Register*, vol. 71.

United States Department of Housing and Urban Development (HUD). (2006, December 27). Announcement of funding award for the housing choice voucher programme. *Federal Register*, vol. 71.

Urban Land Institute. (2003). South Capital Street Corridor. Washington, DC: Implementation Plan. Urban Land Institute.

U.S Department of Housing and Urban Development (HUD). (1996). *Reinvention: From blueprint to action*. Washington, DC: U.S. Department of Housing and Urban Development.

Vagias, W.M. (2006). Likert-type scale response anchors. Clemson International Institute for Tourism & Research Development, Department of Parks, Recreation and Tourism Management. Clemson University.

Vale, L. (1998). Comments on James E. Rosenbaum, Linda, K. Stroh, and Cathy A. Flynn's Lake Parc Place: A study of mixed-income housing. *Housing Policy Debate*, vol. 9, no. 4, pp. 749–756.

Vale, L.J. (2006). Is mixed-income development an antidote to urban poverty? *Housing Policy Debate*, vol. 17. Office of Housing Policy Research, Fannie Mae.

Vale, L. & Shamsuddin, S. (2015). In the US, mixed housing development are not working for low–income families. Cited from http://www.citymetric.com. Accessed on 4th of November, 2015.

Valladares, F., Bastias, C.C., Godoy, O. & Granda, E. (2015, October 14). Species co-existence in a changing world. *Plant Science*, vol. 6.

Valentine, C.A. (1968). *Culture and poverty critique and counter-proposals*. Chicago, IL: University of Chicago Press.

Valladares, L.P. (1978). Working the system: Squatter response to resettlement in Rio de Janeiro. *International Journal of Urban and Regional Research*, vol. 2, no. 1–3, pp. 12–25.

Valladares, L. (2005). *A Invenção da Favela: do Mito de Origem a favela.com*. Rio de Janeiro: FGV.

Van Kempen & Bolt. (2009, December). Social cohesion, social mix, and urban policies in the Netherlands. *Journal of Housing and the Built Environment*, vol. 24, no. 4, pp. 457–475.

Van Kempen, R. & Şule Özüekren, A. (1998). Ethnic segregation in cities: New forms and explanations in a dynamic world. *Urban Studies*, vol. 35, no. 10, pp. 1631–1656.

Van Lindert, P. (1992). *Beyond self-help housing*. London: Mansell Publication Limited.

Van Someren, M., Barnard, Y.F. & Sandberg, J. (1994). *The think aloud method: A practical approach to modelling cognitive*. vol. 11. London: Academic Press, pp. 29–41.

Van Vliet, B.J.M., Chappells, H. & Shove, E. (2005). *Infrastructures of consumption: Environmental innovation in the utility industries*. London: Earthscan/James & James.

Vazquez-Ramos, R., Leahy, M. & Hernandez, N.E. (2007). The Delphi methods in rehabilitation counselling research. *Rehabilitation Counselling Bulletin*, vol. 50, no. 2, pp. 111–118.

Verkade, P.J., Van Meijel, B., Brink, C., Van Os-Medendorp, H., Koekkoek, B. & Francke, A. (2010). Delphi-research exploring essential components and preconditions for case management in people with dementia. *BMC Geriatics*, vol. 10, no. 54, pp. 1471–2318.

von Hoffman, A. (1996). High ambitions: The past and future of American low-income housing policy. *Housing Policy Debate*, vol. 7, no. 3, pp. 423–446.

Wakely, P. (2014). *Urban policy housing strategies in developing countries: Whence and Whither paradigm, policies, programmes and projects*. Development Planning Unit (DPU), University College London. Working Paper Series: Reflection No. 163/60.

Walker, R., Ballard, J., Taylor, C. & Hiller, J. (2003). *The effects of New Living on Indigenous wellbeing: A case study of urban renewal*. Australian Housing and Urban Research Institute (AHURI). Position Paper No. 61.

Ward, P.M. (ed.) (1982). *Self-help housing: A critique*. London: Mansell.

Whetten, D. A. (1989). What constitutes a theoretical contribution? *Academy of Management Review*, vol. 14, no. 4, pp. 490–495.

Whitle, R., Davies, T., Gobey, M. & Simister, J. (2014). Behavioural economics and house prices: A literature review. *Business and Management Horizons*, vol. 2, no. 2, pp. 15–28.

Wikins, C.S. (2002, 4th April). Framing mixed-income housing greatest challenges. In *Paper proceeding presented at the symposium organised by Neighborhood Reinvestment Corporation*, Chicago.

Wilkins, C.S. (2001). Mixed-income rental housing. In *Concept Paper*. Millenial Housing Commission.

Williams, K., Burton, E. & Jenks, M. (1996). Achieving the compact city through intensification: An acceptable option. In *The compact city: A sustainable urban form*, pp. 83–96.

William, K., Burton, E. & Jenks, M. (2000). *Achieving the compact city through intensification: An acceptable options?* London: E & FN Spon.

Williams, P.L. & Webb, C. (1994). The Delphi technique: A methodological discussion. *Journal of Advanced Nursing*, no. 19, pp. 180–186.

Wilson, W.J. (1987). *The truly disadvantaged*. Chicago, IL: University of Chicago Press.

Wilson, W.J. (1991a). Another look at the truly disadvantaged. *Political Science Quarterly*, vol. 106, no. 4, pp. 639–656.

Wilson, W.J. (1991b). Studying inner-city social dislocations: The challenge of public agenda research: 1990 presidential address. *American Sociological Review*, vol. 56, pp. 1–14.

Witte, E. (1972). *Field research on complex decision-making processes–The phase theorem* (pp. 156–182). International Studies of Management and Organization.

Wood, M. (2003). A balance act? Tenure diversification in Australia and the UK. *Urban Policy and Research*, vol. 21, no. 1, pp. 45–56.

Woodside, A.G. (2010). *Case study research: Theory, methods and practice*. Emerald Publishing Limited.

Woodside, A.G. & Wilson, E.J. (2003). Case study research methods for theory building. *Journal of Business & Industrial Marketing*, vol. 18, no. 6/7, pp. 493–508.

Wrigley, N. (2002). "Food deserts" in British cities: Policy context and research priorities. *Urban Studies*, vol. 39, no. 11, pp. 2029–2040.

Wyly, E. & Hammel, D. (1990). Island of Decay in seas of renewal. *Housing Policy Debate*.

Wyly, E.K. & Hammel, J. (1999). Island of decay in seas of renewal: Housing policy and the resurgence of gentrification. *Housing Policy Debate*, vol. 10, no. 4.

Yan, Z. (2004). Wills and ways: Policy dynamics of Hope IV from 1992–2002. Unpublished PhD, Massachusetts Institute of Technology.

Yin, R.K. (1989). *Case study research: Design and methods*. Newbury Park, CA: SAGE.

Yin, R.K. (1994). *Case study research: Design and methods*. 2nd edition. Thousand Oaks, CA: SAGE.

Yin, R.K. (ed.) (2004). *The case study anthology*. Thousand Oaks, CA: SAGE.

Yin, R.K. (2009). *Case study research: Design and methods*. 4th edition. Thousand Oaks, CA: SAGE.

Yin, R.K. (2011). *Case study research: Design and methods (applied social research methods)*. 5th edition. SAGE Publications, Inc.

Yin, R.K. (2014). *Case study research and design*. Vol. 5, 2nd edition. Sage Publications.

Yin, R.K. & Davis, D. (2007). Adding new dimensions to case study evaluations: The case of evaluating comprehensive reforms. *New Directions for Evaluation*, vol. 113, pp. 75–94.

Zemke, R. & Kramlinger, T. (1982). *Figuring things out: A trainer's guide to needs and task analysis*. Reading: Addison-Wesley.

Zenou, Y. & Boccard, N. (2000). Labor discrimination and redlining in cities. *Journal of Urban Economics*, vol. 48, no. 2, pp. 260–285.

Zolingen, S.J. & Klaassen, C.A. (2003). Selection process in a Delphi study about key qualifications in senior secondary vocational education. *Technological Forecasting and Social Change*, vol. 70, pp. 317–340.

Index

Printed and bound by CPI Group (UK) Ltd, Croydon, CR0 4YY

28/02/2024

14460706-0005